SOLITUDE

SOLITUDE

A Return to the Self

Anthony Storr

THE FREE PRESS
A Division of Macmillan, Inc.
NEW YORK

The Free Press
A Division of Macmillan, Inc.
866 Third Avenue, New York, N.Y. 10022

Printed in the United States of America

Library of Congress Cataloging-in-Publication Data

Storr, Anthony.
  Solitude : a return to the self / Anthony Storr.—1st American ed.

    p.   cm.

    1. Solitude—Psychological aspects.   2. Interpersonal relations.
3. Adjustment (Psychology)   I. Title.
BF637.S64S65   1988
155.9′2—dc19   88–7187
                                                       CIP

Acknowledgements

I want to thank Bryan Magee, who first drew my attention to the fact that so many of the great philosophers were predominantly solitary.

I would like to thank my publishers, Erwin A. Glikes and Tom Rosenthal, for some useful suggestions; Howard Davies, for assiduous copy-editing; and Anthony Thwaite, for expert editing and many improvements to my style.

Dr Kay R. Jamison has generously allowed me to use her unpublished work, and has provided many valuable references.

Dr Richard Wyatt, of the National Institute of Mental Health, has saved me from at least one grievous error.

My wife, Catherine Peters, has patiently read the whole typescript and made valuable comments, as well as supplying a great deal of support and encouragement.

Contents

INTRODUCTION

*'Conversation enriches the understanding, but solitude is the school of genius;
and the uniformity of a work denotes the hand of a single artist.'*

Edward Gibbon

Gibbon is surely right. The majority of poets, novelists, composers, and, to a lesser extent, of painters and sculptors, are bound to spend a great deal of their time alone, as Gibbon himself did. Current wisdom, especially that propagated by the various schools of psycho-analysis, assumes that man is a social being who needs the companionship and affection of other human beings from cradle to grave. It is widely believed that interpersonal relationships of an intimate kind are the chief, if not the only, source of human happiness. Yet the lives of creative individuals often seem to run counter to this assumption. For example, many of the world's greatest thinkers have not reared families or formed close personal ties. This is true of Descartes, Newton, Locke, Pascal, Spinoza, Kant, Leibniz, Schopenhauer, Nietzsche, Kierkegaard and Wittgenstein. Some of these men of genius had transient affairs with other men or women: others, like Newton, remained celibate. But none of them married, and most lived alone for the greater part of their lives.

Creative talent of a major kind is not widely bestowed. Those who possess it are often regarded with awe and envy because of their gifts. They also tend to be thought of as peculiar; odd human beings who do not share the pains and pleasures of the average person. Does this difference from the average imply abnormality in the sense of psychopathology? More particularly, is the predilection of the creative person for solitude evidence of some inability to make close relationships?

It is not difficult to point to examples of men and women of genius whose interpersonal relationships have been stormy, and whose personalities have been grossly disturbed by mental illness, alcoholism, or drug abuse. Because of this, it is easy to assume that creative talent, mental instability, and a deficient capacity for making satisfying personal relationships are closely linked. Regarded from this point of view, the possession of creative talent appears as a doubtful blessing: a Janus-faced endowment, which may bring fame and fortune, but which is incompatible with what, for the ordinary person, constitutes happiness.

The belief that men and women of genius are necessarily unstable has been widely held, especially since the time of Freud. It cannot possibly be the whole truth. Not all creative people are notably disturbed; not all solitary people are unhappy. Gibbon, after his initial disappointment in love, enjoyed a particularly happy and equable life which anyone might envy. As he wrote himself:

When I contemplate the common lot of mortality, I must acknowledge that I have drawn a high prize in the lottery of life . . . I am endowed with a cheerful temper, a moderate sensibility, and a natural disposition to repose rather than to activity: some mischievous appetites and habits have perhaps been corrected by philosophy or time. The love of study, a passion which derives fresh vigour from enjoyment, supplies each day, each hour, with a perpetual source of independent and rational pleasure; and I am not sensible of any decay of the mental faculties . . . According to the scale of Switzerland, I am a rich man; and I am indeed rich, since my income is superior to my expense, and my expense is equal to my wishes. My friend Lord Sheffield has kindly relieved me from the cares to which my taste and temper are most adverse: shall I add, that since the failure of my first wishes, I have never entertained any serious thoughts of a matrimonial connection?[1]

As Lytton Strachey wrote in his essay on Gibbon:

> Happiness is the word that immediately rises to the mind at the thought of Edward Gibbon: and happiness in its widest connotation – including good fortune as well as enjoyment.[2]

Some might allege that Gibbon, by renouncing his love for Suzanne Curchod at the behest of his father, had cut himself off from the chief source of human happiness, and should be labelled pathological on this account. Sexual love may have played little part in Gibbon's life, but Gibbon's other relationships were rewarding. Although the immense labour of composing *The Decline and Fall of the Roman Empire* necessitated long periods of solitary study and writing, Gibbon was equally happy in company. When he was in London, he led an active social life, was a member of Boodle's, White's, and Brooks's, as well as of The Literary Club, and was appreciated everywhere as a fascinating talker. In addition, he displayed a touching affection toward his aunt, Mrs Porten, who had largely been responsible for his upbringing, and a gift for friendship which was most clearly manifest in his long and close relationship with Lord Sheffield. Gibbon occasionally laments his solitary state in his correspondence, and toyed with the idea of adopting a female cousin. But the prospect of matrimony was a daydream which he soon dismissed.

> When I have painted in my fancy all the probable consequences of such an union, I have started from my dream, rejoiced in my escape, and ejaculated a thanksgiving that I was still in possession of my natural freedom.[3]

Modern insistence that true happiness can only be found in intimate attachments, more especially in sexual fulfilment, does not allow a place for characters like Gibbon. It is clear that, although his friendships were many, his chief source of self-esteem and of pleasure was his work, as the famous sentence which closes his autobiography makes plain.

In old age, the consolation of hope is reserved for the tenderness of parents, who commence a new life in their children; the faith of enthusiasts who sing Hallelujahs above the clouds, and the vanity of authors who presume the immortality of their name and writings.[4]

Gibbon was a classical artist whose style embodies an attitude toward the follies and extravagances of mankind which is both ironic and detached. Romantics, like Rousseau and Coleridge, detested him for this reason. In his writings, Gibbon's human sympathies certainly appear as limited: sex is generally treated as a subject of amusement; religion dismissed as superstition. But the immensity of the task he set himself demanded such a stance. To impose order upon the turmoil and confusion of so long a period of history required an Olympian perspective. Gibbon's humanity did not, and could not, manifest itself in his great history; but the warmth of his feelings towards his friends and the affection which they showed him demonstrate that the man himself possessed a human heart. By most of the standards adopted in the past, Gibbon would be rated as exceptionally well-balanced. It is only since Freud advanced the notion that heterosexual fulfilment is the *sine qua non* of mental health that anyone would question Gibbon's status as a more than commonly happy and successful human being.

It is not only men and women of genius who may find their chief value in the impersonal rather than in the personal. I shall argue that interests, whether in writing history, breeding carrier pigeons, speculating in stocks and shares, designing aircraft, playing the piano, or gardening, play a greater part in the economy of human happiness than modern psycho-analysts and their followers allow. The great creators exemplify my thesis most aptly because their works remain as evidence. That mysterious being, the ordinary man or woman, leaves little behind to indicate the breadth and depth of interests which may, during a lifetime, have been major preoccupations. The rich may accumulate great collections of the works of others. Enthusiastic gardeners can be notably creative and leave evidence of their passion which lasts for years, if not for as long as a book or a painting. But nothing remains of a passion for windmills or cricket. Yet we must all have known people whose lives were actually made worthwhile by such interests, whether or not their human relationships were satisfactory. The burden of value with which we are at present loading interpersonal relationships is too heavy for those fragile craft to carry. Our expectation that satisfying intimate relationships should, ideally, provide happiness and that, if they do not, there must be something wrong with those relationships, seems to be exaggerated.

Love and friendship are, of course, an important part of what makes life worthwhile. But they are not the only source of happiness. Moreover, human beings change and develop as life goes on. In old age, human relationships often become less important. Perhaps this is a beneficent arrangement of Nature, designed to ensure that the ? ? inevitable parting with loved ones will be less distressing. In any case, there is always an element of uncertainty in interpersonal relationships which should preclude them from being idealized as an absolute or seen as constituting the only path toward personal fulfilment. It may be our idealization of interpersonal relationships in the West that causes marriage, supposedly the most intimate tie, to be so unstable. If we did not look to marriage as the principal source of happiness, fewer marriages would end in tears.

I shall argue that human beings are directed by Nature toward the impersonal as well as toward the personal, and that this feature of the human condition is a valuable and important part of our adaptation. We share with other animals the prime biological necessity of reproducing ourselves; of ensuring that our genes survive, though we do not. But the long span of human life which extends beyond the main reproductive period also has significance. It is then that the impersonal comes to assume a greater importance for the average person, although seeds of such interests have been present from the earliest years.

The great creators, as we shall see, may in some instances have been deflected from human relationships toward their own field of endeavour by adverse circumstances which made it difficult for them to achieve intimacy with others. But this is a matter of emphasis rather than substitution. It does not imply, as some psycho-analysts assume, that creative endeavour is invariably an alternative to human

xiii

relationships. One might argue that people who have no abiding interests other than their spouses and families are as limited intellectually as those who have neither spouse nor children may be emotionally.

Many ordinary interests, and the majority of creative pursuits involving real originality, continue without involving relationships. It seems to me that what goes on in the human being when he is by himself is as important as what happens in his interactions with other people. Something like one third of our total lifespan is, in any case, spent in the isolation of sleep. Two opposing drives operate throughout life: the drive for companionship, love, and everything else which brings us close to our fellow men; and the drive toward being independent, separate, and autonomous. If we were to listen only to the psycho-analytic 'object-relations' theorists, we should be driven to conclude that none of us have validity as isolated individuals. From their standpoint, it appears that we possess value only in so far as we fulfil some useful function vis-à-vis other people, in our roles, for example, as spouse, parent, or neighbour. It follows that the justification for the individual's existence is the existence of others.

Yet some of the people who have contributed most to the enrichment of human experience have contributed little to the welfare of human beings in particular. It can be argued that some of the great thinkers listed above were self-centred, alienated, or 'narcissistic'; more preoccupied with what went on in their own minds than with the welfare of other people. The same is true of many writers, composers, and painters. The creative person is constantly seeking to discover himself, to remodel his own identity, and to find meaning in the universe through what he creates. He finds this a valuable integrating process which, like meditation or prayer, has little to do with other people, but which has its own separate validity. His most significant moments are those in which he attains some new insight, or makes some new discovery; and these moments are chiefly, if not invariably, those in which he is alone.

Although major talent is rare, creative people remain human beings with the same needs and wishes as the rest of us. Because they leave behind records of their thoughts and feelings in their works, they exemplify, in striking fashion, aspects of human striving which are common to us all but which, in the case of ordinary people, escape notice. Perhaps the need of the creative person for solitude, and his preoccupation with internal processes of integration, can reveal something about the needs of the less gifted, more ordinary human being which is, at the time of writing, neglected.

1

The Significance of Human Relationships

'In solitude
What happiness? Who can enjoy alone,
Or all enjoying what contentment find?'

Milton

The current emphasis upon intimate interpersonal relationships as the touchstone of health and happiness is a comparatively recent phenomenon. Earlier generations would not have rated human relationships so highly; believing, perhaps, that the daily round, the common task, should furnish all we need to ask; or, alternatively, being too preoccupied with merely keeping alive and earning a living to have much time to devote to the subtleties of personal relations. Some observers, like Ernest Gellner, suggest that our present preoccupation with, and anxiety about, human relationships has replaced former anxieties about the unpredictability and precariousness of the natural world. He argues that, in modern affluent societies, most of us are protected from disease, poverty, hunger, and natural catastrophes to an extent undreamed of by previous generations. But modern industrial societies are unstable and lacking in structure. Increased mobility has undermined the pillars of society. Because we have more choice as to where we live, what society we should join, and what we should make of our lives, our relations with the other people who constitute our environment are no longer defined by age-old rules and have therefore become matters of increasing concern and anxiety. As Gellner puts it, 'Our

1

OUR environment is now made up basically of relationships with others.'[1]

Gellner goes on to affirm that the realm of personal relations has become 'the area of our most pressing concern'. Our anxieties in this field are compounded by the decline of religious belief. Religion not only provided rules of conduct regarding personal relationships, but also offered a more predictable, stable alternative. Relationships with spouse, children, or neighbours might be difficult, unfulfilling, or unstable; but, so long as one continued to believe in Him, the same could not be said of one's relationship with God.

Although I am far from agreeing with everything which Gellner has to say in his book about psycho-analysis, I think he is right in alleging that psycho-analysis promises a form of salvation; and that this kind of salvation is to be attained by purging the individual of the emotional blocks or blind spots which prevent him from achieving fulfilling interpersonal relationships. Gellner is also right in thinking that psycho-analysis has exerted so widespread an influence that it has become the dominant idiom for the discussion of human personality and personal relationships even by those who do not subscribe to all its doctrines.

Psycho-analysis has changed considerably during the course of the twentieth century. The main change has been the increase in emphasis upon the patient's relationship with the psycho-analyst. Psycho-analysis now insists that analysis of transference, that is, of the patient's emotional response to, and attitude toward, the psycho-analyst, is the most essential feature of psycho-analytic treatment. Indeed, recognition of the importance of transference has been a main factor in creating common ground between psychotherapeutic schools like those of Freud and Jung which in other theoretical ways are still poles apart. Although the status of psycho-analysis as an effective method of curing neurotic symptoms has been questioned in recent years, the influence of concepts derived from psycho-analysis is pervasive. In most varieties of social work, for instance, consideration of the client's capacity to make human relationships is thought to be a vital part of case-work; and attempts are often made to improve this capacity through the agency of the client's relationship with the social worker.

In the early days of psycho-analysis, the emphasis was not so much upon the analysis of transference as upon retracing the course of the patient's psycho-sexual development. The patient was primarily regarded as a separate individual, and his emotional attitude toward the analyst was considered as secondary, or indeed as an obstacle to psycho-analytic investigation. When Freud began his investigation of the origins of neurosis during the last two decades of the nineteenth century, he invariably found disturbances in the sexual lives of his patients. The edifice of psycho-analysis came to rest upon the foundation of the theoretical scheme of sexual development, from infancy onward, which Freud postulated as a consequence of his investigations.

In Freud's view, the various types of neurosis were related to the patient's failure to progress beyond the early stages of sexual development; to fixation at the 'oral', 'anal', or 'phallic' stage, which prevented progress toward 'genitality', as Freud named the stage of sexual maturity. Freud believed that mental life was originally directed by the 'pleasure principle'; that is, by the need to avoid pain and to obtain pleasure. He also believed that the nervous system, and hence the mental apparatus, had the function of reducing the level of intensity of the instinctual impulses which reached it, by finding ways of expressing, and therefore of discharging, those impulses. The idea of psychological health and happiness became linked with the existence, or achievement, of sexual fulfilment.

It became widely assumed that, if a person was happy and healthy, he or she must be enjoying a satisfying sexual life; and, conversely, that if a person was neurotically unhappy, there must be a disturbance in his or her capacity to find sexual release. During Freud's lifetime, the main emphasis was upon instinctual satisfaction; that is, upon the capacity for orgasm. It was tacitly implied that, if partners were able to give each other satisfaction in this way, other aspects of their relationship could be taken for granted. Sex was the touchstone by which the whole relationship could be evaluated. If a patient could overcome the blocks which had caused fixations at immature stages of sexual development, and attain the genital stage, there would then be no obstacle to the establishment of relationships with others on equal and mutually rewarding terms.

3

Freud assumed that neurosis invariably had its origin in the circumstances of the patient's early childhood. The task of the psycho-analyst was to facilitate the recall of early traumatic memories which had been repressed because they were painful or shameful. Following the discovery made by his colleague Breuer, Freud found that, if a patient suffering from hysteria could be persuaded to recall the exact circumstances in which a particular symptom had originated, and could also re-experience the emotions connected with those circumstances, the symptom would disappear. As Freud went on to treat other types of patient, the original emphasis on traumatic incidents somewhat declined in favour of recall of the whole emotional climate in which the patient was brought up; but neurotic symptoms were still assumed to originate from the circumstances of the first five years of life.

Psycho-analysis could therefore be regarded as a process of historical reconstruction; a technique for unearthing the events, feelings, and phantasies of the patient's early childhood. There was little need to examine current relationships, and still less to involve the patient's friends and family in a treatment which was chiefly concerned with subjective responses dating from a period of the patient's life about which they probably knew very little.

Psycho-analysts were often criticized for treating their patients too much as isolated individuals, without reference to their families and friends. The latter, often to their chagrin, were generally discouraged from any participation in the analytic process, and were not usually seen by the psycho-analyst or asked for information about the patient's behaviour and relationships at home. But, if psycho-analytic theory in its original form is accepted, treating the patient without direct involvement of those currently close to him is reasonable. No one except the patient has access to the phantasies and feelings of his early childhood. Even the most detailed account which parents might give of the patient's early years will not disclose what the psycho-analyst is seeking: the patient's subjective reaction to those childhood circumstances rather than the facts themselves.

When Freud first initiated psycho-analytic treatment, he did not anticipate that he would become emotionally important to his patients. He hoped to make psycho-analysis into a 'science of the

4

mind' which would ultimately be based upon, and be as objective as, anatomy and physiology. He saw his own role as that of a detached observer, and assumed that his patients would have the same attitude toward him as they would toward a medical specialist in any other field. When he discovered that this was not the case, that his patients began to experience and to express emotions of love and hate toward himself, he did not accept such emotions as genuine expressions of feelings in the here-and-now, but interpreted them as new editions of emotions from the past which had been *transferred* to the person of the analyst.

Freud originally regarded transference with distaste. As late as 1910, long after he had recognized the importance of transference, he wrote to Pfister:

> As for the transference, it is altogether a curse. The intractable and fierce impulses in the illness, on account of which I renounced both indirect and hypnotic suggestion, cannot be altogether abolished even through psycho-analysis; they can only be restrained and what remains expresses itself in the transference. That is often a considerable amount.[2]

In Lecture 27 of *Introductory Lectures on Psycho-Analysis*, Freud reiterates his conviction that transference must be treated as unreal.

> We overcame the transference by pointing out to the patient that his feelings do not arise from the present situation and do not apply to the person of the doctor, but that they are repeating something that happened to him earlier. In this way we oblige him to transform his repetition into a memory.[3]

Since Freud's day, and, more particularly, since the emergence of the *object-relations* school of psycho-analysis, there has been a shift of emphasis in understanding and interpreting transference. The majority of psycho-analysts, social workers, and other members of the so-called 'helping professions' consider that intimate personal relationships are the chief source of human happiness. Conversely, it is widely assumed that those who do not enjoy the satisfactions provided by such relationships are neurotic, immature, or in some other way abnormal. Today, the thrust of most forms of psycho-therapy, whether with individuals or groups, is directed toward understanding what has gone wrong with the patient's relationships with significant persons in his or her past, in order that the patient can be helped toward making more fruitful and fulfilling human relationships in the future.

Since past relationships condition expectations in regard to new relationships, the attitude of the patient toward the analyst as a new and significant person is an important source of information about previous difficulties and also provides a potential opportunity for correcting these difficulties. To give a simple example, a patient who has experienced rejection or ill-treatment is likely to approach the analyst with an expectation of further rejection and ill-treatment, although the patient may be quite unconscious of the fact that this expectation is affecting his attitude. The realization that he is making false assumptions about how others will treat him, together with the actual experience of being treated by the analyst with greater kindness and understanding than he had expected, may revolutionize his expectations and facilitate his making better relationships with others than had hitherto been possible.

As we have seen, Freud discounted any feelings which the analysand expressed toward the analyst as unreal, and interpreted them as belonging to the past. Today, many analysts recognize that such feelings are not merely facsimiles of childhood impulses and phantasies. In some cases they represent an attempt to make up for what has been missing in the analysand's childhood. The analysand may, for a time, see the analyst as the ideal parent whom he never had. This experience may have a healing effect, and it can be a mistake to dispel this image by premature interpretation or by calling it an illusion.

As we saw earlier, Freud considered that the psycho-analyst's task was to remove the blocks which were preventing the patient from expressing his instinctual drives in adult fashion. If this task could be accomplished, it was supposed that the patient's relationships would automatically improve. Modern analysts have reversed this order. They think first in terms of relationships, second in terms of

6

instinctual satisfaction. If the analysand is enabled to make relationships with other human beings which are on equal terms, and free from anxiety, it is assumed that there will be no difficulty in expressing instinctual drives and attaining sexual fulfilment. Object-relations theorists believe that, from the beginning of life, human beings are seeking *relationships*, not merely instinctual satisfaction. They think of neurosis as representing a failure to make satisfying human relationships rather than as a matter of inhibited or undeveloped sexual drives.

Transference, in the sense of the patient's total emotional attitude or series of attitudes toward the analyst, is therefore seen as a central feature of analytical treatment, not as a relic from the past, nor as 'a curse', nor even, as Freud later regarded it, as 'a powerful ally', because of the power which it gave him to modify the patient's attitudes. Today a psycho-analyst will usually spend a good deal of his time detecting and commenting upon the way in which his patients react to himself, the analyst: whether they are fearful, compliant, aggressive, competitive, withdrawn, or anxious. Such attitudes have their history, which needs to be explored. But the emphasis is different. The analyst studies the analysand's distorted attitude to himself, and by this means perceives the distortions in the analysand's relationships with others. To do this effectively implies the recognition that there is a real relationship in the here-and-now, and that analysis is not solely concerned with the events of early childhood.

The analytical encounter is, after all, unique. No ordinary social meeting allows detailed study of the way in which one party reacts to the other. In no other situation in life can anyone count on a devoted listener who is prepared to give so much time and skilled attention to the problems of a single individual without asking for any reciprocal return, other than professional remuneration. The patient may never have encountered anyone in his life who has paid him such attention or even been prepared to listen to his problems. It is not surprising that the analyst becomes important to him. Recognizing the reality of such feelings is as necessary as recognizing the irrational and distorted elements of the transference which date from the analysand's childhood experience.

7

This concentration upon interpersonal relationships and upon transference is not characteristic of all forms of analytical practice; but it does link together a number of psycho-analysts and psycho-therapists who may originally have been trained in different schools, but who share two fundamental convictions. The first is that neurotic problems are something to do with early failures in the relation between the child and its parents: the second, that health and happiness entirely depend upon the maintenance of intimate personal relationships.

No two children are exactly alike, and it must be recognized that genetic differences may contribute powerfully to problems in childhood development. The same parent may be perceived quite differently by different children. Nevertheless, I share the conviction that many neurotic difficulties in later life can be related to the individual's early emotional experience within the family.

I am less convinced that intimate personal relationships are the only source of health and happiness. In the present climate, there is a danger that love is being idealized as the only path to salvation. When Freud was asked what constituted psychological health, he gave as his answer the ability to love and work. We have over-emphasized the former, and paid too little attention to the latter. In many varieties of analysis, exclusive concentration upon interpersonal relationships has led to failure to consider other ways of finding personal fulfilment, and also to neglecting the study of shifting dynamics within the psyche of the isolated individual.

A number of psycho-analysts contributed to the rise of 'object-relations theory' as opposed to Freud's 'instinct theory'. Amongst these analysts were Melanie Klein, Donald Winnicott, and Ronald Fairbairn. But the most important work in this field has been that of John Bowlby, whose three volumes *Attachment and Loss* are deservedly influential, have inspired a great deal of research, and are widely regarded as having made a major contribution to our understanding of human nature.

Bowlby assumes that the primary need of human beings, from infancy onward, is for supportive and rewarding relationships with other human beings, and that this need for *attachment* extends far beyond the need for sexual fulfilment. The ideas which Bowlby is expressing derive from a welcome synthesis between ethology and psycho-analysis. By emphasizing attachment, which is distinct from sexual involvement, although often associated with it, Bowlby has widened the psycho-analytic view of man and human relationships, bringing it more into line with the findings of workers in other disciplines.

Bowlby's *Attachment and Loss* originated in his work for the World Health Organization on the mental health of homeless children. This led to subsequent study of the effects upon young children of the temporary loss of the mother and to a far greater appreciation of the distress suffered by young children when, for example, they or their mothers have to be admitted to hospital.

Human infants begin to develop specific attachments to particular people around the third quarter of their first year of life. This is the time at which the infant begins to protest if handed to a stranger and tends to cling to the mother or other adults with whom he is familiar. The mother usually provides a secure base to which the infant can return, and, when she is present, the infant is bolder in both exploration and play than when she is absent. If the attachment figure removes herself, even briefly, the infant usually protests. Longer separations, as when children have been admitted to hospital, cause a regular sequence of responses first described by Bowlby. Angry protest is succeeded by a period of despair in which the infant is quietly miserable and apathetic. After a further period, the infant becomes detached and appears no longer to care about the absent attachment figure. This sequence of *protest, despair*, and *detachment* seems to be the standard response of the small child whose mother is removed.

The evidence is sufficiently strong for Bowlby to consider that an adult's capacity for making good relationships with other adults depends upon the individual's experience of attachment figures when a child. A child who from its earliest years is certain that his attachment figures will be available when he needs them, will develop a sense of security and inner confidence. In adult life, this confidence will make it possible for him to trust and love other human beings. In relationships between the sexes in which love and trust has been established, sexual fulfilment follows as a natural consequence.

However, attachment varies in quality and intensity, partly depending upon the mother's reaction to, and treatment of, her infant; and partly, no doubt, upon innate genetic differences. Although the overt response of an infant to the mother's departure may appear to be similar in different instances, the consequences of her prolonged absence may vary considerably from case to case. Research indicates that children brought up in institutions are more disruptive and demanding than children reared in nuclear families. It is likely, though not absolutely proven, that such children are less able to make intimate relationships when grown-up than those who have had the advantage of a close-knit, loving family. Experiments with separating infant monkeys from their mothers indicate that it is not difficult to produce an adult monkey which is incapable of normal social and sexual relationships. However, human beings are extraordinarily resilient, and even children who have been persistently isolated and ill-treated may be able to compensate for this if their environment changes for the better.

In Chapter 12 of the first volume of *Attachment and Loss*, Bowlby discusses the nature and function of attachment from the biological point of view. From his extensive knowledge of attachment behaviour in other species as well as in man, he concludes that the original function of attachment behaviour was protection from predators. First, he points out that isolated animals are more likely to be attacked by predators than animals which stay together in a group. Second, he draws attention to the fact that, in both man and other animals, attachment behaviour is particularly likely to be elicited when the individual is young, sick, or pregnant. These states all make the individual more vulnerable to attack. Third, situations which cause alarm invariably cause people to look around for others with whom to share the danger. In the case of modern man, the danger from predators has receded, but his response to other forms of threat remains the same.

This biological interpretation makes good sense. Modern man seems pre-programmed to respond to a number of stimuli in ways which were more appropriate to the life of a tribal hunter-gatherer than they are to urban Western man at the end of the twentieth century. This is notably so in the case of our aggressive responses to

10

what we consider threat, and also in the case of our paranoid suspicion of strangers. Both kinds of response may have been appropriate for our tribal ancestors, but are dangerous in times when we are menaced by the possibility of a nuclear holocaust.

Bowlby makes the important point that attachment is not the same as dependence. It is true that it takes human beings a very long time to grow up. The period from birth to sexual maturity constitutes nearly a quarter of the total lifespan, which itself is longer than that of any other mammal. Our early helplessness and extended childhood provide opportunity for learning from our elders, which is generally supposed to be the biological reason for the prolongation of immaturity in the human species. Man's adaptation to the world is dependent upon learning and the transmission of culture from one generation to the next. Dependence is at its maximum at birth, when the human infant is most helpless. In contrast, attachment is not evident until the infant is about six months old. Dependence gradually diminishes until maturity is reached: attachment behaviour persists throughout life. If we call an adult dependent, we imply that he is immature. But if he has no intimate attachments, we conclude that there is something wrong with him. In Western society, extreme detachment from ties with others is usually equated with mental illness. Chronic schizophrenics sometimes lead lives in which relationships with others play virtually no part at all. The capacity to form attachments on equal terms is considered evidence of emotional maturity. It is the absence of this capacity which is pathological. Whether there may be other criteria of emotional maturity, like the capacity to be alone, is seldom taken into account.

Anthropologists, sociologists, and psychologists all concur in regarding man as a social being who requires the support and companionship of others throughout his life. In addition to learning, social co-operation has played an essential part in man's survival as a species, just as it has in the survival of sub-human primates, like baboons and chimpanzees. As Konrad Lorenz pointed out, man is neither fleet of foot nor equipped by nature with a tough hide, powerful tusks, claws, or other natural weapons. In order to protect themselves from more powerful species and in order to succeed in hunting large animals, primitive men had to learn co-operation.

11

Their survival depended upon it. Modern man has moved a long way from the social condition of the hunter-gatherer, but his need for social interaction and for positive ties with others has persisted.

There are, therefore, many reasons for giving a high place to attachment in any hierarchy of human needs. Indeed, some sociologists would doubt whether the individual possesses any significance when considered apart from the family and social groups of which he is a member. Most members of Western society assume that close family ties will constitute an important part of their lives; that these ties will be supplemented by other loves and friendships; and that it is these relationships which will give their own lives significance. As Peter Marris has put it:

> The relationships that matter most to us are characteristically to particular people whom we love – husband or wife, parents, children, dearest friend – and sometimes to particular places – a home or personal territory that we invest with the same loving qualities. These specific relationships, which we experience as unique and irreplaceable, seem to embody most crucially the meaning of our lives.[4]

In Marris's view, these unique and irreplaceable relationships act as points of reference which help us to make sense of our experience. We are, as it were, embedded in a structure of which unique relationships are the supporting pillars. We take this so much for granted that we seldom define it, and may hardly be conscious of it until some important relationship comes to an end. As Marris points out, recently bereaved persons often feel, at any rate for a time, that the world has become *meaningless*. When we lose the person who is nearest and dearest to us, we may discover that the meaning of life was bound up with that person to a greater extent than we had supposed. This is the usual pattern; but we must also remember that some people, even after losing a spouse who was dear to them, feel a new sense of freedom and take on a new lease of life.

When Robert S. Weiss studied a number of people whose marriages had recently ended, and who had joined a group for single parents, he found, as might be expected, that, although they gained support from the group, they still complained of loneliness. No amount of friendship was enough to compensate for the loss of close attachment and emotional intimacy which they had experienced in marriage.

But, however crucial such relationships are for most people, it is not only *intimate* personal relationships which provide life with meaning. Weiss also studied married couples who, for one reason or another, had moved a considerable distance from the neighbourhood in which they had been living. Although their intimate attachments to their spouses were unimpaired, they were distressed at no longer feeling part of a group.[5]

In other words, whether or not they are enjoying intimate relationships, human beings need a sense of being part of a larger community than that constituted by the family. The modern assumption that intimate relationships are essential to personal fulfilment tends to make us neglect the significance of relationships which are not so intimate. Schizophrenics, and other individuals who are more or less totally isolated, are rightly regarded as pathological; but many human beings make do with relationships which cannot be regarded as especially close, and not all such human beings are ill or even particularly unhappy.

Social structures of the kind found in the army or in a business may not give individuals the same kind of satisfactions which they might obtain from intimate relationships, but they do provide a setting in which the individual feels he has a function and a place. Gellner's contention, referred to above, that modern society is so mobile and fluid that it has made many people feel disorientated and insecure, is to some extent countered by the fact that many workers are reluctant to abandon a familiar setting even if offered more rewarding opportunities. The fact that a man is part of a hierarchy, and that he has a particular job to carry out, gives his life significance. It also provides a frame of reference through which he perceives his relation with others. In the course of daily life, we habitually encounter many people with whom we are not intimate, but who nevertheless contribute to our sense of self. Neighbours, postmen, bank clerks, shop assistants, and many others may all be familiar figures with whom we daily exchange friendly greetings, but are generally persons about whose lives we know very little. Yet, if such a person disappears and is replaced by another, we feel some sense of loss, however transient. We say that we have become 'used to' so-and-so; but what we miss is mutual recognition, acknowledgement of each other's existence, and thus some affirmation, however slight, that each reciprocally contributes something to life's pattern.

Relationships of this kind play a more important role in the lives of most of us than is generally recognized. When people retire from work in offices or institutions, they miss the familiar figures who used to provide recognition and affirmation. It is generally accepted that most human beings want to be loved. The wish to be recognized and acknowledged is at least as important.

In Western societies today, a large number of people live lives in which intimate relationships play little part, however much they recognize the lack, or attempt to compensate for it in phantasy. Instead of being centred on spouse and children, their lives are based upon the office where, although they may not be loved, they are at least recognized and valued. People who have a special need to be recognized, perhaps because their parents accorded them little recognition in childhood, are attracted to office life for this reason. Although some types of work may require short periods of solitary concentration, most office workers spend relatively little time alone, without human interaction, and, for the majority, this seems to be an attractive feature of office life.

The importance which less intimate, comparatively superficial relationships play in the lives of most of us is also attested by the kind of conversations we have with acquaintances. When neighbours meet in the street, they may, especially in England, use the weather as an opening gambit. But if the exchange is at all prolonged, the conversation is likely to turn to talk of other neighbours. Even the most intellectual persons are seldom averse to gossip, although they may affect to despise it. It would be interesting to know what proportion of conversation consists of talking about the lives of other people, as compared with talking about books, music, painting, ideas or money. Even amongst the highly educated, the proportion cannot be small.

Failure to make, or to sustain, the kind of intimate attachments which the object-relations theorists maintain are the main source of life's meaning and satisfaction does not imply that a person is necessarily cut off from other, less intimate human relationships. Whilst it is certainly more difficult for most people to find meaning in life if they do not have close attachments, many people can and do lead equable and satisfying lives by basing them upon a mixture of work and more superficial relationships. Edward Gibbon, from whom I quoted in the Introduction, is a good example. We should also remember that exceptional people have suffered long periods of solitary confinement without coming to feel that their lives are meaningless, whilst others have deliberately sought weeks or months of solitude for reasons to which we shall return.

Bowlby, in the penultimate paragraph of the third and last volume of *Attachment and Loss*, writes:

> Intimate attachments to other human beings are the hub around which a person's life revolves, not only when he is an infant or a toddler or a schoolchild but throughout his adolescence and his years of maturity as well, and on into old age. From these intimate attachments a person draws his strength and enjoyment of life and, through what he contributes, he gives strength and enjoyment to others. These are matters about which current science and traditional wisdom are at one.[6]

I have been a consistent admirer of Bowlby's work since I first encountered it. Because of his insistence that psycho-analytic observations must be supported by objective studies, and because of his use of ethological concepts, he has done more than any other psycho-analyst to link psycho-analysis with science. But attachment theory, in my view, does less than justice to the importance of work, to the emotional significance of what goes on in the mind of the individual when he is alone, and, more especially, to the central place occupied by the imagination in those who are capable of creative achievement. Intimate attachments are *a* hub around which a person's life revolves, not necessarily *the* hub.

2

The Capacity to be Alone

'We must reserve a little back-shop, all our own, entirely free, wherein to establish our true liberty and principal retreat and solitude.'

Montaigne

In infancy and early childhood, attachment to parents or to parent substitutes is essential if the child is to survive, and secure attachment probably necessary if it is to develop into an adult capable of making intimate relationships with other adults on equal terms. Although broken homes are deplorably common in Western society, parents who are concerned about their children's well-being try to provide them with a stable, loving background which will promote secure attachment and the growth of self-confidence. In addition, most parents will try to ensure that their children have plenty of opportunity to encounter and to play with other children of the same age. In both sub-human primates and in human beings, secure attachment between mother and infant encourages exploratory behaviour. A child who is sure of his mother's availability will generally want to explore his immediate environment, play with toys, and come into contact with whatever else may be in the room, including other children. There is some evidence to suggest that children as young as eighteen months old benefit from being allowed to mix with their peers. It is certain that interaction with children of the same age provides opportunities for learning social skills which are not provided by interaction between parents and child.

For example, rough-and-tumble play, which is important in

16

learning how to handle aggression, is common between children of the same age, but rare between parent and child. Attitudes to sex are generally acquired from other children rather than learned from parents. The study of adults who complain of sexual difficulties often discloses that, as children, they were unusually isolated. Because they did not learn from other children that sexual curiosity and sexual impulses are universal, they grew up feeling themselves to be different from others; perhaps uniquely evil.

In Chapter 1, we saw that most adult human beings want both intimate relationships and the sense of belonging to a community. In childhood, secure attachment to parents or to parent-substitutes is vital; but relationships with other children also provide social experience of a kind which is irreplaceable.

There has been, and continues to be, a great deal of research on these two aspects of child development; but virtually no discussion of whether it is ever valuable for children to be alone. Yet if it is considered desirable to foster the growth of the child's imaginative capacity, we should ensure that our children, when they are old enough to enjoy it, are given time and opportunity for solitude. Many creative adults have left accounts of childhood feelings of mystical union with Nature; peculiar states of awareness, or 'Intimations of Immortality', as Wordsworth called them. Such accounts are furnished by characters as diverse as Walt Whitman, Arthur Koestler, Edmund Gosse, A. L. Rowse and C. S. Lewis. We may be sure that such moments do not occur when playing football, but chiefly when the child is on its own. Bernard Berenson's description is particularly telling. He refers to moments when he lost himself in 'some instant of perfect harmony'.

> In childhood and boyhood this ecstasy overtook me when I was happy out of doors. Was I five or six? Certainly not seven. It was a morning in early summer. A silver haze shimmered and trembled over the lime trees. The air was laden with their fragrance. The temperature was like a caress. I remember – I need not recall – that I climbed up a tree stump and felt suddenly immersed in Itness. I did not call it by that name. I had no need for words. It and I were one.[1]

A. L. Rowse describes similar experiences when he was a school-boy in Cornwall.

> I could not know then it was an early taste of aesthetic sensation, a kind of revelation which has since become a secret touchstone of experience for me, an inner resource and consolation. Later on, though still a schoolboy – now removed downhill to the secondary school – when I read Wordsworth's 'Tintern Abbey' and 'Intimations of Immortality', I realised that that was the experience he was writing about.[2]

Modern psychotherapists, including myself, have taken as their criterion of emotional maturity the capacity of the individual to make mature relationships on equal terms. With few exceptions, psycho-therapists have omitted to consider the fact that the capacity to be alone is also an aspect of emotional maturity.

One such exception is the psycho-analyst, Donald Winnicott. In 1958, Winnicott published a paper on 'The Capacity to be Alone' which has become a psycho-analytic classic. Winnicott wrote:

> It is probably true to say that in psycho-analytical literature more has been written on the *fear* of being alone or the *wish* to be alone than on the *ability* to be alone; also a considerable amount of work has been done on the withdrawn state, a defensive organization implying an expectation of persecution. It would seem to me that a discussion on the *positive* aspects of the capacity to be alone is overdue.[3]

In Chapter 1, I referred to Bowlby's work on the early attachment of the human infant to its mother, and to the sequence of *protest, despair*, and *detachment*, which habitually occurs when the infant's mother is removed. In normal circumstances, if no disastrous severance of the bond between mother and infant has occurred, the child gradually becomes able to tolerate longer periods of maternal absence without anxiety. Bowlby believes that confidence in the availability of attachment figures is gradually built up during the years of immaturity; more particularly during the period from the age of six

18

months to five years, when attachment behaviour is most readily elicited. However, sensitivity to the presence or absence of attachment figures continues until well into adolescence. Many middle-class English children who had experienced total security in early childhood have had their expectations rudely shattered when sent to boarding school at the age of seven or eight.

It is generally recognized that clinging behaviour is indicative of insecurity. The child who will not let the mother leave, even for short periods, is the child who has no confidence in her return. Conversely, the child who has developed trust in the availability of attachment figures is the child who can increasingly experience being left by such figures without anxiety. Thus, the capacity to be alone is one aspect of an inner security which has been built up over the early years. Although there are children who shun company and are pathologically isolated, that is, who are in the 'withdrawn state' referred to by Winnicott, a child who enjoys some measure of solitude should not be confused with such children. Some children who enjoy the solitary exercise of the imagination may develop creative potential.

Building up a sense of security can be seen as a process of conditioning. Repeated confirmation of the presence of attachment figures when needed conditions the child to favourable expectations of their future availability. Psycho-analysts usually refer to this process as *introjecting a good object*; meaning by this that the attachment figure has become part of the individual's inner world, and therefore someone on whom he can rely even though the person concerned is not actually present. This may seem far-fetched, but most people can think of times at which they have said to themselves, 'What would so-and-so do in this situation?' They are then relying upon someone who, although not there in reality, has been incorporated into their imaginative world as someone to turn to in a dilemma.

Winnicott suggests that the capacity to be alone in adult life originates with the infant's experience of being *alone in the presence of the mother*. He is postulating a state in which the infant's immediate needs, for food, warmth, physical contact and so on, have been satisfied, so that there is no need for the infant to be looking to the mother for anything, nor any need for her to be concerned with providing anything. Winnicott writes:

19

I am trying to justify the paradox that the capacity to be alone is based on the experience of being alone in the presence of someone, and that without a sufficiency of this experience the capacity to be alone cannot develop.[4]

Winnicott goes on to make the extremely interesting suggestion that

It is only when alone (that is to say, in the presence of someone) that the infant can discover his personal life.[5]

Infants, because they are immature, need the support of another person if their sense of being 'I', that is, a separate person with a separate identity, is to develop. Winnicott conceives that this begins to happen when the infant is able to be in the relaxed state which is constituted by the experience of being alone in the presence of the mother. After being in this state for a while, the infant will begin to experience a sensation or impulse. Winnicott suggests that

In this setting the sensation or impulse will feel real and be truly a personal experience.

Winnicott contrasts this feeling of personal experience with what he calls

a false life built on reactions to external stimuli.[6]

Throughout most of his professional life, Winnicott was particularly preoccupied with whether an individual's experience was authentic or inauthentic. Many of the patients whom he treated had, for one reason or another, learned as children to be over-compliant; that is, to live in ways which were expected of them, or which pleased others, or which were designed not to offend others. These are the patients who build up what Winnicott called a 'false self'; that is, a self which is based upon compliance with the wishes of others, rather than being based upon the individual's own true feelings and instinctive needs. Such an individual ultimately comes to feel that life is pointless and futile, because he is merely adapting to the world rather than experiencing it as a place in which his subjective needs can find fulfilment.

Although Winnicott's suppositions about the subjective experiences of infants are impossible to prove, I find his conceptions illuminating. He is suggesting that the capacity to be alone originally depends upon what Bowlby would call secure attachment: that is, upon the child being able peacefully to be itself in the presence of the mother without anxiety about her possible departure, and without anxiety as to what may or may not be expected by her. As the secure child grows, it will no longer need the constant physical presence of the mother or other attachment figure, but will be able to be alone without anxiety for longer periods.

But Winnicott goes further. He suggests that the capacity to be alone, first in the presence of the mother, and then in her absence, is also related to the individual's capacity to get in touch with, and make manifest, his own true inner feelings. It is only when the child has experienced a contented, relaxed sense of being alone with, and then without, the mother, that he can be sure of being able to discover what he really needs or wants, irrespective of what others may expect or try to foist upon him.

The capacity to be alone thus becomes linked with self-discovery and self-realization; with becoming aware of one's deepest needs, feelings, and impulses.

Psycho-analysis is also concerned with putting the individual in touch with his or her deepest feelings. The technique employed could be described as encouraging the individual to be alone in the presence of the analyst. This analogy particularly applies to the procedures used in the early days of psycho-analysis, before the analysis of transference became of such central importance (see Chapter 1). The use of the couch not only encouraged relaxation but also precluded eye contact between analysand and analyst. This prevented the analysand from being too preoccupied with the reactions of the analyst to what he was saying, and thus made it easier for him to concentrate upon his own inner world.

Some analysts still believe that providing a secure milieu in which the patient can explore and express his most intimate thoughts and feelings is at least as important as any interpretations which they may offer. One analyst whom I knew personally illustrated this point with the story of a patient whom he saw three times per week over a period of a year. At every session, the patient lay down upon the couch and plunged straight into free association. At the end of the year, the man pronounced himself cured, and proffered his grateful thanks. The analyst declared that, during the whole of this period, he had offered no interpretations whatever. Even if this particular story is slightly exaggerated, the analogy with what Winnicott postulates as taking place between the secure infant and the mother is striking.

As we have seen, patients in analysis can be helped to form better relationships with other people in the outside world by working through and understanding their relationship with the analyst. When a person is encouraged to get in touch with and express his deepest feelings, in the secure knowledge that he will not be rejected, criticized, nor expected to be different, some kind of rearrangement or sorting-out process often occurs within the mind which brings with it a sense of peace; a sense that the depths of the well of truth have really been reached. This process, which in itself contributes to healing, is facilitated by the analyst's providing a suitably secure milieu, but is not necessarily dependent upon the analyst's interpretations. The story of the patient who said he was cured despite, or because of, the silence of the analyst can be seen to contain a strong element of truth. The process of healing, in such cases, is very like the healing which may occur as part of the creative process in solitude.

Integration also takes place in sleep. We are all alone when we are asleep, even though we may be sharing a bed with a loved person. When faced with a problem to which there is no obvious answer, conventional wisdom recommends 'sleeping on it', and conventional wisdom is right. Most people have had the experience of being unable to make up their minds when faced with a difficult decision, and of going to bed with the decision still not taken. On waking in the morning, they often find that the solution has become so obvious that they cannot understand why they could not perceive it on the previous night. Some kind of scanning and re-ordering process has taken place during sleep, although the exact nature of this process remains mysterious.

Another example of integration which requires time, solitude, and, preferably, a period of sleep, is the process of learning. Students find that they cannot easily retain or reproduce material which they have tried to commit to memory immediately before taking an examination. On the other hand, material which has been learned at an earlier stage and 'slept on', is much more easily recalled. Some kind of reverberation around neuronal circuits must be linking new material to old material, and committing new material to the long-term memory store.

Although we spend about a third of our lives asleep, the reasons why we need sleep are not fully understood. That we do need it is certain. As interrogators long ago realized, depriving prisoners of sleep is a relatively quick method of breaking them down. Although a few exceptional people can, without deterioration, survive without sleep for quite long periods, the majority of previously normal human beings exhibit psychotic symptoms like delusions and hallucinations after only a few days and nights without sleep. It is also worth noting that many episodes of mental illness are preceded by periods of insomnia.

The integrating function of sleep may be linked with dreaming. In 1952, Nathaniel Kleitman discovered that there were two kinds of sleep, which can be shown by recording the electrical activity of the brain during sleep to follow a regular cycle. As subjects relax and fall asleep, the fairly rapid electrical waves which are characteristic of the brain's waking activity are replaced by slower, more ample waves. These slower waves are accompanied by slow, rolling eye movements which can easily be seen through the closed eyelids of the sleeper, and which are entirely involuntary. It is possible to record these eye movements at the same time as the brain waves. When people first go to sleep, they enter quite quickly a stage of deep sleep from which it is difficult to rouse them. After about thirty or forty minutes, they begin to sleep more lightly; the sleeper's breathing becomes faster and more irregular; there are small twitches of his face and fingertips, and his eyes make rapid movements as if he was actually looking at something. This phase of rapid-eye-movement sleep, or REM sleep as it is now called, lasts about ten minutes. Then the subject returns to sleeping more deeply. The whole cycle lasts about ninety minutes. Someone who sleeps for seven and a half hours generally spends between one and a half and two hours in this lighter, REM phase of sleep.

A high proportion of people who are awakened during REM sleep recall a dream, whereas very few of those awakened during the deeper phases of sleep do so. In other words, it looks as if most people dream every night for short periods every ninety minutes or so.

Following the discovery of the two varieties of sleep, it became possible to prevent people from dreaming whilst still allowing them an adequate period of sleep. Early experiments in depriving subjects of REM sleep suggested that not allowing dreams to occur produced a variety of symptoms, but later experiments have not confirmed this finding. However, those deprived of dreaming show an increased proportion of REM sleep to deep sleep when dream deprivation is discontinued.

The same phenomenon has been observed in people taking barbiturates, amphetamines, or alcohol. When the drugs are stopped, a rebound phenomenon occurs. The subject shows an increase in REM sleep as if he were trying to make up for what had been missing. According to William C. Dement, schizophrenics in remission show a particular need for REM sleep. After only two nights of dream deprivation they showed an excessive REM rebound. When not in remission, that is, when experiencing overt symptoms of schizophrenia like hallucinations and delusions, or when exhibiting types of bizarre behaviour characteristic of the illness, schizophrenics do not show REM rebound after two nights of deprivation.[7] If further experiments confirm that the overtly psychotic do not need dreams to the same extent as normal people, the old idea that schizophrenic illness is 'dreaming whilst being awake' becomes even more convincing. Conversely, although normal mortals do not become psychotic even if totally deprived of REM sleep, entering the mad world of dreams each night probably promotes mental health in ways we do not fully understand.

It seems clear that some kind of scanning or re-programming takes place in dreams which has a beneficial effect upon ordinary mental functioning. Dreaming seems to be biologically adaptive. Stanley Palombo suggests that dreams are concerned with matching past and present experience. He thinks that

> the dream compares the representation of an emotionally significant event of the past with the representation of an emotionally significant aspect of the previous day's experience.[8]

This information-processing function of the dream is concerned with allotting the new experience to the right slot in the permanent memory. Whether this model accounts for all dreams is dubious; but it goes some way to explaining why it is that in dreams, time is so often out of joint. If past and present are being compared, it is not surprising that, in the dream, they so often appear to be confused.

Another example of some kind of re-ordering process taking place in the brain can be discerned in the stage of the creative process which Graham Wallas called *incubation*. Wallas's first stage is *preparation*. The creative person develops some preliminary interest in a particular subject, collects material, and reads everything he can find about it. Next, a period of time intervenes during which the accumulated material simmers, or is unconsciously scanned, compared with other mental contents, organized, or elaborated. We do not understand what goes on during this period of incubation, but it is a necessary prelude to the next stage, that of *illumination*. This is the time at which the creative person has a new insight, discovers a solution to his problem, or in some other way finds that he can order the material which he has accumulated by employing an overriding principle or an all-embracing conception.

The time taken for incubation can vary from a few minutes to months or even years. Brahms said that, when a new idea occurred to him, he would turn to something else and perhaps think no more of the new idea for several months. When he took it up again, he would find that the idea had unconsciously assumed a different form at which he would begin working.

It would be absurd to suggest that the new idea was reverberating through the networks of the brain for several months to the exclusion of all else. The brain is highly complicated, and capable of carrying out a great many operations simultaneously. But the parallel with the scanning or sorting process which occurs spontaneously in dreams, or which is deliberately encouraged by prayer or meditation, is striking. What takes place in the circuitry of the brain is a mystery; but it can be confidently asserted that these processes require time, passivity, and preferably solitude. Creative people may or may not need the peace of being physically alone. Schubert and Mozart, for example, could concentrate on their ideas in circumstances which others would find distracting. But observers have generally noted that such people are greatly absorbed with their own thoughts even when in company. Winnicott's paradoxical description of 'being alone in the presence of' may be relevant not only to the infant with its mother, but also to those who are capable of intense concentration and preoccupation with their own inner processes even when surrounded by other people.

The fact that mental processes of the kind discussed above require time, and that incubation resulting in new insights may need long periods of gestation, may also be related to one factor which some researchers have singled out as characteristic of human intelligence. Intelligent behaviour has been defined as 'behaviour that is adaptively variable within the lifetime of the individual'.[9] It is the opposite of the kind of behaviour governed by pre-programmed patterns which is characteristic of many species further down the evolutionary scale. Behaviour determined by built-in responses to environmental stimuli is both automatic and immediate. Human behaviour, which is in most circumstances much more flexible, not only depends upon learning, and hence upon memory, but also upon the capacity *not* to respond immediately and automatically to a given stimulus. Stenhouse suggests that, if intelligent behaviour is to evolve from instinctive behaviour, three basic factors must be developed.

The most important factor is that which gives the individual animal the power *not to respond* in the usual way to the stimulus situation which previously initiated an instinctive sequence culminating in a consummatory act. This power not to respond may be absolute, or may be merely the ability to delay the

26

response – withhold it provisionally, as it were – but its absence would negate the very possibility of adaptive variability in behaviour.[10]

If the individual is to produce a new response to a given situation, he must be capable of learning and also of storing what he has learned. Stenhouse's second factor is the development of a central memory store in which items which are functionally related can be filed, and against which new experiences can be measured. We have already encountered Palombo's idea that dreams may be concerned with the process of sorting and comparing new experiences with past experiences.

Stenhouse's third factor is the development of some capacity to abstract or to generalize.

> There must be an ability for seeing similarities and differences, if some memory items rather than others are to be selected to act as modifiers of present behaviour.[11]

This capacity is present to some degree in all animals capable of learning from experience, but is particularly highly developed in man.

The idea that intelligent behaviour is dependent upon not responding immediately to any given situation can also be linked with the phenomena of dreaming. In dreams we may picture ourselves travelling, walking, running, fighting, or, in any number of other ways, being physically active. Yet in reality dreamers show little movement other than rapid eye movements and a few twitches of their limbs. There is an inhibition of the motor centres of the brain at the same time that the cortex shows increased electrical activity. Experiments in cats have shown that, if the part of the brain responsible for inhibiting the motor centres is destroyed, the animal will act out its dreams by showing aggressive or playful behaviour even whilst asleep. The inhibition of motor activity which occurs in dreams can be seen as one way of delaying immediate responses so that some kind of sorting activity can occur in the brain.

A comparable inhibition of motor activity occurs when we are awake and engaged in *thinking*. Thinking can be regarded as a

27

preliminary to action; a scanning of possibilities, a linking of concepts, a reviewing of possible strategies. Eventually, thinking results in some sort of physical action, even if this is no more energetic than pressing the keys of a typewriter. Whilst thinking is going on, this eventual action must be postponed. Many people find this postponement difficult, and engage in some kind of displacement activity whilst thinking, like walking up and down, smoking, or playing with a pencil. Thinking is predominantly a solitary activity, although others may be present when an individual is concentrating upon his own thoughts.

Another analogy to Winnicott's concept of the capacity to be alone is prayer. Prayer goes far beyond merely asking for benefits for oneself or for others. Prayer can be a public act of worship; but the person who prays in private feels himself to be alone in the presence of God. This is another way of putting the individual in touch with his deepest feelings. In some religions, no response to prayer from any supernatural being is even expected. Prayer is undertaken, not with the intention of influencing a deity, nor with any hope of prayers being directly answered, but in order to produce a harmonious state of mind. Prayer and meditation facilitate integration by allowing time for previously unrelated thoughts and feelings to interact. Being able to get in touch with one's deepest thoughts and feelings, and providing time for them to regroup themselves into new formations and combinations, are important aspects of the creative process, as well as a way of relieving tension and promoting mental health.

It appears, therefore, that some development of the capacity to be alone is necessary if the brain is to function at its best, and if the individual is to fulfil his highest potential. Human beings easily become alienated from their own deepest needs and feelings. Learning, thinking, innovation, and maintaining contact with one's own inner world are all facilitated by solitude.

3

The Uses of Solitude

'Dans le tumulte des hommes et des événements, la solitude était ma tentation. Maintenant, elle est mon amie. De quelle autre se contenter quand on a rencontré l'Histoire?'

Charles de Gaulle

The capacity to be alone is a valuable resource when changes of mental attitude are required. After major alterations in circumstances, fundamental reappraisal of the significance and meaning of existence may be needed. In a culture in which interpersonal relationships are generally considered to provide the answer to every form of distress, it is sometimes difficult to persuade well-meaning helpers that solitude can be as therapeutic as emotional support.

One distressing change in circumstances which is almost universally experienced is bereavement; of spouse, child, parent, or sibling. Research has confirmed the common-sense supposition that coming to terms with bereavement takes time; and has also disclosed that the process of mourning may be hindered by the various defensive measures which human beings employ when they wish to avoid experiencing painful feelings.

Some of these measures are reinforced and hallowed by the distaste which the English upper and middle classes traditionally show for overt expression of emotion. The man who has just lost a dearly loved wife, but who nevertheless goes to the office as usual, makes no reference to his loss, and perhaps works longer hours than usual, tends to be admired. This is partly because we prize stoicism; and partly because the sufferer who says nothing about his feelings is saving his fellows embarrassment. Many people do not know what to say to a bereaved person. If such a one himself behaves as if nothing has happened, his friends may thankfully conclude that he does not want them to express sympathy.

Admiration for the courage which such a person is displaying is misplaced. Every psychotherapist will have had the experience of treating patients in whom mourning has been delayed and uncompleted because they had tried to deal with their loss by adopting a stiff upper lip or a mask of indifference. When the dead person is mentioned during the course of psychotherapy, the patient will sometimes exhibit uncontrollable grief, although the loss may have taken place some months or years previously.

Objective studies have demonstrated that widows who do not show emotion shortly after bereavement suffer from more physical and psychological symptoms during the subsequent month; remain disturbed for longer; and, thirteen months after their loss, are still showing more disturbance than those who were able to 'break down' during the first week.[1]

Many cultures provide for a period of mourning by preventing the bereaved person from going to work or engaging in ordinary activities. In the last chapter, mention was made of certain psychic processes, like incubation, which require long periods of time for their completion. Mourning is another example of a process which may be very prolonged indeed. In rural Greece, bereaved women mourn for a period of five years. During this time, the bereaved woman wears black, visits the grave of the deceased daily, and begins by conducting conversations with the departed. Often, the grave is personified: rather than talk of visiting or tending the grave, a woman will speak of visiting her husband or daughter. The rituals demanded have the effect of emphasizing the reality of the loss.

Many Greek villagers subscribe to what can be called an indigenous theory of catharsis. They recognize that in spite of the desirability of immersing oneself fully in the emotions of pain, grief, and sorrow, the ultimate goal of a woman in mourning is to rid herself of these emotions through their repeated expression.[2]

The end of mourning, the final acceptance of death, takes place after the body is exhumed. The bones of the dead person are then collected, placed in a metal box, and join the bones of other villagers in the local ossuary.

A new social reality is constructed which enables the bereaved to inhabit more fully a world in which the deceased plays no part... This process is brought about through a gradual reduction in the intensity of the emotions associated with death, through the formation of new social relationships with new significant others, and through the constant confrontation with the objective facts of death, climaxing in the exhumation of the bones of the deceased. The result of this process is as complete an acceptance of the final and irreversible nature of death as is possible.[3]

Following bereavement, orthodox Jews are expected to stay at home, apart from a daily visit to the synagogue, whilst others feed and care for them. Although Murray Parkes casts some doubt upon how effective Jewish customs may be in some families, my own limited experience suggests that partial segregation of the mourner and the prohibition of normal working activities is beneficial. Coming to terms with loss is a difficult, painful, and largely solitary process which may be delayed rather than aided by distractions. Any rituals which underline the fact that bereavement is a profoundly traumatic event are helpful. In Great Britain today, religion is in decline, and there are few guidelines to indicate what is expected of mourners. When conventional periods of mourning were decreed, and the state of the mourner proclaimed by the adoption of black clothes, it was probably easier for the bereaved person to make the adjustment needed.

Although the support and sympathy of relatives and friends is helpful to bereaved persons, coming to terms with the loss of a loved person who was very close to one can only partially be shared. The process is essentially private, because it is so much concerned with intimacies which were not, and could not be, shared with others when the deceased partner was alive. The work of mourning is, by its very nature, something which takes place in the watches of the night and in the solitary recesses of the individual mind.

Mourning is one example of a long drawn out mental process leading to an eventual change of attitude. Instead of regarding life as necessarily bound up with, or even constituted by, the existence of an intimate relationship with the deceased person, the mourner comes to see matters differently. The mourner may or may not form new, intimate ties; but whether he or she does so or not, the mourner usually comes to realize that the significance of life is not entirely constituted by personal relationships; that the life of a person without intimate relationships also has meaning.

Changes of attitude take time because our ways of thinking about life and ourselves so easily become habitual. In the early days of psycho-analysis, analysts were reluctant to take on patients who were in their fifties or older, because it was thought that the possibility of bringing about changes in attitude were slender. In subsequent years, it has been realized that even elderly people are capable of change and innovation. Some people find it hard to adapt to any kind of change in circumstances; but this rigidity is more a characteristic of the obsessional personality than it is of being old.

Whether in young or old, changes of attitude are facilitated by solitude and often by change of environment as well. This is because habitual attitudes and behaviour often receive reinforcement from external circumstances. To take a trivial example, anyone who has attempted to give up smoking comes to realize that the wish for a cigarette often depends upon cues from the environment which recur at intervals. Finishing a meal; sitting down to work at a familiar desk; reaching for a drink after work is over – such trivial reinforcing stimuli are well known to everyone who has struggled with the habit. This is why many people find it easier to give up smoking when they go on holiday. In an unfamiliar place, where one no longer does the same thing at the same time each day, cues from the environment either disappear or lose some of their significance.

Holidays are escapes from the routine of ordinary day-to-day existence. When we feel in need of a holiday, we often refer to needing 'a change'. Holidays and the capacity to change march hand in hand. The word 'retreat' carries similar overtones of meaning.

Although retreat in the face of the enemy may precede defeat, it does not necessarily do so: *reculer pour mieux sauter* applies to a variety of mental and physical manoeuvres including sleep, rest, and recreation. The word 'retreat' itself may be used to indicate a period of time, and by extension a place, which is especially designed for religious meditation and quiet worship. The Retreat was the name given to one of the most famous British mental hospitals, founded in 1792 and still flourishing, in which the pioneer Samuel Tuke instituted a regime of tolerance, kindness, and minimum restraint. By providing a safe 'asylum' from the harassments of the world, it was hoped that salutary change in the disturbed minds of the mentally ill would come about.

This, too, was the concept underlying the 'rest cure' for mental disturbances promoted by Silas Weir Mitchell, an American neurologist who practised during the latter part of the nineteenth century. Its twentieth-century successor was 'continuous narcosis', a technique of keeping patients asleep by means of drugs for twenty or more hours out of the twenty-four. As we have seen, drugs, by inhibiting REM sleep, tend to prevent sleep from knitting up 'the ravell'd sleave of care' as effectively as it does unaided, which may be one reason why this treatment is no longer in use.

Both the 'rest cure' and continuous narcosis involved removal from relatives and partial isolation. Today, the fact that isolation can be therapeutic is seldom mentioned in textbooks of psychiatry. The emphasis is upon group participation, 'milieu therapy', ward meetings, staff–patient interaction, occupational therapy, art therapy, and every other means which can be devised of keeping the mentally ill constantly occupied and in contact with one another as well as with doctors and nurses. In the case of schizophrenic patients, who are too easily inclined to lose contact with the external world altogether, this ceaseless activity is probably beneficial. I am less persuaded of its value in depressed patients; and regret that the average mental hospital can make little provision for those patients who want to be alone and who would benefit from being so.

That solitude promotes insight as well as change has been recognized by great religious leaders, who have usually retreated from the world before returning to it to share what has been revealed

33

to them. Although accounts vary, the enlightenment which finally came to the Buddha whilst he was meditating beneath a tree on the banks of the Nairanjana river is said to have been the culmination of long reflection upon the human condition. Jesus, according to both St Matthew and St Luke, spent forty days in the wilderness undergoing temptation by the devil before returning to proclaim his message of repentance and salvation. Mahomet, during the month of Ramadan, each year withdrew himself from the world to the cave of Hera. St Catherine of Siena spent three years in seclusion in her little room in the Via Benincasa during which she underwent a series of mystical experiences before entering upon an active life of teaching and preaching.

Contemporary Western culture makes the peace of solitude difficult to attain. The telephone is an ever-present threat to privacy. In cities, it is impossible to get away from the noise of motor traffic, aircraft, or railways. This, of course, is not a new problem. City streets, before the invention of the automobile, may, intermittently, have been even noisier than our own. The iron-bound wheels of carts travelling over cobbles make more noise than rubber tyres on asphalt. But the general continuous level of noise in cities is constantly increasing, despite the attempts of legislation to curb it.

Indeed, noise is so ubiquitous that many people evidently feel uncomfortable in its absence. Hence, the menace of 'Muzak' has invaded shops, hotels, aircraft, and even elevators. Some car drivers describe driving as relaxing, simply because they are alone and temporarily unavailable to others. But the popularity of car radios and cassette players attests the widespread desire for constant auditory input; and the invention of the car telephone has ensured that drivers who install it are never out of touch with those who want to talk to them. In the next chapter, we shall look at some aspects of 'sensory deprivation'. As noise abatement enthusiasts have discovered, its opposite, sensory overload, is a largely disregarded problem. The current popularity of techniques like 'transcendental meditation' may represent an attempt to counterbalance the absence of silence and solitude which the modern urban environment inflicts upon us.

Removing oneself voluntarily from one's habitual environment promotes self-understanding and contact with those inner depths of being which elude one in the hurly-burly of day-to-day life. In the ordinary way, our sense of identity depends upon interaction both with the physical world and with other people. My study, lined with books, reflects my interests, confirms my identity as a writer, and reinforces my sense of what kind of person I consider myself to be. My relationships with my family, with colleagues, friends, and less intimate acquaintances, define me as a person who holds certain views and who may be expected to behave in ways which are predictable.

But I may come to feel that such habitually defining factors are also limiting. Suppose that I become dissatisfied with my habitual self, or feel that there are areas of experience or self-understanding which I cannot reach. One way of exploring these is to remove myself from present surroundings and see what emerges. This is not without its dangers. Any form of new organization or integration within the mind has to be preceded by some degree of disorganization. No one can tell, until he has experienced it, whether or not this necessary disruption of former patterns will be succeeded by something better.

The desire for solitude as a means of escape from the pressure of ordinary life and as a way of renewal is vividly illustrated by Admiral Byrd's account of manning an advanced weather base in the Antarctic during the winter of 1934. He insisted on doing this alone. He admits that his desire for this experience was not primarily the wish to make meteorological observations, although these constituted the ostensible reason for his solitary vigil.

> Aside from the meteorological and auroral work, I had no important purposes. There was nothing of that sort. Nothing whatever, except one man's desire to know that kind of experience to the full, to be by himself for a while and to taste peace and quiet and solitude long enough to find out how good they really are.[4]

Byrd was not escaping from personal unhappiness. He describes himself as having an extraordinarily happy private life. Nevertheless, the pressures of organizing a variety of expeditions during the previous fourteen years, combined with anxiety about raising money

35

for them and the inevitable publicity which surrounded his achievements, induced what he called 'a crowding confusion'. He reached a point at which his life appeared to him aimless. He felt that he had no time to read the books he wanted to read; no time to listen to the music he wanted to hear.

I wanted something more than just privacy in the geographical sense. I wanted to sink roots into some replenishing philosophy.[5]

He also admits that he wanted to test his powers of endurance in an existence more rigorous than anything he had yet experienced. His hopes for finding a new meaning in life were realized. In his diary for 14 April, he records:

Took my daily walk at 4 p.m. today in 89° of frost . . . I paused to listen to the silence . . . The day was dying, the night being born – but with great peace. Here were imponderable processes and forces of the cosmos, harmonious and soundless. Harmony, that was it! That was what came out of the silence – a gentle rhythm, the strain of a perfect chord, the music of the spheres, perhaps.

It was enough to catch that rhythm, momentarily to be myself a part of it. In that instant I could feel no doubt of man's oneness with the universe. The conviction came that that rhythm was too orderly, too harmonious, too perfect to be a product of blind chance – that, therefore, there must be purpose in the whole and that man was part of that whole and not an accidental off-shoot. It was a feeling that transcended reason; that went to the heart of man's despair and found it groundless. The universe was a cosmos, not a chaos; man was as rightfully a part of that cosmos as were the day and night.[6]

On another occasion, he refers to feeling 'more *alive*' than at any other time in his life. Unfortunately, Byrd became ill, poisoned by the fumes of a faulty stove. The latter part of his account is largely concerned with his fight against physical weakness rather than with his oceanic, mystical experience. But in spite of the nearly fatal outcome of his experience, Byrd, four years after his ordeal was over, was able to write:

> I did take away something that I had not fully possessed before: appreciation of the sheer beauty and miracle of being alive, and a humble set of values . . . Civilization has not altered my ideas. I live more simply now, and with more peace.[7]

What Byrd is describing is a mystical experience of unity with the universe which is familiar to those who have read similar accounts furnished by religious adepts. As William James wrote in *The Varieties of Religious Experience*,

> This overcoming of all the usual barriers between the individual and the Absolute is the great mystic achievement. In mystic states we both become one with the Absolute and we become aware of our oneness.[8]

In his paper *Civilization and Its Discontents*, Freud refers to the correspondence which he had with Romain Rolland, to whom he had sent his book dismissing religion, *The Future of an Illusion*. Rolland complained that Freud had not understood the true source of religious sentiments, which Rolland affirmed to be 'a sensation of "eternity", a feeling as of something limitless, unbounded – as it were, "oceanic" '. Freud states that he can find no trace of any such feeling in himself. He goes on to say that what Rolland was describing was 'a feeling of an indissoluble bond, of being one with the external world as a whole'.[9]

Freud proceeds to compare this feeling with the height of being in love, in which a man may feel that he is one with his beloved. As might be expected, Freud regards the oceanic feeling as a regression to an earlier state: that of the infant at the breast, at a period before the infant has learned to distinguish his ego from the external world. According to Freud, this is a gradual process.

He must be very strongly impressed by the fact that some

sources of excitation, which he will later recognize as his own bodily organs, can provide him with sensations at any moment, whereas other sources evade him from time to time – among them what he desires most of all, his mother's breast – and only reappear as a result of his screaming for help. In this way, there is for the first time set over against the ego an 'object', in the form of something which exists 'outside' and which is only forced to appear by a special action.[10]

Freud is not impressed with Rolland's claim that the oceanic feeling is the source of religious sentiments. Freud claimed that man's need for religion originated with the infant's sense of helplessness: 'I cannot think of any need in childhood as strong as the need for a father's protection.'[11] However, he admits that the oceanic feeling may have become connected with religion at a later stage, and surmises that 'oneness with the universe' is

a first attempt at a religious consolation, as though it were another way of disclaiming the danger which the ego recognizes as threatening it from the external world.[12]

Although we are all subject to self-deception and to a variety of wish-fulfilling illusions, Freud's account of the oceanic feeling and its meaning is less than satisfactory. It seems a more important experience than he admits. Defensive strategies and escapist wish-fulfilments generally appear superficial and partially inauthentic even to those who are employing them. But those who have experienced the states of mind recorded by Byrd and by William James record them as having had a permanent effect upon their perception of themselves and of the world; as being the profoundest moments of their existence. This is true both of those who have felt the sense of unity with the universe and of those who have felt the sense of unity with a beloved person.

Freud was right in seeing a close similarity between these two varieties of unity, but wrong in dismissing them as merely regressive. Such feelings are intensely subjective, and are hardly susceptible of measurement or scientific scrutiny. But to feel totally at one with another person, or totally at one with the universe, are such deep experiences that, although they may be transient, they cannot be dismissed as mere evasions or defences against unwelcome truths.

It is certainly possible that the oceanic feeling may be related to early infantile experience of unity with the mother. Merging of subject and object, of the self with Nature or with a beloved person, may be a reflection of the original unity with the mother with which we all begin life and from which we gradually become differentiated as separate entities. But Freud, perhaps because he himself denies ever having had such an experience, treats it as illusory; whilst those who describe ecstatic feelings of unity usually portray them as more intensely real than any other feelings which they can recall.

Ecstatic experiences of unity are sometimes connected with an acceptance of, or even a wish for, death. Wagner, who idealized erotic passion as the prototype of ecstatic unity, ends *The Flying Dutchman* with the redemption of the wanderer by Senta's love and suicide. The original stage directions demand that the transfigured couple shall be seen rising toward heaven in the glow of the setting sun above the wreck of the Dutchman's ship. *Götterdämmerung*, the last of the four operas which comprise *The Ring of the Nibelung*, ends with Brünnhilde mounting her horse and leaping into the flames of Siegfried's funeral pyre to join him in death. *Tristan und Isolde* ends with the *Liebestod*; with Isolde expiring in ecstasy on the corpse of Tristan. Wagner himself wrote of this:

> one thing alone left living: desire, desire unquenchable, longing forever rebearing itself – a fevered craving; one sole redemption – death, surcease of being, the sleep that knows no waking! . . . Its power spent, the heart sinks back to pine of its desire – desire without attainment; for each fruition sows the seeds of fresh desire, till in its final lassitude the breaking eye beholds a glimmer of the highest bliss: it is the bliss of quitting life, of being no more, of last redemption into that wondrous realm from which we stray the furthest when we strive to enter it by fiercest force. Shall we call it death? Or is it not night's wonder world, whence – as the story says – an ivy and a vine sprang up in locked embrace o'er Tristan and Isolde's grave?[13]

39

In his book *Beyond Endurance*, Glin Bennet describes the oceanic feelings of being at one with oneself and with the universe which accompany solitary journeys. The search for such experiences constitutes one reason for such journeys; but they may carry with them the temptation of suicide. Bennet quotes the case of Frank Mulville, a single-handed sailor who, in the Caribbean, had an overwhelming desire to look back at his beautiful yacht, and let himself over the side in order to do so. The sight so inspired him that he was seriously tempted to let go the rope and merge himself for ever with the sea.[14]

Bennet gives another example of the same danger which was recorded by Christiane Ritter. She spent a number of days entirely alone in a hut in the north-western part of Spitzbergen, when her husband and his companion were away hunting. She described a variety of illusions and hallucinations, including a feeling that she was somehow identified with the moonlight. She had a dream of water flowing under the ice which seemed to be enticing her. After being alone for nine days, she did not dare venture out of the hut.[15]

Keats captures both ecstasy and its link with death in his 'Ode to a Nightingale'.

> Darkling I listen; and for many a time
> I have been half in love with easeful Death,
> Call'd him soft names in many a mused rhyme,
> To take into the air my quiet breath;
> Now more than ever seems it rich to die,
> To cease upon the midnight with no pain,
>   While thou art pouring forth thy soul abroad
>   In such an ecstasy![16]

The association of ecstatic states of mind with death is understandable. These rare moments are of such perfection that it is hard to return to the commonplace, and tempting to end life before tensions, anxieties, sorrows, and irritations intrude once more.

For Freud, dissolution of the ego is nothing but a backward look at an infantile condition which may indeed have been blissful, but which represents a paradise lost which no adult can, or should wish to, regain. For Jung, the attainment of such states are high achievements; numinous experiences which may be the fruit of long struggles to understand oneself and to make sense out of existence. At a later point in this book, Jung's concept of individuation, of the union of opposites within the circle of the individual psyche, will be further explored.

4

Enforced Solitude

'The worst solitude is to be destitute of sincere friendship.'
Francis Bacon

In the last chapter, some of the beneficent effects of freely chosen solitude were outlined. Solitude which is imposed by others is a different matter. Solitary confinement is generally perceived as a harsh penalty, and when solitary confinement is accompanied by threats, uncertainty, lack of sleep and other measures, the victim may suffer disruption of normal mental function without being able to muster any compensatory reintegration. On the other hand, less rigorous conditions of imprisonment have sometimes proved fruitful. Being cut off from the distractions of ordinary life encourages the prisoner with creative potential to call upon the resources of his imagination. As we shall see, a variety of authors have begun writing in prison, where this has been allowed; or have passed through periods of spiritual and mental turmoil which have later found expression in their works.

Punitive imprisonment for criminals was initially conceived as a method of enforcing repentance; a humane alternative to horrific physical punishments like amputation, branding, flogging, breaking on the wheel and other tortures or brutal methods of execution. Local jails, in which vagrants, alcoholics, beggars and other nuisances could be temporarily confined were in widespread use for centuries. Jails were also used to house accused persons awaiting

trial, and convicted criminals awaiting punishment. But imprisonment as a specific punishment for serious offenders is a comparatively recent sanction. Norval Morris claims that

> the prison is an American invention, an invention of the
> Pennsylvania Quakers of the last decade of the eighteenth
> century... In their 'penitentiary' the Quakers planned to
> substitute the correctional specifics of isolation, repentance, and
> the uplifting effects of scriptural injunction and solitary Bible
> reading for the brutality and inutility of capital and corporal
> punishments. These three treatments – removal from corrupt-
> ing peers, time for reflection and self-examination, the guidance
> of biblical precepts – would no doubt have been helpful to the
> reflective Quakers who devised the prison, but relatively few of
> them ever became prisoners. The suitability of these remedies
> for the great mass of those who subsequently found their way to
> the penitentiary is more questionable.[1]

This is, of course, ironic understatement. Today, imprisonment is
generally recognized as being worse than useless in the fight against
crime. Its deterrent effect is dubious, its reforming effect negligible.
Prisons reinforce a criminal subculture by herding offenders
together. Long sentences, by separating criminals from their families,
lead to the break-up of family ties. Since the availability of family and
social support after release is one of the few factors known to make
reconviction for further crimes less likely, protracted imprisonment
actually increases the probability that subsequent offences will be
committed. Availability of suitable employment after release is
another factor which has been shown to diminish the chances of
reconviction. But most societies are so unwilling to spend money on
prisons that programmes for retraining prisoners or teaching them
new industrial skills are quite inadequate.

In ordinary British prisons, solitary confinement is seldom used
except as a comparatively brief punishment for serious violence. In
France, at least until recently, solitary confinement was used during
the initial part of life sentences, though tempered with some
participation in group activities. Originally, isolation was supposed to

encourage remorse and subsequent reform by forcing the convict to confront his own conscience. The single cells in which sentences were served were modelled upon those of the monastery. But prison authorities came to realize that isolation imposed considerable stress upon prisoners, and led to mental instability and unruly behaviour. Although association with other criminals carried the likelihood of reinforcing the choice of crime as a way of life, this disadvantage came to be considered the lesser of two evils. Long periods of isolation became recognized as cruel as well as ineffective.

Moreover, since the Second World War, prisons in Britain have become so permanently overcrowded that solitary meditation upon the evils of their crimes is no longer a practical possibility for prisoners, even if it were thought desirable. Today, cells designed for one prisoner have to be occupied by three. This contravenes the Standard Minimum Rules for the Treatment of Prisoners adopted by the United Nations Congress of 1955, which states that each prisoner shall occupy by night a cell or room by himself, except in conditions of *temporary* overcrowding.

In Denmark, a high proportion of detainees awaiting trial for criminal offences are kept in solitary confinement whilst their cases are being investigated. No other European country uses isolation in pre-trial detention to this extent, although there have been recent complaints of similar practices in Sweden. Periods of isolation vary from two weeks to four weeks or more; but several instances are known of detainees spending between one and two years in isolation.

Detainees spend twenty-three out of every twenty-four hours in a small cell. They are allowed two half-hour periods of exercise alone, but their solitude is otherwise interrupted only by visits to the lavatory and the delivery of meals. In spite of being allowed books, radio and television, letters, and, in some cases, supervised visits, even this degree of isolation often has deleterious effects upon mental functioning. Many detainees complain of restlessness, insomnia, inability to concentrate, and partial failure of memory. They find it difficult to measure the passage of time, and invent obsessional rituals to mark the hours and give structure to the day. When these rituals are interrupted by interrogation or by visits from a lawyer, they become intensely anxious. Self-mutilation and suicidal attempts are common. In 1980, seven out of ten successful suicides in prison were those of pre-trial detainees. If isolation is prolonged beyond a few weeks, many detainees complain of inexplicable fatigue. Some become almost totally apathetic; others lose control of their emotions to the point of believing that they are going mad. Even when removed from isolation, many symptoms persist. Detainees complain that they cannot remember what they read; that they cannot even follow a television programme. It is hardly surprising that some make inaccurate or contradictory statements to the police when being interrogated. After prolonged periods of isolation, many fear resuming social relationships and dare not risk intimacy. Such impairment of the ability to relate to others may persist for years.[2]

If such dire mental sequelae follow short periods of isolation which, in other respects, are comparatively humane, it is not hard to imagine how much worse are the effects of solitary confinement by totalitarian regimes in which the most elementary human rights are disregarded. The paper by Lawrence Hinkle and Harold Wolff on the techniques of interrogation and indoctrination employed by Communist states has become a classic, and I have drawn heavily on their account.[3]

The usual procedure is as follows. A person suspected of crimes against the State, that is, of being a political dissident, is placed under surveillance. So are his friends and associates. The suspect often becomes aware of this scrutiny, and suffers acute anxiety as a consequence. When sufficient 'evidence' has been accumulated, the state police proceed to arrest him. Anyone thus arrested is assumed to be guilty, although the crimes of which he is accused are never specified. The arrest usually takes place in the middle of the night. Prisoners whose cases are relatively unimportant may be confined in cells with other prisoners, who are often informers. But prisoners from whom information is required, or who are destined for public trial, are placed in solitary confinement. The cell is small. It usually has only one window which is placed above eye-level so that the prisoner can see nothing of the external world. But the door of the cell contains a peep-hole through which the prisoner can be observed at any time without his knowledge:

45

At all times except when he is eating, sleeping, exercising, or being interrogated, the prisoner is left strictly alone in his cell. He has nothing to do, nothing to read, and no one to talk to. Under the strictest regimen, he may have to stand or sit in his cell in a fixed position all day. He may sleep only at hours prescribed for sleep. Then he must go to bed promptly when told, and must lie in a fixed position upon his back with his hands outside the blanket. If he deviates from this position, the guard outside will awaken him and make him resume it. The light in his cell burns constantly. He must sleep with his face constantly toward it.[4]

Usually, the temperature of the cell is too cold for comfort, although it may sometimes be overheated. The food provided is unpalatable, and hardly enough to maintain nutrition. The combination of partial starvation, deprivation of sleep, uncomfortable temperatures, and continuous, intense anxiety combine to undermine the resistance of all but the most robust of prisoners.

During the first three weeks of this regime, most prisoners become intensely anxious and restless. They are not allowed to talk to the guards, nor to have any contact with other prisoners. They are given no information about what is to happen to them, and no information about what may happen to their families and friends. Many prisoners find that *uncertainty* is the worst torment which they experience.

After about four weeks, most prisoners realize that their protests, enquiries and requests are entirely fruitless. They are experiencing in reality what, for most of us, is only a phantasy; the basic human nightmare of being entirely helpless in the hands of malignant persecutors. This, I believe, is one of the fundamental fears of mankind; dating perhaps from earliest infancy, when every human being is totally dependent upon, and at the mercy of, persons who are much more powerful than himself.

At this point, many prisoners become profoundly depressed. Some become confused and hallucinated. Others cease from any kind of spontaneous activity, stop caring about their personal appearance and habits, and enter upon a state resembling depressive stupor.

Since the only human relationship available is that with the interrogator, many prisoners at first welcome sessions of interrogation and seek to prolong them. When the prisoner discovers that the interrogator is invariably dissatisfied with the account he has given of himself and his 'crimes', and begins to suffer under various forms of coercion applied to him, interrogation sessions become a nightmare rather than a welcome relief from isolation. Prolonged standing, which causes excruciating pain, followed by impairment of the circulation and renal failure, is commonly used. Cruder methods of physical torture, though officially forbidden, may also be employed. These periods of hostile interrogation and intense pressure alternate with periods of apparently relaxed friendliness, in which the prisoner is better treated. Since the interrogator remains the only human being with whom the prisoner has any contact, a relationship springs up between them. The prisoner may even develop feelings of sympathy toward the interrogator, who may have persuaded him that he is only doing his duty; that it is as distasteful to himself as it is to the prisoner, and that, if only the prisoner will sign a full confession of the 'crimes' attributed to him, the unpleasant business of interrogation will be over. Hinkle and Wolff write:

> There are instances of prisoners who signed depositions largely out of sympathy for their interrogators, because they felt that these men would be punished if a proper deposition were not forthcoming. In other words, the warm and friendly feelings which develop between the prisoner and the interrogator may have a powerful influence on the prisoner's behavior.[5]

Even when positive feelings towards the interrogator are not involved, nearly all prisoners will, in the end, sign a deposition admitting what Communist laws define as 'crimes against the State', rather than face further interrogation, isolation, and torture.

These techniques for eliciting confessions were developed empirically over many years. They are refinements of methods employed by the Czarist secret police. Isolation plays a prominent part in the procedure. Firstly, it brings about a partial disruption of mental functioning; and secondly, it encourages dependence upon the interrogator, and thus inclines the prisoner toward compliance.

Although very few prisoners thus treated refuse to sign a confession, there are some notable exceptions. Dr Edith Bone has left a record of her extraordinary toughness and resilience in her book *Seven Years Solitary*.[6]

Dr Bone was over sixty when she was arrested in Hungary in 1949. A notable linguist, she had been invited to Hungary to translate English scientific books into Hungarian. She herself had joined the Communist Party in 1919. She was accused of being a British agent, but refused to make a false confession or in any way to collaborate with her interrogators. This elderly lady spent seven years in prison before she was finally released in November 1956. For three of those years she was denied access to books or writing materials. The cell in which she was first confined was bitterly cold and had no window. Worse was to come. For five months she was kept in a cellar in total darkness. The walls ran with water or were covered with fungus; the floor was deep in excrement. There was no ventilation. Dr Bone invented various techniques for keeping herself sane. She recited and translated poetry, and herself composed verses. She completed a mental inventory of her vocabulary in the six languages in which she was fluent, and went for imaginary walks through the streets of the many cities which she knew well. Throughout these and other ordeals, Dr Bone treated her captors with contempt, and never ceased to protest her innocence. She is not only a shining example of courage which few could match, but also illustrates the point that a well-stocked, disciplined mind can prevent its own disruption.

Similar techniques for preserving normal mental functions were employed by Christopher Burney, who describes his imprisonment in France in his book *Solitary Confinement*.[7] He also used imaginary walks and inventories to keep his mental faculties employed. In addition, he noted the vital importance for prisoners of keeping some area of decision, however small, which is entirely their own. Even the prisoner who agrees to be totally at the mercy of his captors can retain some degree of autonomy: by for example deciding whether to eat the bread he is given, or to save it for future consumption. On such apparently trivial decisions may depend whether or not the prisoner retains any sense of being an independent entity.

Although, for the most part, prisoners in the Nazi concentration

48

camps were not held in solitary confinement, the importance of retaining some capacity for independent decision-making is also stressed by Bruno Bettelheim. From his own observations when he was a prisoner in Dachau and Buchenwald, Bettelheim concluded that the prisoners who gave up and died were those who had abandoned any attempt at personal autonomy; who acquiesced in their captors' aim of dehumanizing and exercising total control over them.

In the concentration camps, efforts to deprive the prisoners of even the smallest remnants of their autonomy were particularly vicious and all-pervasive. Nevertheless the system succeeded only to various degrees, affecting some aspects of one's life more than others. In the measure that the prisoner was deprived of autonomy it brought about a commensurately severe personality disintegration, both in his inner life and in his relations to others.[8]

Another wonderful example of the deliberate exercise of recall in a well-furnished mind in order to prevent breakdown is given by Yehudi Menuhin. At the end of the war, when the Germans were rounding up the Jews in Budapest, the mother of Antal Dorati, the conductor,

found herself herded into a small room with dozens of others, where they were kept for many days with no food and no facilities of any kind. Most of the others went out of their minds, but she kept sane by methodically going through the four parts of each of the Beethoven quartets, which she knew individually by heart.[9]

Part of the mental disruption caused by imprisonment, and more especially by solitary confinement, is the result of what has come to be known as *sensory deprivation*. During waking hours, the brain only functions efficiently if perceptual stimuli from the external world are being received. Our relationship to the environment and our understanding of it depend upon the information we gain through our senses. When asleep, our perceptions of the external world are greatly reduced, although significant sounds, like the cry of a child, may still arouse us. We enter the fantastic world of dreams; an hallucinatory, subjective world which is not dependent upon memory in the here-and-now, but which is governed by our previous experience, by our wishes, our fears, and our hopes.

Research into sensory deprivation began in the early 1950s, as part of an enquiry into Communist methods of obtaining confessions by so-called 'brainwashing'. Volunteers were confined in sound-proof, darkened rooms, and required to lie still on a bed, except when eating or using the lavatory. In more stringent experiments, subjects were suspended in warm water and required to inhibit all movement so as to receive as little information as possible from the skin and muscles, as well as being deprived of sight and sound. Since the subjects were volunteers, arrangements were made by which they could terminate the experiment at will if they found such conditions intolerable.

Although the results of such experiments varied to some extent according to the methods employed, the general consequences can be summarized.

First, intellectual performance deteriorated, especially if subjects were asked to undertake anything new or 'creative'. Many reported difficulty in concentration, and were unable to pursue a connected train of thought. Some complained of insistent, obsessional thoughts which they could not control. Others abandoned any attempt at coherent thought and gave themselves up to daydreams.

Second, suggestibility was greatly increased. In one experiment, susceptibility to propaganda was shown to increase eightfold as compared with subjects under normal conditions exposed to the same material. When a person is receiving very little information, what he does receive makes a more powerful impression; a fact well appreciated by totalitarian regimes which control the Press.

Third, many volunteers experienced visual hallucinations, and a few reported auditory or tactile hallucinations.

Fourth, a number of volunteers experienced panic attacks. Some suffered from irrational fears; for example, of becoming blind. Others became convinced that the experimenters had abandoned them. One volunteer demanded early release because his mind became flooded with such unpleasant memories of childhood that he could not bear it. Not even voluntarily chosen isolation is always tolerable.

At Princeton, where some of the most extensive studies of sensory deprivation were carried out on their own students, the researchers ran out of volunteers during the summer, when most Princeton students were away. Volunteers were recruited from other colleges which, unlike Princeton, ran summer schools. This venture proved a failure. In spite of being paid for their time, the volunteers from outside Princeton nearly all demanded early release from the conditions of sensory deprivation. Whereas the Princeton students knew and trusted the experimenters who were in charge of the investigation, the volunteers from further afield had no such confidence.

This last point is worth emphasis. It illustrates the fact that the same conditions of isolation or sensory deprivation can have a very different impact according to circumstances.

Certain kinds of illness or injury demand treatment which involves reduction of sensory input. This may cause mental distress of a severe kind. For example, the treatment of a badly burned patient may involve complete immobilization and extensive bandaging, sometimes including bandages over the eyes. Patients in this condition may have to have all their physical needs attended to by nurses. Psychotic episodes have often been reported in such patients.

Eye surgery is well known to provoke psychiatric symptoms, especially when both eyes have to be covered, and when immobilization is also required, as after repair of a torn retina.

Heart surgery sometimes involves prolonged immobilization, helplessness, and being connected to a number of life-support machines. Oxygen tents may isolate the patient still further from normal sensory input. Under such circumstances, it is not surprising that delirious states have been reported.

Blindness and deafness have both been recognized as causal agents in mental illness. Deafness, especially, is apt to provoke paranoid ideas of being talked about, disparaged, or cheated. In contrast, partial sensory deprivation of this kind, by compelling the

51

subject to look inward, may produce positive effects similar to those described by Admiral Byrd.

Beethoven's deafness probably began in 1796, when he was twenty-six years old. It took some time for it to become severe, and Beethoven continued to perform in public, with increasing difficulty, until around 1814. He began to use an ear trumpet in 1816. The Conversation Books, used so that visitors could communicate with him in writing, date from 1818. During the first two or three years of the nineteenth century, Beethoven went through agonies of anxiety about his hearing and his health in general, which he expressed in letters to friends and in the famous Heiligenstadt Testament of 1802, addressed to his brothers, and found amongst his papers after his death.

> But what a humiliation for me when someone standing next to me heard a flute in the distance and *I heard nothing*, or someone heard a *shepherd singing* and again I heard nothing. Such incidents drove me almost to despair; a little more of that and I would have ended my life – it was only *my art* that held me back.[10]

Beethoven's deafness increased his mistrust of other human beings, his irascibility, and his difficulty in making close relationships. However, one of his recent biographers writes:

> But there may be a sense in which deafness played a positive role in his creativity, for we know that deafness did not impair and indeed may even have heightened his abilities as a composer, perhaps by its exclusion of piano virtuosity as a competing outlet for his creativity, perhaps by permitting a total concentration upon composition within a world of increasing auditory seclusion. In his deaf world, Beethoven could experiment with new forms of experience, free from the intrusive sounds of the external environment; free from the rigidities of the material world; free, like the dreamer, to combine and recombine the stuff of reality, in accordance with his desires, into previously undreamed-of forms and structures.[11]

Some of Beethoven's later experiments are discussed in Chapter 11.

Goya is another example of a creative man of genius whose art owed a good deal of its originality to deafness. Born in 1746, Goya became the most fashionable and successful artist in Spain; a court painter, and deputy director of painting at the Royal Academy of Madrid. But, in 1792, Goya contracted an illness which left him deaf. He turned from painting portraits to works in which, as he himself wrote, he found more scope for invention and phantasy. His satirical etchings, *Los Caprichos*, were succeeded by *Los Desastres de la guerra*, representing his reaction to the horrors of the Napoleonic invasion. During 1820–23, he decorated the walls of his house, the Quinta del Sordo (House of the Deaf Man), with the so-called 'black paintings' now in the Prado. André Malraux writes:

> To allow his genius to become apparent to himself it was necessary that he should dare to *give up aiming to please*. Cut off from everyone by deafness he discovered the vulnerability of the spectator, he realized that the painter has only to struggle with himself and he will become, sooner or later, the conqueror of all.[12]

Goya had a horrific imagination. His isolation, induced by deafness, impelled him to record his nightmare visions, his despair at human folly and wickedness, his hatred of tyranny, and his compassion for human suffering, with an intensity achieved by no other artist. His ghastly picture of 'Saturn devouring his Children' adorned a wall of his dining-room. It is difficult to understand how a man obsessed with such horrors could live with himself; but Goya was as tough a man as has ever existed. At the age of eighty-two he wrote that he could neither see nor write nor hear: 'I have nothing left but the will – and that I have in abundance.'[13]

We saw earlier that, under conditions of partial sensory deprivation, doubts about the integrity of persons to whom one has entrusted oneself as patient or as paid volunteer are easily aroused. It is therefore not surprising that enforced solitude imposed by enemies often has devastating effects. Intense anxiety and uncertainty about the future combine with fear of torture and isolation to disrupt the normal functions of the mind. The effects of such disruption may persist for months or years.

In Northern Ireland, sensory deprivation was deliberately used as part of the technique employed in the interrogation of suspected terrorists. The procedures were as follows. The heads of the detainees were covered with a thick black hood, except when they were being interrogated. They were subjected to a continuous, monotonous noise of such volume that communication with other detainees was impossible. They were required to stand facing a wall with legs apart, leaning on their fingertips. In addition, they were deprived of sleep during the early days of the operation, and given no food or drink other than one round of bread and one pint of water at six-hourly intervals. If they sought rest by propping their heads against the wall they were prevented from doing so. If they collapsed, they were picked up and compelled to resume the required posture.

Sound-proof, light-proof rooms of the kind used in research into sensory deprivation are very expensive; but the techniques employed in Northern Ireland proved to be effective substitutes. The hoods prevented the men from receiving any visual information. A machine ensured that they received no auditory information other than a loud, monotonous noise. The posture against the wall reduced kinaesthetic information from skin and muscles. Thus, the detainees were effectively isolated and perceptually deprived, in spite of being subjected to these techniques in the same room as others.

The effects were devastating. Partial starvation, which causes rapid loss of weight, combined with deprivation of sleep and an uncomfortable posture are by themselves enough to cause extreme stress and some disruption of brain function, even without additional deprivation of auditory and visual information. Subject to breaks for bread and water and visits to the lavatory, some men were kept against the wall continuously for fifteen or sixteen hours. Many experienced hallucinations and believed that they were going mad. Afterwards, some said that they would prefer to die rather than face further interrogation.

Psychiatric examination of these men after their release revealed persistent symptoms: nightmares, waking tension and anxiety, suicidal thoughts, depression, and a variety of physical complaints like headaches and peptic ulcers which are commonly considered to be connected with stress. Responsible psychiatric opinion considered that some, at least, of the hooded men would never recover from their experience.

When the facts about these interrogation procedures began to be known, protests were made from many sides by people who were deeply shocked that Britain should be employing methods of breaking down detainees which amounted to torture. It appeared that the use of such methods had developed gradually, without official authorization. Eventually the Prime Minister (then Edward Heath) forbade any further employment of these techniques in the interrogation of prisoners or suspects.

Although in Britain and similar countries long prison sentences seldom involve long periods of solitary confinement, they do deprive the prisoner of most of the stimuli from the outside world which make life worth living, and can therefore be said to enforce some degree of sensory deprivation in the widest sense. The monotonous environment of the prison, the limited access to exercise and to the open air, the invariable routine, the absence of both social and sexual intimacy with loved ones – these are all deprivations which, in the case of long prison sentences, have a permanently deleterious effect upon the mind of the prisoner.

Until recently, 'life' sentences were usually terminated by parole after a maximum of nine or ten years' incarceration, because it was realized that longer periods of confinement made it unlikely that the prisoner, when released, would be able to cope with life outside. In Britain, those who have received life sentences can be released at any time, but remain on parole licence until death. This means that, during the remainder of their lives, they can be recalled to prison if the authorities consider it necessary. Today, many judges, when sentencing offenders who have committed heinous crimes like rape or murder, recommend that the criminal should be confined for twenty years or more. Such recommendations are taken very seriously. If they are implemented, it follows that an increasing number of offenders will be permanently disabled and rendered unfit to live in the community.

Deprivation of external stimuli is particularly severe in prisons in which 'maximum security' is enforced, because the prisoners contained there are regarded as dangerous or likely to attempt escape. These, of course, are also the prisoners who are most likely to have received extended sentences. Although there are a few instances of prisoners serving very long sentences who have survived intact, like the Birdman of Alcatraz, deterioration and 'institutional neurosis' is common. Long-term prisoners become withdrawn, apathetic, and uninterested in their own appearance and surroundings. In their book *Psychological Survival*, Stanley Cohen and Laurie Taylor give an excellent review of these effects, based upon their study of long-term prisoners in the maximum security block of Durham prison, now fortunately abolished. The authors had been recruited to give weekly classes in social science to long-term prisoners. Although the classes aroused considerable interest in those inmates who had not been in prison very long, few prisoners who had already served many years attended. However, one prisoner who had served fourteen years came regularly. Afterwards he wrote to the authors:

Can you imagine what it is like being a prisoner for life, your dreams turn into nightmares and your castles to ashes, all you think about is fantasy and in the end you turn your back on reality and live in a contorted world of make-believe, you refuse to accept the rules of fellow-mortals and make ones that will fit in with your own little world, there is no daylight in this world of the 'lifer', it is all darkness, and it is in this darkness that we find peace and the ability to live in a world of our own, a world of make-believe.[14]

The examples cited in this chapter demonstrate that separation from the stimuli of ordinary, day-to-day existence can be therapeutic or disruptive according to circumstances: more especially, according to whether such separation is imposed or voluntary. Length of time is also important. It is probable, though not definitely established, that prolonged periods of removal from ordinary life have permanently deleterious effects, whether enforced by others or not.

However, conditions of imprisonment vary widely, and, in the past, were sometimes less rigorous than they are today. Several notable examples exist which demonstrate that partial solitude and estrangement from normal life, even in prison, can encourage creative production.

The Roman philosopher Boethius attained the important position of *magister officiorum* under the Ostrogothic king Theodoric. This involved being head of the civil service and chief of the palace officials, a position which can have left little time for his favourite pursuit, the study of philosophy. But Theodoric's trust in Boethius did not persist. The philosopher was accused of treason, arrested, condemned, and sent into exile to await execution. While imprisoned in Pavia, Boethius composed *The Consolation of Philosophy*, the work by which he is now chiefly remembered. He was tortured and then bludgeoned to death in 524 or 525 AD.

Sir Thomas More, Henry VIII's Chancellor from 1529, was imprisoned in the Tower of London for refusing to repudiate papal supremacy and to accept the King as head of the Church of England. More spent over a year in prison before his trial and execution in 1535. During this period he wrote *A Dialoge of Cumfort against Tribulacion* which has been described as a masterpiece of Christian wisdom.

Sir Walter Raleigh, being accused of treason, was sentenced to death. But his death sentence was suspended, and he was imprisoned in the Tower of London from 1603 to 1616. As in the case of Sir Thomas More, we may suppose that the conditions imposed were not too rigorous, for, during these years, Raleigh wrote *The History of the World*. This spanned the period from the Creation to the second century BC and was published in 1614. On his release, Raleigh undertook a second expedition to Guiana. Unfortunately, this was unsuccessful. The promised gold was not forthcoming; Raleigh's suspended death sentence was revived, and he was executed in 1618.

John Bunyan, who had joined the Bedford Separatist Church in about 1655, preached his unorthodox beliefs without hindrance until the Restoration of Charles II in 1660. On 12 November of that year, he was brought before the magistrates accused of holding services not in conformity with those of the Church of England. In January 1661, he was committed at the assizes to Bedford county jail, where he remained until March 1672. However, the conditions of his imprisonment were sufficiently liberal to allow him visits to his friends and family, and even occasional preaching. During the twelve years of his confinement, he wrote his spiritual autobiography, *Grace Abounding* (1666), and almost certainly composed a considerable part of *The Pilgrim's Progress*. The Declaration of Indulgence to Non-conformists issued by Charles II which allowed Bunyan's release was later withdrawn, and Bunyan was again imprisoned for illegal preaching in 1677.

On Christmas Day 1849, Dostoevsky began the long journey from St Petersburg to Siberia where he was to spend the next four years in a prison camp. Together with other members of the Petrashevsky circle, he had been arrested in April 1849, and had already spent eight months as a prisoner in the Peter and Paul fortress. During this initial period, he was in solitary confinement, and at first was not allowed books or writing materials. In spite of this, he discovered that he had inner resources which enabled him to tolerate captivity far better than he had initially expected. His arrest may even have saved him from breakdown, rather than precipitating it; for there is evidence that his participation in an underground revolutionary organization had been preying on his mind during the previous winter, and had brought him to the edge of collapse.

When, at the beginning of July, the prisoners were allowed to receive books from the library of the fortress, Dostoevsky fell upon them. He also wrote to his brother Mikhail telling him that he had thought out three stories and two novels. The famous incident of the mock execution in Semenovsky Square, when Dostoevsky faced a firing squad, only to be reprieved at the last minute, followed on 22 December. In Siberia, Dostoevsky's only literary activity was to keep a surreptitious notebook in which he noted down the phrases and expressions used by his fellow convicts. He managed to give the notebook to one of the medical assistants who returned it to him on his release. Its contents were used in *House of the Dead*, the book which described Dostoevsky's prison camp experience.

This experience was horrific, not only because of the appalling physical conditions in which the convicts were housed, and the perpetual threat of flogging under which they lived, but because

Dostoevsky found himself, as a 'gentleman', totally rejected by the brutish peasant prisoners whose cause he had espoused and for whose sake, as a potential revolutionary, he was suffering exile and imprisonment. During the time of his imprisonment, Dostoevsky underwent a conversion experience in which his total disillusion with the peasantry was replaced by an almost mystical belief in their essential goodness. This was based upon an involuntary memory which came back to him from his childhood of an incident in which one of his father's serfs, Marey, had comforted him when he was terrified. Although Dostoevsky suffered deeply from never being physically alone whilst in the prison camp, his emotional isolation and lack of companionship had had the effect of turning his attention inward, and allowing his mind to wander in the past.

All through his four years in camp he had employed this technique of involuntary association, which probably served somewhat the same purpose as psychoanalysis or drug therapy in releasing repressed memories and thereby relieving his psychic blockages and morbid fixations. This technique also served the additional and reassuring function of keeping alive his artistic faculties under conditions where he was forbidden to put pen to paper.[15]

Dostoevsky's experience of penal servitude permanently influenced his view of human nature and hence permeated his novels. More particularly, his experience of seeing convicts who for years had been ruthlessly crushed suddenly break out and assert their own personalities, often in violent and irrational fashion, made him feel that individual self-expression or self-realization was a basic human need, a need which did not accord with the subordination of individuality to the collective demands of the State required by Socialism.

There are also less admirable examples of literary endeavour being furthered by imprisonment. The Marquis de Sade was recurrently imprisoned throughout his life until he was finally confined in the asylum at Charenton, where he died on 2 December 1814, at the age of seventy-four. His perverse imagination flourished in captivity, and it is to the fortresses of Vincennes and the Bastille that we owe such works as *Justine* and *Les 120 Journées de Sodome*.

Sade's infatuation with absolute power found echoes in the writings of Adolf Hitler, another author whose works owed something to imprisonment. After the failure of his *putsch* in Munich, Hitler was confined in the old fortress of Landsberg. Although he received a five-year sentence, he spent less than nine months in prison, where he was treated as an honoured guest. It was during this period that he began to dictate *Mein Kampf* to Rudolf Hess.

'Without my imprisonment,' Hitler remarked long afterward, '*Mein Kampf* would never have been written. That period gave me the chance of deepening various notions for which I then had only an instinctive feeling.'[16]

In contrast to most of the examples given in this chapter, it is occasionally recorded that even solitary confinement imposed by enemies can be the trigger for psychological experiences of lasting value. Anthony Grey, who experienced solitary confinement in China, and Arthur Koestler, who was similarly imprisoned in Spain, discussed their experiences together on television. The transcript of their discussion appears in Koestler's collection of essays, *Kaleidoscope*.

Both men were grateful that they did not have to share a cell with another prisoner. Both felt that solitude enhanced their appreciation of, and sympathy with, their fellow men. Both had intense experiences of feeling that some kind of higher order of reality existed with which solitude put them in touch. Both felt that trying to put this experience into words tended to trivialize it, because words could not really express it. Although neither man subscribed to any orthodox religious belief, both agreed that they had felt the abstract existence of something which was indefinable or which could only be expressed in symbols.

Anthony Grey thought that his experience had given him a new awareness and appreciation of normal life. Koestler concurred, but added that he had also become more aware of horrors lurking under the surface. Koestler also refers to a feeling of inner freedom, of being alone and confronted with ultimate realities instead of with your bank statement. Your bank statement and other trivialities are again a kind of confinement. Not in space but in spiritual space . . . So you have got a dialogue with existence. A dialogue with life, a dialogue with death.

Grey comments that this is an area of experience into which most people do not enter. Koestler rightly affirms that most people have occasional confrontations of this kind

when they are severely ill or when a parent dies, or when they first fall in love. Then they are transferred from what I call the trivial plane to the tragic or absolute plane. But it only happens a few times. Whereas in the type of experience which we shared, one has one's nose rubbed into it, for a protracted period.[17]

So, occasionally, good can come out of evil. Anthony Grey recalled being shown a painting by a Chinese friend in which a beautiful lotus flower is growing out of mud. The human spirit is not indestructible; but a courageous few discover that, when in hell, they are granted a glimpse of heaven.

5

The Hunger of Imagination

'Were it not for imagination, Sir, a man would be as happy in the arms of a chambermaid as of a Duchess.'

Samuel Johnson

We have seen that the capacity to be alone is a valuable resource. It enables men and women to get in touch with their deepest feelings; to come to terms with loss; to sort out their ideas; to change attitudes. In some instances, even the enforced isolation of prison may encourage the growth of the creative imagination.

Imagination, it is safe to say, is more highly developed in human beings than in any other creature. Although animals dream, and sub-human primates certainly show some capacity for invention, the range of human imagination far outstrips that exhibited by even the cleverest ape. It is clear that the development of human imagination is biologically adaptive; but it is also the case that we have had to pay a certain price for this development. Imagination has given man flexibility; but in doing so, has robbed him of contentment.

The behaviour of creatures lower down the evolutionary scale than ourselves is often largely governed by pre-programmed patterns. Some of these patterns, like the display of the bower-bird, or the hunting habits of wasps, are beautiful and elaborate. So long as the animal follows these age-old patterns, its behaviour is fitted to the environment as closely as a key fits a lock. If the environment remains constant, the animal's basic needs, for survival and for reproduction, will be provided for in more or less automatic fashion. (I am tempted to engage in anthropomorphism, and to say that such an animal could be considered 'happy'.) But if the environment changes, the animal whose behaviour is governed by pre-programmed patterns is at a disadvantage, for it cannot easily adapt to changing circumstances.

Human beings, because their behaviour is principally governed by learning and by the transmission of culture from generation to generation, are much more flexible. Babies are provided with a certain number of built-in responses in order to ensure their survival; but the most distinctive feature of human behaviour is that so much is learned, so little innately determined. This is what has enabled men to survive in extreme climates, from the Equator to the Poles, in places which provide little or nothing of what they need. Men have even managed to leave the earth altogether, and learned how to exist for long periods in space. Such environments demand the exercise of ingenuity and skill. Survival cannot be ensured unless intelligence and imagination take over from innate patterns in making provision for basic needs.

But the price of flexibility, of being released from the tyranny of rigid, inbuilt patterns of behaviour, is that 'happiness', in the sense of perfect adaptation to the environment or complete fulfilment of needs, is only briefly experienced. 'Call no man happy till he dies,' said Solon. When individuals fall in love, or cry 'Eureka' at making a new discovery, or have the kind of transcendental emotion described by Wordsworth as being 'surprised by joy', they feel blissfully at one with the universe: but, as everyone knows, such experiences are transient.

In a previous book, I suggested that dissatisfaction with what is, or 'divine discontent', was an inescapable part of the human condition. As Samuel Johnson pointed out, the present passes so quickly that we can hardly think at all except in terms of the past or the future. When the philosopher Imlac takes Rasselas to visit the Great Pyramid, he speculates upon why the pyramid was ever built.

The narrowness of the chambers proves that it could afford no retreat from enemies, and treasures might have been reposited at far less expense with equal security. It seems to have been erected only in compliance with that hunger of imagination

63

which preys incessantly upon life, and must be always appeased by some enjoyment. Those who have already all that they can enjoy must enlarge their desires.[1]

What Johnson calls that 'hunger of imagination' is also a necessary feature of human adaptation. Man's extraordinary success as a species springs from his discontent, which compels him to employ his imagination. The type of modern man who exhibits more discontent than any other, Western man, has been the most successful.

There are, at first sight, some exceptions to what I have just written. In certain parts of the world, small communities still exist in which traditional ways of life have continued unchanged for centuries. Without knowing more about their inner imaginative lives, it is impossible to tell how much the members of such communities suffer from discontent; but even the best adapted probably imagine a heaven in which they will be protected from danger and released from toil. What is tragically certain is that such groups are always at risk, because, like animals governed by inbuilt patterns of behaviour, they find it hard to adapt to the impact of Western civilization. It is always the dissatisfied who triumph. Western man has treated with appalling cruelty the aborigines of Australia, the Indians of both North and South America, the inhabitants of Africa and India, and many other groups. But, given the restless inventiveness of the West, displacement of traditional groups of men is probably inevitable, even when segregation and extermination have not been deliberately employed.

Discontent, therefore, may be considered adaptive because it encourages the use of the imagination, and thus spurs men on to further conquests and to ever-increasing mastery of the environment. At first sight, this proposition appears to concur with Freud's conception of phantasy. For Freud wrote, in his paper 'Creative Writers and Day-Dreaming',

We may lay it down that a happy person never phantasies, only an unsatisfied one. The motive forces of phantasies are unsatisfied wishes, and every single phantasy is the fulfilment of a wish, a correction of an unsatisfying reality.[2]

However, Freud's view of phantasy is that it is essentially escapist, a turning away from reality rather than a preliminary to altering reality in the desired direction, as I am proposing. Freud considered that phantasy was derived from play, and that both activities not only pertained to childhood, but were also a denial of reality.

The growing child, when he stops playing, gives up nothing but the link with real objects; instead of *playing*, he now *phantasies*. He builds castles in the air and creates what are called *day-dreams*.[3]

Freud believed that infants were originally dominated by the pleasure principle: that is, by the need to avoid pain and to obtain pleasure. When instinctive needs, for food, warmth, or comfort, disturbed the infant's rest, the infant would react by hallucinating what it needed.

Whatever was thought of (wished for) was simply presented in a hallucinatory manner, just as still happens today with our dream-thoughts every night. It was only the non-occurrence of the expected satisfaction, the disappointment experienced, that led to the abandonment of this attempt at satisfaction by means of hallucination. Instead of it, the psychical apparatus had to decide to form a conception of the real circumstances in the external world and to endeavour to make a real alteration in them. A new principle of mental functioning was introduced; what was presented to the mind was no longer what was agreeable but what was real. This setting-up of the *reality principle* proved to be a momentous step.[4]

Freud considered that the pleasure principle was only gradually replaced by the reality principle. Since no mental content is ever completely expunged, traces of the pleasure principle lingered on and could, so Freud believed, be detected not only in dreams, but also in play. As we have seen, Freud thought that later forms of phantasy were derived from play.

Freud seems to assume that the real world can or should be able to provide complete satisfaction and that, ideally, it should be possible for the mature person to abandon phantasy altogether. Freud was too realistic, hard-headed and pessimistic a man to believe that this ideal could ever be reached. Nevertheless, he did consider that phantasy should become less and less necessary as the maturing individual approached rational adaptation to the external world. Phantasy, in Freud's conceptual scheme, was linked with hallucination, with dreaming, and with play. He considered that all these forms of mental activity were escapist: ways of evading reality which were dependent upon the infantile form of mental functioning which he designated 'primary process', and which were governed by the pleasure principle rather than by the reality principle. Freud's somewhat puritanical vision was that proper, mature adaptation to the world was governed by deliberate thought and rational planning. He would not have countenanced our present proposition: that an inner world of phantasy is part of man's biological endowment, and that it is the inevitable discrepancy between this inner world and the outer world that compels men to become inventive and imaginative.

Yet Freud's own achievement bears witness to what I have just written. Almost up to the time of his death at the age of eighty-three, Freud was revising his ideas. Although he believed that he had discovered the fundamental principles of a new science, he did not consider the edifice of psycho-analysis complete. Like every creative person, whether he be artist or scientist, Freud was unable to rest upon his laurels. The gulf between what he imagined psycho-analysis might become and what it actually was remained unbridged.

If, unlike Freud, we assume that an inner imaginative world is part of man's biological endowment, and that man's success as a species has depended upon it, we can see that we should not merely strive to replace phantasy by reason, as Freud would have us do. Instead, we should use our capacity for phantasy to build bridges between the inner world of the imagination and the external world. The two worlds will never entirely coincide, as we might suppose happens in the case of animals whose life-cycles are chiefly governed by innate patterns of behaviour. But that is not a matter for regret. If our reach did not exceed our grasp, we should no longer be human. A race of men which lacked the capacity for phantasy would not only be unable to imagine a better life in material terms, but would also lack religion, music, literature, and painting. As Goya wrote:

> Phantasy abandoned by reason produces impossible monsters; united with her, she is the mother of the arts and the origin of their marvels.[5]

Even science depends more upon phantasy than Freud acknowledged. Many scientific hypotheses take origin from flights of the imagination which at first seem wild, but which later stand up to sober scrutiny and detailed proof. Newton's notion that gravity was a universal which acted at enormous distances was a leap of the imagination which must have seemed absurd until he was able to demonstrate it mathematically. Kekulé's discovery of the ring structure of organic molecules originated from a dream-like vision of atoms combining in chains which then formed into coils like snakes eating their own tails. Einstein's special theory of relativity depended upon his being able to imagine how the universe might appear to an observer travelling at near the speed of light. These are examples of phantasies which, although originating in the imagination, nevertheless connected with the external world in ways which illumined it and made it more comprehensible.

Other phantasies giving rise to supposedly scientific hypotheses have lacked this connection with the external world. Such creations of the imagination are ultimately discarded as delusions. Throughout the eighteenth century, for example, the standard explanation of combustion was the theory of *phlogiston*. Phlogiston was considered to be the material principle of combustibility. When something burned, it was supposed to lose phlogiston, which was thought of as an imponderable fluid. It was finally demonstrated that phlogiston existed only in the imagination; that nothing in the external world corresponded to it.

We see, therefore, that in the field of science, there are two kinds of phantasy. The first reaches out to the external world and, by maintaining a connection with that world which corresponds to its real workings, becomes a fruitful hypothesis. The second, making no such connection with the external world, is ultimately dismissed as a delusion.

These two kinds of phantasy can also be distinguished in the arts. When a great writer like Tolstoy uses his imagination to tell a story and to invent characters which both deeply move us and which become immortal, we rightly suppose that his phantasies are connecting with external reality and illuminating that reality for us. On the other hand, we recognize that the phantasies of lesser writers, perhaps manifesting themselves as 'thrillers' or 'romantic' novels, have little to do with the real world and may, indeed, be no more than an attempt to escape from it.

In his paper 'Formulations on the Two Principles of Mental Functioning' from which I have already quoted, Freud seems partially to agree with this when he writes:

Art brings about a reconciliation between the two principles in a peculiar way. An artist is originally a man who turns away from reality because he cannot come to terms with the renunciation of instinctual satisfaction which it at first demands, and who allows his erotic and ambitious wishes full play in the life of phantasy. He finds a way back to reality, however, from this world of phantasy by making use of special gifts to mould his phantasies into truths of a new kind, which are valued by men as precious reflections of reality. Thus in a certain fashion, he actually becomes the hero, the king, the creator, or the favourite he desired to be, without following the long roundabout path of making alterations in the external world. But he can only achieve this because other men feel the same dissatisfaction as he does with the renunciation demanded by reality, and because that dissatisfaction, which results from the replacement of the pleasure principle by the reality principle, is itself a part of reality.[6]

The confusion which is evident in this passage arises because Freud cannot discard his proposition that phantasy is something which ought, in the mature adult, to be superseded by hard-headed, rational thought. Freud goes some way toward recognizing that phantasy is not entirely escapist wish-fulfilment when he refers to the artist moulding his phantasies into 'truths of a new kind', but he does not really follow this up. If he had done so, he would surely have concluded that, whilst some kinds of phantasy are escapist, others foreshadow new and fruitful ways of adapting to the realities of the external world.

There are good biological reasons for accepting the fact that man is so constituted that he possesses an inner world of the imagination which is different from, though connected to, the world of external reality. It is the discrepancy between the two worlds which motivates creative imagination. People who realize their creative potential are constantly bridging the gap between inner and outer. They invest the external world with meaning because they disown neither the world's objectivity nor their own subjectivity.

This interaction between inner and outer worlds is easily seen when we observe children at play. Children make use of real objects in the external world, but invest these objects with meanings which derive from the world of their own imagination. This process begins very early in the child's life. Many infants develop intense attachments to particular objects. D. W. Winnicott was the first psychoanalyst to draw attention to the importance of such attachments in his paper 'Transitional Objects and Transitional Phenomena'.[7] These phenomena are closely connected with the beginnings of independence and with the capacity to be alone.

According to Winnicott, the age at which infants first exhibit attachment to external objects varies, but it may be from as early as four months old. Infants at first use their own thumbs or fists as comforters. Later, they may substitute a piece of blanket, a napkin, or a handkerchief. It may happen that a particular blanket or eiderdown, and later on, a doll or teddy-bear, becomes vitally important to the child, especially when going to sleep. The object becomes a defence against anxiety; a comforter which to some extent is a substitute for the mother's breast, or for the mother herself as a secure attachment figure. Such objects may become almost inseparable from the infant; at times, even more important than the mother herself.

Winnicott calls such objects 'transitional' because he considers them to represent intermediate stages between the child's attachment to the mother and its attachment to later 'objects'; that is, to people whom the child comes to love and to depend upon. Winnicott considers that such objects mediate between the inner world of the imagination and the external world. The blanket, doll, or teddy-bear is clearly a real object which exists as a separate entity from the child: but, at the same time, it is heavily invested with subjective emotions which belong to the child's inner world. This process of mediation between inner and outer might be described as the child's first creative act.

Winnicott makes the important point that the use of transitional objects is not pathological. Although such objects provide security and comfort, and can therefore be said to be substitutes for the mother, they are not developed because the mother is inadequate. Transitional objects only appear when the infant can invest them with supportive or loving qualities. In order to be able to do this, the infant must have experienced actual support and love. Only when the mother has been introjected as at least a partially good object can those qualities be projected upon a transitional object. The capacity to develop attachments to transitional objects is, therefore, a sign of health rather than a sign of deprivation, just as the capacity to be alone is a sign of inner security rather than an expression of a withdrawn state. This is supported by the observation that institutionalized children whose capacity for forming human attachments may be impaired rarely form attachments to cuddly toys.[8]

Moreover, it is the secure infant who later exhibits the greatest interest in toys and other impersonal objects in the environment. As we noted earlier, independent exploratory investigation is characteristic of the secure infant, whilst anxious clinging to the mother typically indicates an infant who is not securely attached.

The use of transitional objects suggests that the positive functions of imagination begin very early in life. In the Introduction, it was suggested that there were two opposing drives in human nature: the drive toward closeness to other human beings, and the drive toward being independent and self-sufficient. May it not be that the first manifestation of the latter drive is the development of transitional objects? For the use of such objects demonstrates that the young child can, at least temporarily, dispense with the actual presence of the mother. Transitional objects may, therefore, be connected both with the capacity to be alone, and with the development of the imagination.

The existence of such objects also supports the suggestion made in the Introduction that human beings are directed toward the impersonal as well as toward the personal. These very early manifestations of investing impersonal objects with significance are evidence that man was not born for love alone. The meaning attaching to such objects may later become invested in objects of scientific enquiry, or in any of the manifold aspects of the external world which engage adult attention.

Transitional objects gradually lose their emotional charge as the child grows older. Often such objects become linked with a variety of other objects and are used in play. Children easily transmute a broomstick into a horse, an armchair into a house. At a later stage overt play is replaced by phantasy, in which no external objects are needed to speed the flow of the imagination.

Freud was right in linking play and phantasy, but he was surely wrong in believing that play and phantasy should be abandoned in favour of rationality. When I suggested that people who realized their creative potential were constantly bridging the gap between inner and outer worlds, I was not referring only to the creation of works of art or to the construction of scientific hypotheses, but to what Winnicott has aptly called 'creative apperception'. Creative apperception depends upon linking subjective and objective; upon colouring the external world with the warm hues of the imagination. Winnicott wrote:

> It is creative apperception more than anything else that makes the individual feel that life is worth living.[9]

It seems probable that there is always an element of play in creative living. When this playful element disappears, joy goes with it, and so does any sense of being able to innovate. Creative people not infrequently experience periods of despair in which their ability to create anything new seems to have deserted them. This is often because a particular piece of work has become invested with such

71

overwhelming importance that it is no longer possible to play with it. What Gibbon referred to as 'the vanity of authors' sometimes makes them regard their work with such desperate seriousness that 'playing around' with it becomes impossible. Kekulé, describing the vision which led to the discovery of the ring structure of organic molecules referred to above, said: 'Let us learn to dream, gentlemen.' He might equally well have said: 'Let us learn to play.'

The subjective can be so over-emphasized that the individual's inner world becomes entirely divorced from reality. In that case we call him mad. On the other hand, as Winnicott points out, the individual can suppress his inner world in such a way that he becomes over-compliant with external reality. If the individual regards the external world merely as something to which he has to adapt, rather than as something in which his subjectivity can find fulfilment, his individuality disappears and his life becomes meaningless or futile.

An inner world of phantasy must be regarded as part of man's biological inheritance. Imagination is active in even the best adjusted and happiest human being; but the extent of the gap between inner and outer worlds, and hence the ease or difficulty with which the gap is bridged, varies greatly in different individuals. Some of these differences are examined in subsequent chapters.

6

The Significance of the Individual

'No man ever will unfold the capacities of his own intellect who does not at least checker his life with solitude.'

De Quincey

An inner world of phantasy exists in every human being, and finds expression in an infinite variety of different ways. The man who goes racing or who eagerly watches football on television is giving rein to phantasy, although he may not be creating or producing anything. Hobbies and interests are often aspects of a human being which most clearly define his individuality, and make him the person he is. To discover what really interests a person is to be well on the way to understanding them. Sometimes such interests as the playing of team games are only practicable by interacting with other people; but often they reflect what the individual does when he is alone, or when communication and interaction are at a minimum. In Britain, every weekend sees the banks of rivers and canals lined with fishermen, who keep a discreet distance from one another, and seldom converse. Theirs is essentially a solitary sport, in which so little happens that phantasy must be particularly alive. The same applies to gardening, and to many other interests, whether obviously 'creative' or not, which occupy the leisure of those whose basic physical needs have been provided for. Everyone needs interests as well as interpersonal relationships; and interests, as well as relationships, play an important part in defining individual identity and in giving meaning to a person's life.

Bowlby's statement that intimate attachments are the hub around which a person's life revolves, and Marris's assertion that specific relationships embody most crucially the meaning of a person's life, leave out of account not only interests, which may be crucially important, but also the need which many people feel for some scheme, religion, philosophy, or ideology which makes sense of life.

In an essay on 'The Concept of Cure' I suggested that there were two main factors in the analytical process which promoted recovery from neurotic distress.

> The first factor is that the patient adopts some scheme or system of thought which appears to make sense out of his distress. The second is that he makes a relationship of a fruitful kind with another person.[1]

Both factors enter into all our lives, but some natures are more inclined toward finding the meaning of life chiefly in interpersonal relationships; others toward finding it in interests, beliefs, or patterns of thought.

However important personal relationships may be for the creatively gifted person, it is often the case that his particular field of endeavour is still more important. The meaning of his life is constituted less by his personal relationships than it is by his work. If he is successful, the public will concur with this estimate. Although most people are interested in the private lives of the great originals, we generally regard their creative achievements as far more important than their personal relationships. If they behave badly toward their spouses, lovers, or friends, we are likely to be more indulgent toward them than toward ordinary people. Wagner was notoriously unscrupulous; but his sexual and financial misdemeanours pale into insignificance beside the vastness and originality of his compositions. Strindberg behaved intolerably badly toward his three wives and toward many of his erstwhile friends; but his ability to portray his predilection for quarrelling and his hatred for women in such plays as *The Father* and *Miss Julie* make us inclined to forget his personal vindictiveness.

Analysts spend their lives listening to people who have encountered problems in their intimate relationships. It is surely remarkable that, when they came to write their autobiographies, the two most original analysts of the twentieth century devoted scarcely any space to their wives and families, or indeed to anything save the development of their respective ideas. Both Freud's *An Autobiographical Study* and Jung's *Memories, Dreams, Reflections* are exceptionally uninformative about their authors' relations with others. We may applaud their discretion, and sympathize with their desire for privacy; but we may also justly conclude that their own accounts of themselves demonstrate where their hearts were centred.

It is true that many creative people fail to make mature personal relationships, and some are extremely isolated. It is also true that, in some instances, trauma, in the shape of early separation or bereavement, has steered the potentially creative person toward developing aspects of his personality which can find fulfilment in comparative isolation. *But this does not mean that solitary, creative pursuits are themselves pathological.* Even those who have the happiest relationships with others need something other than those relationships to complete their fulfilment.

The development of imagination in human beings has made it possible for them to use the impersonal, as well as the personal, as a principal means of self-development, as a primary path toward self-realization. The great original creators are demonstrating one aspect of a human potential which can be found in everyone, albeit in embryo form in most of us. Although we may strive to do so, none of us develops our various potentialities equally; and many creative people appear to nurture their talents more carefully than they do their personal relationships.

The idea that individual self-development is an important pursuit is a comparatively recent one in human history; and the idea that the arts are vehicles of self-expression or can serve the purpose of self-development is still more recent. At the dawn of history, the arts were strictly functional; and functional for the community, not for the individual artist. The Palaeolithic artists who drew and painted animals on the walls of their cave dwellings were not making works of art in order to express their personal way of looking at the world, but were attempting to work magic. As Germain Bazin writes:

75

The primitive artist was a magician whose drawing had all the virtue of a magic spell, an incantation.

Bazin believes that early man painted and carved natural forms 'to ensure the fertility of his prey, to entice it into his traps, or to acquire its strength for his own purposes'.[2] Herbert Read refers to cave paintings as exemplifying 'the desire to "realize" the object on which magical powers were to be exercised'.[3]

The act of drawing sharpens the perceptions of the draughtsman; an idea passionately advanced by Ruskin, who believed that it was only by trying to capture the external world in form and colour that the artist learns to apprehend it. In the case of early man, we can be sure that the more accurately he drew his potential prey, the more he could be said to 'know' the animal which he was depicting. The more knowledge he had, the more likely he was to be successful in the hunt.

If naming things is the first creative act, as Bazin alleges, perhaps drawing is the second. Drawing is comparable with forming concepts. It enables the draughtsman to experiment with images separate from the object which originally engaged his interest, and thus gives him a sense of mastery over that object. Belief in the power of the image was probably the reason that Egyptian sculptors made effigies of the dead. The image was believed to guarantee survival after death. Bazin tells us that, in the Nile valley, 'the sculptor was known as "He-who-keeps-alive" '.[4]

When anthropologists study the art of other cultures today, they describe it as being social in character. Raymond Firth states that

> the primitive artist and his public share essentially the same set of values . . . In contrast to what is generally the case in Western societies, the artist is not divorced from his public.[5]

The majority of pre-industrial societies seem not to have a word signifying 'art' as such, although they of course have words for particular artistic activities like singing or carving. As Western civilization developed, belief in the magical power of the image declined, but painting and sculpture continued to serve communal, rather than individual, interests. Artists were craftsmen who were not expected to be original, but to carry out the orders of their patrons. Their chief task was to remind worshippers, who were often illiterate, of the tenets of the Christian religion; and, to this end, they painted the walls of churches with scenes from the life of Christ and the saints. The medieval artist was recruited from the lower ranks of society. Because painting and sculpture involved manual labour, the visual arts were regarded as inferior to literature and the theoretical sciences. It was only from about the middle of the thirteenth century AD that the names of individual painters began to be recorded.

Moreover, even when artists painted portraits of particular people, the individuality of the subject was considered less important than his rank or office in society. Colin Morris writes:

> We must admit from the beginning that it is not possible to be certain, with any portrait before 1200, that it is in our sense a personal study.[6]

Jacob Burckhardt claims that, in Europe, consciousness of individuality first developed in Italy.

> In the Middle Ages both sides of human consciousness – that which was turned within as that which was turned without – lay dreaming or half awake beneath a common veil. The veil was woven of faith, illusion, and childish prepossession, through which the world and history were seen clad in strange hues. Man was conscious of himself only as a member of a race, people, party, family, or corporation – only through some general category. In Italy this veil first melted into air; an *objective* treatment of the State and of all the things of this world became possible. The *subjective* side at the same time asserted itself with corresponding emphasis; man became a spiritual *individual*, and recognized himself as such.[7]

The art of representational portraiture of recognizable individuals became highly developed before self-portraiture became at all common. As Peter Abbs notes in his thesis 'The Development of

Autobiography in Western Culture', the Renaissance artist often followed the convention of including himself amongst the figures depicted in a commissioned painting, or used himself as a model for one of the saints or other holy figures whom he was portraying. But self-portraiture as a means of self-exploration, or of boldly displaying the true inner man, only began to develop in the late fifteenth century, reaching its zenith in the seventeenth century in the long series of Rembrandt's self-portraits.

Music also began by serving communal purposes. E. O. Wilson supposes that, just as birdsong has the function of communicating information about the singer to other members of the species, so human music originally furthered the ends of human tribes. 'Singing and dancing serve to draw groups together, direct the emotions of the people, and prepare them for joint action.'[8]

Raymond Firth writes that, in the kind of communities which he studied,

> Even songs, as a rule, are not composed simply to be listened to for pleasure. They have work to do, to serve as funeral dirges, as accompaniments to dancing, or to serenade a lover.[9]

He might have added that rhythm co-ordinates muscular action, lightens the toll of manual labour, and postpones fatigue. Our own Western music is a legacy of the Church. It must be remembered that, for centuries, the church was the central meeting-place of every town and village. The function of music was collective: the evocation of group emotion as part of the act of worship.

Pre-industrial societies have little notion of a person as a separate entity. A Nigerian psychiatrist told me that, when a psychiatric clinic was first set up in a rural district of Nigeria to treat the mentally ill, the family invariably accompanied the sufferer and insisted upon being present at the patient's interview with the psychiatrist. The idea that the patient might exist as an individual apart from the family, or that he might have personal problems which he did not want to share with them, did not occur to Nigerians who were still living a traditional village life. In his book *Social Anthropology*, Sir Edmund Leach refers to the ethos of individualism which is central to the contemporary Western society but which is notably absent from most of the societies which social anthropologists study.[10]

The growth of individualism, and hence of the modern conception of the artist, was hastened by the Reformation. Although Luther was an ascetic who attacked wealth and luxury, he was also an individualist who preached the supremacy of the individual conscience. Until the sixteenth century, the ultimate standard of human institutions and activities was not only religious, but promulgated by a universal Western Church. As Tawney eloquently demonstrates in *Religion and the Rise of Capitalism*, however often men exhibited personal greed and ambition, there was none the less a generally agreed conception of how the individual *ought* to behave. The idea that anyone should pursue his personal economic ends to the limit, provided that he kept within the law, was foreign to the medieval mind, which regarded the alleviation of poverty as a duty, and the private accumulation of wealth as a danger to the soul.

The Reformation made possible the growth of Calvinism, and the establishment of the Protestant work ethic. It was not long before poverty was regarded as a punishment for idleness or fecklessness, and the accumulation of wealth as a reward for the virtues of industry and thrift.

Durkheim later pointed out that the growth of individualism was also related to the division of labour. As societies grew larger and more complex, occupational specialization led to greater differentiation between individuals. The growth of cities furthered looser, less intimate social relations; and, whilst the individual gained personal freedom by being emancipated from the intimate ties which characterize smaller societies, he became vulnerable to *anomie*, the alienation which results from no longer conforming to any traditional code.

In the thesis to which I have already referred, Abbs points out that, according to the *Oxford English Dictionary*, it was not until 1674 that the word 'self' took on its modern meaning of 'a permanent subject of successive and varying states of consciousness'. He goes on to list a number of instances of 'self' forming compounds with other words which all entered the language at roughly the same time.

Self-sufficient (1598), self-knowledge (1613), self-made (1615), self-seeker (1632), selfish (1640), self-examination (1647), selfhood (1649), self-interest (1649), self-knowing (1667), self-deception (1677), self-determination (1683), self-conscious (1687).[11]

Abbs also remarks that the word *individual* originally denoted *indivisible*, and could, for example, be used of the Trinity or of a married couple, meaning 'not to be parted'. Abbs writes:

The gradual inversion of meaning for the word 'individual', moving from the indivisible and collective to the divisible and distinctive, carries quietly within itself the historical development of self-consciousness, testifies to that complex dynamic of change which separated the person from his world making him self-conscious and self-aware, that change in the structure of feeling which during the Renaissance shifted from a sense of unconscious fusion with the world towards a state of conscious individuation.[12]

In societies in which the function of the artist, whether painter, sculptor, musician, or story-teller, was to serve the community by giving expression to traditional wisdom, his skills were valued, but his individuality was not. Today, we demand that he shall display originality, and that what he produces shall bear the unmistakable imprint of his uniqueness. We treat a genuine Titian with reverence; but if some art historian tells us that it is only a copy, however beautiful, we are likely to pass by on the other side. The commercial value of a work of art depends upon its demonstrable authenticity rather than upon its intrinsic merit. Art has become an individual statement and, for the artist himself, a means whereby he can pursue his own self-realization.

Autobiography developed from the confessional. St Augustine provided the model in his *Confessions*. However, the word 'autobiography' was not introduced until much later. A quotation from Southey dated 1809 is the first example of the word's use given by the *Oxford English Dictionary*. Over the centuries, autobiography changed from being a narrative of the soul's relation with God to an enterprise far more like that of psycho-analysis. In recounting the circumstances of his life from childhood onward, the autobiographer sought to define the influences which had shaped his character, to portray the relationships which had most affected him, to reveal the motives which had impelled him. In other words, the autobiographer became a writer who was attempting to make a coherent narrative out of his life, and, in the process of doing so, hoping perhaps to discover its meaning.

The modern psycho-analyst is concerned to make coherent sense out of his patient's life-story in much the same way. As I suggested earlier, this is an important aspect of the therapeutic endeavour. Psycho-analysis is not necessarily successful in ridding people of neurotic symptoms or in altering the basic structure of personality; but any enterprise which promises to make sense of the chaotic aspects of an individual's life will continue to appeal to people on that ground alone.

The literary genre of autobiography is now so popular that men and women of little interest and no distinction feel impelled to record their life-stories. It may be the case that, the less a person feels himself to be embedded in a family and social nexus, the more he feels that he has to make his mark in individual fashion. Originality implies being bold enough to go beyond accepted norms. Sometimes it involves being misunderstood or rejected by one's peers. Those who are not too dependent upon, or too closely involved with, others, find it easier to ignore convention. Primitive societies find it difficult to allow for individual decisions or varieties of opinion. When the maintenance of group solidarity is a prime consideration, originality may be stifled. Bruno Bettelheim studied Israeli adolescents who had been brought up in kibbutzim. He found that the high value placed upon shared group feelings was inimical to creativity.

I believe they find it nearly impossible to have a deeply personal opinion that differs from the group's, or to express themselves in a piece of creative writing – not because of the repression of feelings alone, but because it would shatter the ego. If one's ego is a group ego, then to set one's private ego against the group

81

ego is a shattering experience. And the personal ego feels too weak to survive when its strongest aspect, the group ego, gets lost.[13]

A manual on how to rear children which has had a wide circulation in the Soviet Union, stresses the need for fostering obedience in young children, since this 'provides the basis for developing that most precious of qualities: self-discipline'. The author goes on to ask:

What about developing independence in children? We shall answer; if a child does not obey and does not consider others, then his independence invariably takes ugly forms.[14]

Soviet children are reported to be, on the whole, better behaved, less aggressive, and less delinquent than their Western counterparts. Whether they are less original is a question which I cannot answer; but judging from the way in which Soviet artists and musicians have, in the past, been forced to conform to collective norms, it seems improbable that originality, in a collectively-based society, is either prized or encouraged.

What has been called 'the culture of poverty' includes amongst other characteristics crowded living quarters, forced gregariousness, and an absence of privacy. Although many other factors, including lack of education, may be operating, such communal living may be one reason why the very poor lack spokesmen in the shape of writers. Writers come predominantly from the middle class in which privacy is more easily obtainable, and in which solidarity with friends and neighbours is not so stringently demanded.

It is not only the highly creative who would not whole-heartedly agree with Bowlby's contention that intimate attachments to other human beings are the hub around which a person's life revolves. For the deeply religious, and especially for those whose vocation demands celibacy, attachment to God takes precedence over attachment to persons. Although such people may succeed in loving their neighbours as themselves, the injunction 'Thou shalt love the Lord thy God with all thy heart and with all thy soul, and with all thy mind' is truly 'the first and great commandment'.[15] Throughout most of

Europe's recorded history, it was assumed that ultimate happiness was not to be expected from human relationships and institutions, but could only be found in man's relation with the divine.

Indeed, many of the devout believed that human relationships were an obstacle to communion with God. The founders of the monastic movement were the hermits of the Egyptian desert, whose ideal of perfection was only to be achieved through renunciation of the world, mortification of the flesh, and a solitary life of contemplation and rigorous discipline. It was recognized very early that the life of the anchorite was not possible for everyone, and so the 'coenobitic' tradition arose in which monks no longer lived alone but shared the life of dedication to God in communities. Intimate attachments, or desires for such attachments, are not unknown within the walls of monasteries, but they are regarded as intrusive distractions and firmly discouraged.

Although learning was not a necessary feature of monastic life, the libraries of the monasteries preserved the learning of the past, and attracted those monks who had scholarly interests. In the twelfth and thirteenth centuries, the monasteries led an intellectual revival, and were pre-eminent in history and biography.[16] Perhaps monastic discipline and the absence of close personal ties not only facilitated the individual's relation with God, but also fostered scholarship.

It would, I think, be quite wrong to assume that all those who have put their relation with God before their relations with their fellows are abnormal or neurotic. Some of those who choose the monastic or celibate life certainly do so for the 'wrong' reasons: because their human relationships have failed, or because they dislike taking responsibility, or because they want a secure haven from the world. But this is not true of all; and even if it were so, would not imply that a life in which intimate attachments to other human beings played little part was necessarily incomplete or inferior.

The religious person might argue that modern psycho-analysts have idealized intimate attachments; that human relationships are, because of the nature of man, necessarily imperfect; and that encouraging people to look for complete fulfilment in this way has done more harm than good. As I suggested in the Introduction, the increasing prevalence of divorce in Western countries has come about not only because there has been a decline in the numbers of those who apply Christian standards to marriage, but also because people have been encouraged to believe in the possibility of finding the 'right' person and the ideal relationship.

Many fortunate people do make intimate relationships which continue until death, and which constitute their major source of happiness. But even the closest relationship is bound to have flaws and disadvantages, and it is often because people do not accept this that they are more unhappy than they need be, and more inclined to abandon one another. If it is accepted that no relationship is ever ideal, it makes it easier to understand why men and women need other sources of fulfilment. As we have seen, many creative activities are predominantly solitary. They are concerned with self-realization and self-development in isolation, or with finding some coherent pattern in life. The degree to which these creative activities take priority in the life of an individual varies with his personality and talents. Everyone needs some human relationships; but everyone also needs some kind of fulfilment which is relevant to himself alone. Provided that they have friends and acquaintances, those who are passionately engaged in pursuing interests which are important to them may achieve happiness without having any very close relationships.

7

Solitude and Temperament

'In extraversion and introversion it is clearly a matter of two antithetical, natural attitudes or trends, which Goethe once referred to as diastole and systole.'

C. G. Jung

Most psychiatrists and psychologists agree that human beings differ in temperament, and that such differences are largely inborn, however much they may be fostered or suppressed by the circumstances of childhood and by subsequent events in a person's life. This is especially true when considering the individual's reaction to solitude. At the very least, we all need the solitude of sleep; but, in waking life, people vary widely in how much they value experiences involving human relationships and how much they value what happens when they are alone.

Jung introduced the terms *extravert* and *introvert* in his book *Psychological Types*, which was first published in 1921. Following his break with Freud in 1913, Jung went through a long period of mental upheaval which was so intense that he described himself as 'being menaced by a psychosis'.[1] This is vividly described in his autobiography. During the next eight years, he published very little, since he was primarily preoccupied with recording and interpreting the stream of visions, dreams, and phantasies which threatened to overwhelm his reason. However, in the course of passing through this period of turmoil, Jung was able to forge from it his own, independent point of view; and the first fruits of this was *Psychological Types*.

Jung claims that he became interested in the problem of types when he was trying to understand the alternative interpretations of human nature advanced by Sigmund Freud and Alfred Adler. How was it that psychiatrists faced with the same psychological material could furnish such different explanations of its origin and meaning? Jung gives some illuminating examples of how particular cases can be explained by either point of view. He writes:

> For if we examine the two theories without prejudice, we cannot deny that both contain significant truths, and, contradictory as these are, they should not be regarded as mutually exclusive . . . Now, since both theories are in a large measure correct – that is to say, since they both appear to explain their material – it follows that a neurosis must have two opposite aspects, one of which is grasped by the Freudian, the other by the Adlerian theory. But how comes it that each investigator sees only one side, and why does each maintain that he has the only valid view?[2]

Jung concluded that the fundamental difference lay in the way the two investigators regarded the relation between subject and object. In Jung's view, Freud saw the subject as being dependent upon, and largely shaped by, significant objects; more especially by parents and other important influences in early childhood. Hence, the patient's difficulties in object-relationships follow patterns established in the first few years. These are repeated in the transference situation which, as we have already observed in Chapter 1, has become the central preoccupation of analysts from a variety of different schools.

According to Jung, Adler sees the subject as having to protect himself against the undue influence of significant objects.

> Adler sees how a subject who feels suppressed and inferior tries to secure an illusory superiority by means of 'protests', 'arrangements', and other appropriate devices directed equally against parents, teachers, regulations, authorities, situations, institutions, and such. Even sexuality may figure amongst these devices. This view lays undue emphasis upon the subject, before which the idiosyncrasy and significance of objects entirely vanishes.[3]

Jung continues:

> Certainly both investigators see the subject in relation to the object; but how differently this relation is seen! With Adler the emphasis is placed upon a subject who, no matter what the object, seeks his own security and supremacy; with Freud the emphasis is placed wholly upon objects, which, according to their specific character, either promote or hinder the subject's desire for pleasure.[4]

There are certain objections to categorizing Freud and Adler in this way which need not detain us here. But Jung's description makes it clear that Freud's attitude, which he calls *extraverted*, conceives the subject as primarily in search of, and moving *toward*, objects. Adler, on the other hand, takes the *introverted* attitude of conceiving the subject as primarily needing to establish autonomy and independence, and hence moving *away* from objects.

Jung thought of extraversion and introversion as temperamental factors operating from the beginning of life, and as co-existing in everyone, although in varying measure. No doubt the ideal person would exhibit both attitudes in balanced fashion, but, in practice, one or other attitude generally predominated.

According to Jung, neurosis followed if either extraversion or introversion became exaggerated. Extreme extraversion led to the individual losing his own identity in the press of people and events. Extreme introversion threatened the subjectively preoccupied individual with loss of contact with external reality. When this kind of exaggeration occurred, an unconscious process would be set in motion which would attempt to compensate for the individual's one-sided attitude. We need not pursue Jung's further subdivision of types at this point; but we shall return to his view of the psyche as a self-regulating system in a later chapter, since this is very much concerned with the internal development of the individual as a separate entity, and hence related to the principal subject of this book.

Other observers have advanced classifications which, although they may emphasize different traits of personality, appear to be closely connected with the extravert–introvert dichotomy.

The art historian, Wilhelm Worringer, wrote a dissertation in 1906, which became his famous *Abstraction and Empathy*. It is the subject of a chapter in *Psychological Types*, but deserves to be read in its own right. Worringer stated that modern aesthetics was based upon the behaviour of the contemplating subject. He wrote:

Aesthetic enjoyment is objectified self-enjoyment. To enjoy aesthetically means to enjoy myself in a sensuous object diverse from myself, to empathise myself into it.[5]

But Worringer perceived that the concept of empathy was not applicable to long periods of art history, nor to every variety of art.

Its Archimedian point is situated at *one* pole of human artistic feeling alone. It will only assume the shape of a comprehensive aesthetic system when it has united with the lines that lead from the opposite pole.

We regard as this counter-pole an aesthetics which proceeds not from man's urge to empathy, but from his urge to abstraction. Just as the urge to empathy as a pre-assumption of aesthetic experience finds its gratification in the beauty of the organic, so the urge to abstraction finds its beauty in the life-denying inorganic, in the crystalline or, in general terms, in all abstract law and necessity.[6]

Worringer regarded abstraction as originating from anxiety; an attempt by man to create order and regularity in the face of a world in which he felt himself to be at the mercy of the unpredictable forces of Nature. The polarity is between trust in Nature and fear of Nature. Worringer perceived that extreme empathy led to 'losing oneself' in the object – the danger already mentioned in connection with exaggerated extraversion. Geometric form, on the other hand, represented an abstract regularity not found in Nature. Worringer wrote of primitive man:

In the necessity and irrefragability of geometric abstraction he could find repose. It was seemingly purified of all dependence upon the things of the outer world, as well as from the contemplating subject himself. It was the only absolute form that could be conceived and attained by man.[7]

Thus, abstraction is linked with detachment from the potentially dangerous object, with safety, and with a sense of personal integrity and power. This is also the kind of satisfaction which the scientist experiences in his encounters with Nature. A new hypothesis leading to a law which will predict events originates from perceived regularities, from the ability of the scientist to detach himself, his own subjective feelings, from whatever phenomena he is studying, and, when proven, gives an enhanced power over Nature. For example, recent work suggests that measuring changes in gravity in the vicinity of volcanoes may lead to an increased capacity to predict eruptions, which are still some of the most powerful and unpredictable natural events threatening the lives of men.

Abstraction, then, is connected with self-preservation; with the Adlerian, introverted need to establish distance from the object, independence and, where possible, control.

These two attitudes or poles of human nature are also reflected in Liam Hudson's classification of human beings into *divergers* and *convergers*. Hudson became interested in the preferences of clever schoolboys; whether they were principally attracted toward the arts or the sciences. He found that these preferences were linked with a number of other traits of character which supported the popular notion that the Scientist and the Artist are different sorts of person.

Convergers, who tend to specialize in the 'hard' sciences, or possibly in the classics, have the kind of intelligence which shows at its best in conventional intelligence tests of the kind in which there is only one correct answer to a question. They are less good at 'open-ended' tests in which a variety of answers are possible. In their spare time, convergers pursue mechanical or technical hobbies and show comparatively little interest in the lives of other people. They have conventional attitudes to authority, are emotionally inhibited, and seldom recall their dreams.

Divergers, in contrast, choose the arts or biology as their preferred

89

subjects. They are less good at conventional intelligence tests, better at open-ended tests where creative phantasy is demanded. Their spare-time activities are connected with people rather than with things. They have unconventional attitudes to authority, are emotionally uninhibited, and often recall dreams.

Modern elaborations of tests purporting to measure extraversion and introversion as defined in textbooks of psychology do not necessarily show such close parallels between extraversion and divergence, and between introversion and convergence as one might expect; but we are here concerned with only one major aspect; the relation between subject and object. Divergers, like extraverts, seem able easily to identify with other people, and to be open toward them. Convergers, like introverts, seem to withdraw from others, and to be more at ease with inanimate objects or with abstract concepts than they are with people. This is a generalization from extremes. No human being is all convergent, or all divergent; but these attitudes do seem to be manifested early in life, and to be remarkably persistent.

Another dichotomy which marches hand in hand with those we have just outlined is given by Howard Gardner in his book on the significance of children's drawings. He discerns two types of children whom he calls *patterners* and *dramatists*. Both groups are described as being of equal intelligence and charm, but as exhibiting 'strikingly different approaches to their daily experience'. These differences are detectable from the age of three and a half; that is, from about the time when the child first begins to link the act of drawing with his actual perception of the world about him, rather than simply scribbling whatever subjectively occurs to him. Gardner writes:

> On the one hand we have encountered a cadre of young children whom we have come to call *patterners*. These youngsters analyze the world very much in terms of the configurations they can discern, the patterns and regularities they encounter, and, in particular, the physical attributes of objects – their colors, size, shape, and the like. Such patterners enthusiastically arrange blocks on top of one another, endlessly experiment with forms on the table or in their drawings, constantly match objects with one another, build pairs and trios and the like; but they

90

spend little time re-enacting familiar scenes in play and they engage in relatively little social conversation (though they certainly understand what is said).

Sharply contrasted with these youngsters is the population we have touted as *dramatists*. These children are keenly interested in the structure of events that unfold in their vicinity – the actions, adventures, clashes, and conflicts that befall the world of individuals, as well as the fantastic tales describing even more gripping events, which they ask to hear over and over again. While patterners cling to the activities of drawing, modeling with clay, and arrangement of numerical arrays, the dramatists prefer to engage in pretend play, in storytelling, in continuing conversation and social exchange with adults and peers. For them, one of life's chief pleasures inheres in maintaining contact with others and celebrating the pageantry of interpersonal relations. Our patterners, on the other hand, seem almost to spurn the world of social relations, preferring instead to immerse (and perhaps lose) themselves in the world of (usually visual) patterns.[8]

Although Gardner does not use these terms himself, I think it is clear that the patterners could be described as predominantly introverted, or perhaps as potential convergers; whilst the dramatists are predominantly extraverted, perhaps potential divergers. Moreover, the patterners, who are less concerned with, or even avoidant of, people, resemble convergers in being preoccupied with finding or imposing order. The dramatists resemble divergers in being more concerned with people and with telling stories.

It is tempting to hazard a guess that, if any of these children later show creative potential, the dramatists will become novelists, poets, or playwrights, whilst the patterners will incline toward the sciences or philosophy. Only research involving years of following the growth and development of the two types of children will confirm or disprove this supposition. We are not even sure that these attitudes are quite as persistent as they appear to be. Perhaps those who begin as patterners later develop more of the characteristics of the dramatists, and vice versa.

What is important to realize is that Gardner's observations are another indication that the current emphasis upon relationships as the major determinant of mental health may be misplaced. There is no reason to suppose, from Gardner's descriptions, that the more introverted children, who were primarily concerned with pattern-making rather than with other people, were neurotic or abnormal; and the same holds true of Liam Hudson's convergers. Perhaps the ability to distance oneself from over-involvement with others, and the capacity to make a coherent pattern of one's life, are also important factors in attaining peace of mind and maintaining mental health.

In the previous chapter, reference was made to two factors which promoted a person's recovery from neurotic disorders: first, the adoption of some scheme or system of thought which appeared to make sense of the patient's distress; secondly, the achievement of a fruitful relationship with another person.

The need to make sense of one's experience is, of course, not confined to neurotic distress, but is an essential part of man's adaptation as a species. The development of intelligence, of consciousness, of partial emancipation from the governance of instinctive patterns, has made man into a reflective animal who feels the need to interpret, and to bring order to, both the world of external reality and the inner world of his imagination. Much of the emphasis placed on the transference situation in psycho-analysis is due to its being an element common to different psycho-analytic schools. The factor of making sense of the patient's experience is underemphasized partly because different analysts may view the same experience in very different ways.

In the end, one has to make sense of one's own life, however influential guidance from mentors may have been. The pattern made is not necessarily 'true' in any provable fashion, although it is possible to say that some views are closer to what is objectively known of the world than are others. But the need is there; and if it appears more obviously in the psychology of introverts, convergers, and patterners than it does in the psychology of extraverts, divergers, and dramatists, this does not mean that it is not present in the latter group as well as in the former. Even the most introverted persons need some human relationships; even the most extraverted persons need some pattern and order in their lives.

Temperamental differences between human beings may be chiefly determined genetically, but are, of course, influenced by a variety of environmental factors during the individual's development. We have so far been considering varieties of temperament which are 'normal', but neurotic attitudes, and psychotic attitudes also, are but exaggerations of normal human tendencies. At the time of writing, it is generally considered that the highly introverted person is more pathological than the very extraverted person. This is because of the current emphasis upon object relationships, and the disregard of processes which take place in solitude. However, there is a link between extraversion and introversion and two different types of personality which can be labelled pathological, and which may be disturbed in any degree from the slightly cranky to the psychotic. I shall refer to these two varieties of personality as *depressive* and *schizoid*. All such classifications of personality are inadequate, since they fail to do justice to man's infinite variety. But if we are to make any attempt to understand the different ways in which different kinds of individuals experience the world, we must use classifications as guidelines. What is particularly relevant to our present purposes is that both types of person have an especial need to be alone, although for different reasons.

Chapter 2 was concerned with the capacity to be alone. The *need* to be alone differs from the *capacity* to be alone in its suggestion that, at times, other people constitute a hindrance, interference, or threat.

At first sight, it may seem odd to write of extraverts needing to be alone since, by definition, extraverts are open, sociable people whose whole way of life is characterized by their confident relationship with others. However, as we hinted earlier, extraverts may lose contact with their subjective needs by becoming over-involved with, or losing themselves in, their objects. This is especially so of the type of extraverted person I call *depressive*, but is also part of the experience of most of us.

Most members of Western cultures have had the experience of finding particular social occasions exhausting, and have welcomed the opportunity of a retreat into privacy in order to recover and 'be themselves' again. If society is to function smoothly, there are bound to be occasions when one has to pretend; be welcoming when one is tired; smile when one wants to groan; or in other ways put on an act. Such dissimulation is fatiguing.

The Victorian lady used regularly to retire for a 'rest' in the afternoon. She needed to do so because convention demanded that she should constantly be empathically alert to the needs of others without regard to any needs of her own. Her afternoon rest allowed her to recuperate from the social role of dutiful listener and ministering angel; a role which allowed no scope for self-expression. Even Florence Nightingale, who was far from being merely a ministering angel, found that the only way in which she could study and write was to develop a neurotic illness which released her from the burden of household duties and enabled her to retire to the solitude of the bedroom.

Social pretences are temporary and deliberate examples of the device of the false self, based upon compliance, which Winnicott described, and which was discussed in Chapter 2. Winnicott was concerned with patients who had habitually adopted this mask from early childhood; who had lost touch with their true, inner feelings, and who were therefore unaware that they were living lives which were inauthentic. But most well-behaved adults feel that, on some social occasions, they need to be more than usually compliant, and remain well aware that the *persona* which they are presenting does not reflect their true feelings. There is always some discrepancy between an individual's public face and what he is in private.

People vary considerably in the degree to which they can be their true selves in company. Some enviable mortals seem able, from their earliest years, to express whatever they are feeling in the presence of comparative strangers without fear of being rebuffed, disapproved of, contradicted, or made to feel foolish. It seems likely that this kind of security springs from repeated experiences of the kind which Winnicott describes: of having been able, as an infant, to be alone in the presence of the mother without anxiety; and, in later childhood, of feeling loved and unconditionally accepted.

Other individuals find it difficult to be authentically themselves even in the presence of their spouses, lovers, or closest friends and relatives. Such individuals, whilst not going so far as to construct a false self which entirely replaces the true self at a conscious level, have an especial need to be alone which goes beyond the occasional demand for solitude referred to above. One possibility, plausible but as yet unproven, is that this especial need to be alone in adult life is derived from, or has been enhanced by, some degree of insecure attachment in early childhood. The child who has not, in infancy, formed secure bonds of trust with attachment figures, may react to parents, and later to other people, in a variety of ways; but I suggest that these variants are founded upon two basic themes. The first is *placation*; the second, *avoidance*. I shall try to show that placation is associated with the development of a depressive personality, whilst avoidance is associated with the development of a schizoid personality.

We are not yet in a position to determine all the factors which govern whether or not an infant becomes securely attached. As noted in Chapter 1, attachment varies in quality and in intensity. It is certain that insecure attachment, though sometimes the result of injudicious handling, lack of affection, or rejection by the mother, is not always to be blamed on her. Infants differ genetically, and some may be incapable of forming secure bonds of attachment, however much loving care they are given. This is true of some children who are later termed 'autistic'.

One common pattern of parent–child interaction which leads to insecurity and over-compliance can be outlined. A child who is not spurned nor in any way ill-treated may yet grow up to feel that his parents' love for him is conditional. Such a child comes to believe that continuance of his parents' love for him, and hence his security, depends, not upon being his authentic self, but upon being what his parents require him to be. Parents who induce this kind of belief in their children are often deeply concerned about their welfare, but are apt to demand impossibly high standards of 'good' behaviour, making the child believe that its instinctive drives and spontaneous responses are wrong. In extreme instances, this leads to the formation of a false self built on identification with the parent, and the total repression of the true self. In less extreme cases, the child displays a false self when in the company of others, but maintains a true self which only

95

emerges when he is alone. This is one reason for developing an especial need to be alone.

A child who shows this kind of partial compliance is clearly not going to incorporate the inner sense of his own worth which develops in children who are certain that their parents' love for them will be unconditionally continued. Confidence that one is of value and significance as a unique individual is one of the most precious possessions which anyone can have. Whether or not genetic factors are concerned with the development of this kind of confidence, it is certainly furthered or hindered by the quality of love which parents extend.

Children who feel that they have to be compliant to the extent of partially denying or repressing their true natures are bound to remain dependent on external sources for the maintenance of self-esteem. Such a child will develop into an adult who will continue to feel that he has to be successful, or good, or approved of by everyone, if he is to retain any sense of his own value. This necessarily makes him especially vulnerable to the reverses in life which we all have to endure: to failure in an examination or in competition for a job; to rejection by an actual or potential lover; to bereavement or to any other form of loss. Such unpleasant events make all of us temporarily resentful or low-spirited or both; but, in the case of those who possess little or no built-in self-esteem, may precipitate a devastating plunge into the hell of severe depression.

People who react to disapproval, failure, or loss by becoming so severely depressed that they are clearly 'ill', seem to lack any inner resources to which they may turn in the face of misfortune. For them, hazards which to others are challenges precipitate feelings of total hopelessness and helplessness. Some business men who become bankrupt set to and start a new enterprise. Others cast themselves from a window on the thirtieth floor. The latter variety behave as though there were no second chances in life; as though they were entirely dependent for maintaining their self-esteem upon the success of whatever enterprise was currently engaging them, without taking into account past blessings or future possibilities. It is as if any love or recognition which they had won in the past counted for nothing; as if there were nothing inside themselves to which to turn, no sense of being *intrinsically* worthwhile.

Patients suffering from depression of such severity that they are labelled psychotic often complain that they feel *empty*; that there is something missing, a void within which can never be filled. Utterances of this kind, especially when accompanied by fears of organic disease, are often dismissed as hypochondriacal delusions. It is more appropriate to consider such statements as metaphors which express a psychological truth. Severely depressed patients really *do* lack something within which other, less vulnerable people possess; an incorporated sense of their own value as persons.

People who can be precipitated into severe depression in this way are those referred to earlier as *depressive personalities*. It must be emphasized that this is a shorthand description which does not include every variety of potentially depressed person, but which can be aptly applied to those displaying this common type of vulnerability.

People of this temperament, or possessing this psychopathology, usually adopt a placatory attitude toward others because they cannot afford to disagree or risk anything which might cause offence or incur disapproval. Because the price of approval is compliance, which must involve some degree of dissimulation, this type of individual needs to get away from other people in order to be himself unimpeded by the need to please.

A 'masochistic', submissive stance toward others must involve the repression of aggression. The person who cannot stand up to other people, or assert himself when this is appropriate, represses his hostility. When he becomes depressed, his hostility toward others is displaced and becomes directed against himself in the form of self-reproach. As Freud pointed out in his classic paper, 'Mourning and Melancholia', the reproaches which the depressed person levels against himself are usually explicable as reproaches which he would like to have directed at someone close to him, but which he dared not express for fear of antagonizing a person upon whose love he depends.[9]

People of this kind constitute a considerable fraction of psychiatric practice. They also respond well to psychiatric treatment. It is easier to facilitate self-assertion in the timid than it is to induce humility in the overweening. But it must be emphasized that not all patients who suffer from recurrent depression are of the type just described. So-called 'bipolar', manic-depressive patients, who suffer from episodes of mania or hypomania as well as depression, are generally less inhibited, compliant, and self-effacing than the vulnerable people who only suffer from recurrent depression.

If a person with a depressive personality is in any way gifted, he may find that he can best express his true self in some form of creative work rather than in interaction with others. Since people of this temperament are predominantly extraverted, dramatists rather than patterners, divergers rather than convergers, it is likely that any gifts which they possess will be channelled in the direction of story-telling, plays, poetry, opera, or toward other creative pursuits which are chiefly concerned with human beings, although the people with whom they are involved may be creatures of their imagination.

It has sometimes been remarked that writers are disappointing to meet. This is often because their true personalities only emerge in their writings, and are concealed during the ordinary interchanges of social life. This does not apply to all writers; only to those who exhibit the temperament which has just been described. Writers, like other artists, display a variety of temperaments, from the flamboyance of a Balzac to the withdrawal of a Kafka; but the depressive temperament is particularly common amongst them.

The second variety of person who shows a special need to be alone is introverted, and, when disturbed or clearly pathological, is labelled *schizoid*. It was suggested earlier that there may be a link between the development of this kind of personality and the type of infantile behaviour which attachment theorists call *avoidance*. Once again, it must be emphasized that such a link is speculative and would not, even if established by research, solve the problem of how far that personality type is determined by nature and how far by nurture.

In Chapter 1, we touched on Bowlby's work on the behaviour of young children who have been separated from the mother. When reunited with the mother after a period of separation, infants show avoidance by averting their gaze, by turning the back toward the mother, and by moving away from contact. If picked up, the infant displaying avoidance may scream and struggle, only ceasing to do so when put down. Alternatively, without struggling and screaming, it may stretch out toward some object in the room, and when set down, occupy itself with this object rather than with the mother. Such avoidance behaviour is usually only temporary and disappears after a period of time which depends partly on the duration of the separation and partly upon the infant's previous relationship with the mother.

But separation is not the only circumstance prompting avoidance behaviour. According to Mary Main and Donna R. Weston, mothers who show aversion to physical contact with the infant during the first three months of the infant's life are likely to induce avoidance behaviour in the infant by the end of its first year. Mothers who demonstrate angry or threatening behaviour also induce avoidance in their infants.

> Mothers of mother-avoidant infants mocked their infants or spoke sarcastically to or about them; some stared them down.[10]

Mothers who go further and actually batter their babies produce infants who, as compared with controls, are

> more avoidant of peers and care-givers in response to friendly overtures, more likely to assault and threaten to assault them, and more likely to show unpredictable aggressive behaviour toward care-givers.[11]

In addition, mothers who are coldly unresponsive, that is, who show neither pleasure in response to their infants nor any reaction even when attacked by them, cause avoidance behaviour in their infants. None of these descriptions of maternal behaviour implies that such behaviour is the *only* cause of avoidance in the infant. Genetic differences, or brain damage, may also be implicated.

More research is needed before a confident interpretation of the biological purpose of avoidance behaviour can be given; but one interesting idea, particularly relevant to the main theme of this book, is that avoidance may permit the infant to maintain control over, flexibility in, and organization of, its own behaviour. Mary Main and Donna Weston write:

What is 'behavioral disorganization'? Behavior can be called disorganized when it vacillates between opposite extremes without reference to changes in the environment or when it appears repeatedly in an environment that does not call for it.[12]

When mothers both threaten their infants and also reject physical contact with them, they place them in an impossible position. Threats of any kind, from any source, stimulate an intense need for attachment on the part of the infant, because the prime function of attachment is protection from the threat of danger. But if the source of the threat is the very person to whom the infant must turn for protection, the infant is faced with a conflict which cannot be resolved. Placed in such a situation, the infant exhibits vacillation between approach, avoidance, and angry behaviour. This disorganization of behaviour can only be alleviated by the infant turning away from everything to do with the mother.

It is clear that avoidance implies a deeper disturbance in the relation between the infant and its mother than does compliance. This may be connected with the fact that avoidance is manifested at an earlier stage in the infant's development than the more sophisticated behaviour of compliance. Avoidance is connected with the fear of being damaged or destroyed by hostility. Compliance is concerned with the fear of love being withdrawn. Avoidance suggests doubt as to whether love has ever been proffered. Compliance implies recognition that love is available, but doubts whether it will last.

These patterns of behaviour are most obviously manifested in the pathological types of personality which warrant the labels 'schizoid' or 'depressive', but can also be detected as underlying factors in the attitudes of 'normal' people toward others. Students of the work of Melanie Klein will at once link these ideas with yet another dichotomy: the stages of infant development which she described as the 'paranoid-schizoid position' and the 'depressive position'. Although many of Melanie Klein's concepts remain unproven and unprovable, her belief that 'psychotic' mechanisms underlie and affect the emotional attitudes of 'normal' people is convincing. For example, it is only if we accept the existence of a latent paranoid potential lurking in the recesses of the normal mind that we can

100

explain the mass delusions which led to the persecution of witches and the Nazi slaughter of the Jews. Vast numbers of ordinary men and women held beliefs about witches and Jews which, if they had been expressed by one or two individuals instead of by whole communities, would have been dismissed as paranoid delusions. There are extremely primitive, irrational mental forces at work in the minds of all of us which are usually overlaid and controlled by reason, but which find overt expression in the behaviour of those whom we call mentally ill, and which also manifest themselves in the behaviour of normal people when under threat or other forms of stress. No one is so exquisitely well-balanced that he or she does not use avoidance or compliance to some extent in encounters with other people. Yet these attitudes can justifiably be linked with the very early varieties of behaviour in infants which were described above, and also with the pathological phenomena characteristic of the insane.

One of the most characteristic traits of the people whom psychiatrists label schizoid is their inability to make close relationships with people without feeling threatened. The typical schizoid dilemma is a desperate need for love combined with an equally desperate fear of close involvement. Kafka was a writer who vividly portrayed this dilemma in extreme form, and who also used avoidance in adult life in order that he could employ his writing as a means of preventing 'behavioral disorganization'.

Although Kafka, during his brief life, made a number of friends who were deeply fond of him and who sometimes idealized him, he said that, even with his closest friend and later biographer, Max Brod, he had never been able to hold a prolonged conversation in which he had really revealed himself. Strangers always constituted a threat. In a letter dated June 1913, Kakfa wrote:

But if I am in an unfamiliar place, among a number of strange people, or people whom I feel to be strangers, then the whole room presses on my chest and I am unable to move, my whole personality seems virtually to get under their skins, and everything becomes hopeless.[13]

During childhood and adolesence, Kafka was deeply ashamed of his body, which he considered disgracefully skinny and weak. It was not until he was twenty-eight years old that he felt able to appear in public swimming pools without embarrassment. His alienation from the body, which is characteristic of schizoid personalities, contributed to his doubts about the validity of his own existence, and to his fears that other people would overwhelm or destroy him. Even when he was afflicted with stomach ache, he imagined the pain as being caused by a stranger who was attacking him with a club. This paranoid phantasy is exactly comparable to those attributed by Melanie Klein to infants who are still in the paranoid-schizoid phase of development. According to her account, the human infant, because of its helplessness, reacts to frustration as if it were persecution, and fears its own destruction by the powerful parents on whom it depends. According to the Kleinian view, infants attribute to those who care for them intensely destructive impulses which are really part of their own psychology; that is, they employ the psychological mechanism of paranoid projection. In later life, suffering is liable to resuscitate these early emotions, and is therefore experienced as an attack upon the self from outside rather than as an internal experience. Whether or not one accepts Melanie Klein's view of the infant's psyche during the first months of life, Kafka's account of his reaction to strangers and to his own pain certainly attests the persistence and importance of paranoid projection in his psychology.

Given this temperament, it is not surprising that Kakfa had difficulties in his relationships with women. For five years, he was deeply involved with a girl called Felice Bauer, to whom he proposed marriage in June 1913. But, during the whole of this period, the couple, who lived respectively in Prague and Berlin, met on no more than nine or ten occasions, often for no more than an hour or two. The relationship was almost entirely epistolary. Kafka's letters, which are frequently distressing, display an intense need for Felice and a painful anxiety about her whereabouts, even about what she is wearing or eating. He demands instant replies to his daily letters, and becomes acutely distressed if he does not hear from her. But Felice's actual presence is treated as threatening, at least when Kafka is writing:

You once said that you would like to sit beside me while I write. Listen, in that case I could not write at all. For writing means revealing oneself to excess; that utmost of self-revelation and surrender, in which a human being, when involved with others, would feel he was losing himself, and from which, therefore, he will always shrink as long as he is in his right mind – for everyone wants to live as long as he is alive – even the degree of self-revelation and surrender is not enough for writing. Writing that springs from the surface of existence – when there is no other way and the deeper wells have dried up – is nothing, and collapses the moment a truer emotion makes that surface shake. That is why one can never be alone enough when one writes, why there can never be enough silence around one when one writes, why even night is not night enough.[14]

Needless to say, the marriage did not take place.

Kafka's need to be alone when writing might, at first sight, be interpreted simply as a reluctance to let anyone else see or criticize the self which his writing is revealing 'to excess'. He may certainly have considered that he needed to revise and edit what he felt to be so intensely personal before he would let even his beloved Felice read it. But his anxiety goes further than this. Actual proximity threatened to undermine the fragile organization of his psyche. Kafka hovered on the brink of psychosis. Erich Heller writes:

Of course, this is a disposition akin to madness, separated only from it by a writing table, an imagination capable of holding together what appears to have an irresistible tendency to fall apart, and an intelligence of supreme integrity.[15]

This pattern of intense emotional involvement on paper combined with actual distance from the beloved was repeated in his later relationship with Milena Jesenská. It was not until the last year of his life, when he was dying of tuberculosis, that Kafka was actually able to move in and live with a woman, Dora Dymant. Even then, he referred to this step as

103

a reckless move which can only be compared to some great historical event, like Napoleon's Russian campaign.[16]

Kafka's fear was that close involvement would threaten the one thing that kept him sane; his ability to keep the conflicting parts of his personality together by means of his writing. Without this, 'Things fall apart; the centre cannot hold.'[17] The person whom Kafka most needed was also a perpetual threat.

I suggested above that introverted or schizoid personalities, when possessed of creative abilities, were more likely to be drawn to philosophy or the hard sciences than toward fiction, since they are concerned with pattern-making rather than with story-telling. Kafka is so moving an example of what I have called the schizoid dilemma that I could not forbear to quote him, even though, at first sight, he may appear not to fit this hypothesis. But Kafka's terrifying fictional world is hardly concerned with real people. Many of his characters are not even given names, but are simply distinguished by their functions; as doorkeeper, warder, or officer. Kafka's world is essentially that of the human being threatened by impersonal forces which he can neither understand nor master; the state of affairs which, in Worringer's view, produced abstraction rather than empathy.

Another question remains. Kafka's ambivalence toward Felice and Milena inevitably reminds one of the avoidant infant who fears the very person upon whom he most depends. But is there really any justification for linking adult personality traits with infantile behaviour? I think that there is, although I am also aware that some research demonstrates that children may change considerably over the years in response to different sets of circumstances.

There is a curious paradox connected with this problem which is worth noting. Geneticists, and many psychologists, assume that inheritance is far more important than environment in determining adult personality. Psycho-analysts believe that environmental factors, especially those obtaining in infancy and early childhood, are the paramount forces shaping what people become. But the two camps join hands in supposing that these different factors act upon the individual early in life, and that the very young child is necessarily father to the man or mother to the woman, without taking much account of the possibility that later events in childhood and adolescence are also important determinants of adult personality.

8

Separation, Isolation, and the
Growth of Imagination

*'I think I could turn and live with animals, they are so
placid and self-contain'd,
I stand and look at them long and long.'*

Walt Whitman

In Chapter 6, it was suggested that an inner world of phantasy exists
in every human being, and that interests in which imagination plays
a part are, in many individuals, as important as interpersonal
relationships in giving meaning to their lives. There is nothing
pathological in the employment of imagination. We cannot dispense
with phantasy: if we could, we should lose much of what makes us
distinctively human. But, as one would expect, imaginative capacity
tends to become particularly highly developed in gifted individuals
who, for one reason or another, have passed rather solitary child-
hoods. We have already noted that the effects of solitude can be
damaging or rewarding according to circumstances. Unless those
circumstances are so inimically severe that they cause mental
disintegration, absence of, or partial deprivation of, interpersonal
relationships encourages imagination to flourish.

Imagination is generally recognized to be particularly active in
childhood, and is an especially evident resource in children who
either spend a good deal of time alone because other children are not
available, or who do so because they find it difficult to make
relationships with their peers. The people who later devote their lives
to pursuits in which imagination plays a major role have often started
to do so in childhood to a greater extent than the average because

circumstances of separation, loss, or enforced isolation have impelled them in that direction. Isolated children often invent imaginary companions. Others go further, and invent stories in which a variety of imaginary persons take part.

Various types of deprivation in early life may make it difficult for those who suffer them to achieve intimate attachments. But the development of an imaginary world can sometimes serve as a retreat from unhappiness, a compensation for loss, and a basis for later creative achievement. Some bereaved or very isolated children abandon any hope of making lasting intimate attachments, and only risk embarking upon relationships which are not so close. The relationships made by some creatively gifted people may be limited, incomplete, or stormy. Creative artists are quite likely to choose relationships which will further their work, rather than relationships which are intrinsically rewarding, and their spouses may well find that marital relations take second place. But this sequence of events is not invariable. There are examples of people who, as children, led isolated lives, but who nevertheless were able to make close relationships when adult. It is also not unknown for creative people, once they have achieved an intimate relationship, to lose some of their imaginative drive.

Anthony Trollope is one instance of a novelist who himself attributed the development of his creative imagination to early isolation. In his autobiography, Trollope describes the misery of his schooldays at Harrow and Winchester. As a result of his father's poverty, his school bills were not paid, and his pocket-money was stopped. The facts became known to his schoolfellows. Large, awkward, ugly, he became what he describes as 'a Pariah', who had no friends and who was despised by his companions. He took refuge in phantasy.

As a boy, even as a child, I was thrown much upon myself. I have explained, when speaking of my school-days, how it came to pass that other boys would not play with me. I was therefore alone, and had to form my plays within myself. Play of some kind was necessary to me then, as it has always been. Study was not my bent, and I could not please myself by being all idle.

Thus it came to pass that I was always going about with some castle in the air firmly built within my mind.

Trollope describes these compensatory romances as occupying six or seven years of his life before he left school and started work in the Post Office, and as continuing in his mind even after he had started work.

There can, I imagine, hardly be a more dangerous mental practice; but I have often doubted whether, had it not been my practice, I should ever have written a novel. I learned in this way to maintain an interest in a fictitious story, to dwell on a work created by my own imagination, and to live in a world altogether outside the world of my own material life.[1]

Trollope's pejorative appraisal of his daydreams as 'dangerous' recalls Freud's puritanical vision of phantasy as both childish and escapist. Yet Trollope's phantasy life later turned out to be so closely connected with the external world that some critics have dismissed his novels as being earthbound, pedestrian, and lacking in imagination. However, C. P. Snow calls him 'the finest natural psychologist of all nineteenth-century novelists'.[2]

Snow is surely right in attributing Trollope's capacity for empathy to his early unhappiness. Feeling rejected, as we shall see in other instances, often leads to watchfulness; to a wary appraisal of the feelings and behaviour of others who may inflict further pain if one does not learn to please them. In this way, the budding novelist learns to observe human beings and to gauge their motives.

Beatrix Potter is an interesting example of a writer who had a predominantly isolated childhood which, though not actively unhappy, caused her to grow up exceedingly shy and tongue-tied in company. Margaret Lane's biography of her, *The Tale of Beatrix Potter*, was first published in 1946. Humphrey Carpenter, in his chapter on Beatrix Potter in *Secret Gardens*, accuses Margaret Lane of exaggerating the writer's early loneliness and difficulties in making human relationships.[3] Carpenter points out that, in 1946, Beatrix Potter's secret journals, written in a code of her own invention, had not been deciphered; and claims that, if they had been available, Margaret Lane would have painted a different picture of her. However, a second edition of Margaret Lane's biography appeared in 1968 in which she makes considerable use of the journals and gives full acknowledgement to Leslie Linder, who broke Beatrix Potter's code and spent nine years transcribing what she had written.

Beatrix Potter was born on 28 July 1866, and remained an only child for her first five years. Attentive parents can sometimes compensate for the loneliness of an only child by sending the child to kindergarten, inviting other children to the house, and in other ways ensuring that opportunities for mixing with contemporaries are easily available. No such amenities were thought necessary for Beatrix Potter. She was provided with a Scottish nurse, given luncheon in the nursery, and taken for a walk in the afternoon. What more could a middle-class child, brought up in the well-to-do surroundings of Kensington, possibly want?

She was never sent to school, did not share her parents' life to any great extent, and was given no opportunity of mixing with other children, apart from occasional encounters with cousins. Her parents did not entertain guests at home; the atmosphere was stiflingly respectable; and no attempt was made to meet the needs of children. Beatrix Potter was nineteen before she saw the Horse Guards, the Admiralty and Whitehall, for the Potter carriage seldom left the immediate environs of South Kensington. It is not surprising that she grew up to be ill-at-ease in company. Her only escapes from this 'Victorian mausoleum', as a cousin called it, were visits to her paternal grandmother at a house near Hatfield, occasional visits to other relatives, and an annual family holiday in Scotland, where she began to take an interest in, and weave phantasies around, the lives of animals. She learned to read from the Waverley novels of Scott. Her first literary efforts seem to have been hymns and 'sentimental descriptions of Scottish scenery'.[4]

A younger brother, Bertram, made his appearance in due course but, as soon as he was old enough, was despatched to boarding school. A governess, Miss Hammond, became an encouraging presence who fostered Beatrix Potter's interest in nature and in drawing, but she left in the girl's early 'teens, saying that her pupil had already outstripped her. Although visiting governesses came to teach her German and French, most of Beatrix Potter's hours were spent without human companionship. But she did manage to acquire pets: a rabbit, a couple of mice, some bats, and a family of snails. Margaret Lane writes:

> She had made friends with rabbits and hedgehogs, mice and minnows, as a prisoner in solitary confinement will befriend a mouse.[5]

It is interesting that, when her coded journal was finally deciphered, no secrets which appeared to require concealment were revealed. Margaret Lane writes, very perceptively:

> No hidden self-communings, no secret fantasy, even singularly few complaints. She seems to have embarked on this labour of many years almost in spite of herself, driven by a restless urge to use her faculties, to stretch her mind, to let nothing of significance escape, to create *something*.[6]

The journal was kept up until Beatrix Potter was thirty. Although its contents were unexciting, the fact that she wrote it assiduously for so many years argues that, for her, it was an important affirmation of her identity as an individual. In a household where little acknowledgement of a child's separate individuality was offered, such affirmation of identity can seem to the child to be opposition to parents and therefore wrong. This may be the reason why the journal had to be encoded.

Her other creative activity was drawing, at which, as her books show, she became delightfully accomplished.

When she was seventeen, Beatrix Potter was taught German by Annie Carter, with whom she became very friendly. When Miss Carter married, Beatrix Potter continued to correspond with her, and to take an interest in her children. The eldest of these, a boy called Noel, developed a long illness when he was five years old. In order to entertain him, Beatrix Potter sent him a long, illustrated letter recounting the adventures of Peter Rabbit. This was privately printed as a book in 1901, and then brought out publicly in 1902, by Warne & Co.

During the next ten years, *The Tale of Peter Rabbit* was followed by *The Tale of Squirrel Nutkin*, *The Tale of Jemima Puddleduck*, and by the tales of all the other charming creatures who became familiar to, and beloved by, subsequent generations of children. Beatrix Potter's drawings of animals are so exquisite that, some years ago, there was a special exhibition of them in London. It is interesting to observe that her drawings of people never reached the same high standard. Why should they? People, at that stage in her life, had never meant as much to her as the tiny pets to whom she had given her heart, and whom she therefore observed more closely.

It is also interesting that the creative period in which all her best books were written lasted a mere ten years. In 1913, in spite of bitter opposition from her parents, Beatrix Potter married a solicitor, and settled down to farming in the Lake District. In 1913 also, Beatrix Potter reached the age of forty-seven. It could be argued that, as age renders childhood increasingly remote, creativity based upon childhood phantasy is bound to decline. It could also be surmised that, when another human being became for the first time the emotional centre of Beatrix Potter's life, the intensity of feeling with which she had invested the lives of animals diminished, and her motive for inventing stories about them disappeared. She is not the only example of a writer whose interest in imaginative invention seems to have declined in similar fashion; but other women writers, like Trollope's mother, carried on writing in spite of marriage and maternity.

At the beginning of his chapter on Beatrix Potter to which we have already referred, Humphrey Carpenter postulates

a stereotype in many people's minds of the typical children's writer of the late Victorian and Edwardian period. He or she is supposed to have been a lonely, withdrawn, introverted individual, scarcely able to achieve normal human relationships, and only capable of communicating his or her deepest feelings by talking to children or writing books for them.[7]

I share Carpenter's dislike of stereotypes; but it is nevertheless quite often the case that adults who find it difficult to make relationships with their contemporaries are more at ease with children or animals, whether or not they happen to be writers. Let us briefly look at some examples of writers who showed these character-istics and whose emotional development and choice of career were partly determined by early separation from their parents.

Edward Lear, whose nonsense rhymes and comic drawings have entertained both adults and children for over a hundred years, was the twentieth child of his parents. When his father ran into debt, the family split up. At the age of four, in order to ease the burden on his mother, Lear was entrusted to the care of his elder sister, Ann. From then on, his mother had nothing further to do with his upbringing. Vivien Noakes writes:

> He was a rather ugly, short-sighted, affectionate little boy, and he was bewildered and hurt by her unaccountable rejection of him.[8]

Although his sister proved an affectionate guardian, and the family were later reunited, Lear seems never to have formed close ties with either parent, and, from the age of seven onward, was subject to recurrent attacks of depression which he called 'the Morbids'. His psychological disturbance was further complicated by epilepsy and asthma. He grew up to become a lonely adult, predominantly homosexual, but probably never consummating his desires.

> His search was not for physical love, but for someone who would want him as a person in the way that his parents had not wanted him as a child. Through his sensibility and charm he was sought after as a friend, and he loved to be with children because they liked him and showed it. But what he was searching for, and never found, was real spiritual involvement with another person.[9]

Vivien Noakes subtitles her biography 'The Life of a Wanderer', for Lear spent much of his life in travel, making his living as a painter.

112

Perpetual travel, or frequent moves of house, are often engaged in by the maternally deprived or by those who, for other reasons, find it difficult to create a place which they can consider 'home'. Lear, in spite of his charm and the lovable qualities which brought him many friends, never overcame his essential loneliness.

Rudyard Kipling is a particularly striking example of a writer whose early deprivation and unhappiness had a profound effect upon his future. Kipling was born in Bombay on 30 December 1865. His father, John Lockwood Kipling, was principal of a school of art in that city. On 15 April 1871, Kipling's father and mother, together with his younger sister, who had been born on 11 June 1868, returned to England for a six-month leave of absence. In those days, it was customary for the children of English parents living in India to be sent home for their education. This was partly to avoid the risks of disease and premature death, which were certainly greater in the hot climate of India, and partly for snobbish reasons. Children brought up by Indian 'ayahs' were less likely to acquire the habits and manners of the English middle-class.

Kipling, just before his sixth birthday, was left with his sister in the care of a retired naval captain and his wife, Captain and Mrs Holloway. The parents did not inform their children that they were returning to India without them. Kipling was not to see his mother again until April 1877. The five years which he spent in what he later called 'The House of Desolation' marked him for life. He was bullied by the Holloways' son, a boy some six years older, and ruthlessly punished, both by beatings and by enforced isolation, at the hands of the hateful Mrs Holloway. He was also bullied at the local day-school to which he was sent, and at which he performed badly. Every night he was cross-examined as to how he had spent his day. Each contradiction which the frightened, sleepy child produced was treated as a deliberate lie, and further proof of punishable wicked-ness. One of Kipling's biographers, Charles Carrington, remarks that his long years of suffering at the hands of Mrs Holloway taught him

the stoic lessons that the mind must make its own happiness, that any troubles can be endured if the sufferer has resources of his own to sustain him.[10]

In his story 'Baa, Baa, Black Sheep', Kipling gives an autobiographical account of this dreadfully unhappy part of his life. Angus Wilson writes:

> The writing of it was extremely painful to him as we know from his friend, Mrs Hill, in whose house in Allahabad he was living when he wrote it.[11]

Kipling referred to his treatment by Mrs Holloway as 'calculated torture'; but he also said that its effect was to make him pay careful attention to the lies which he had to tell, and concluded that this was the foundation of his literary effort.

The art of fiction may in part spring from the capacity to make lies convincing, but this is not its only source, and Kipling is being unnecessarily self-deprecating in suggesting it. What he also records is his delight in discovering that, if only adults left him alone, he could, through reading, escape into a world of his own.

As an adult, Kipling remained elusive and shunned publicity. He resented enquiry into his private life, wishing to be judged on his writings alone. His marriage was of a kind characteristic of creative people whose principal wish is not close intimacy, but the freedom to pursue their imaginative work without interruption. Carrie Balestier, whom Kipling married in 1892, was a capable woman who protected him from visitors, took over the running of the household, and managed his business affairs and correspondence. Although he enjoyed his fame and had widespread social contacts, Kipling remained reserved, and was apt to retreat into reverie on social occasions. Carrington thinks that the marriage was more satisfactory on his side than it was on his wife's.

Kipling's inner tension revealed itself in insomnia and duodenal ulcer. Like Edward Lear, he was at his best and most relaxed with children. He also exhibited an extraordinary capacity for inspiring confidence in others, who found themselves telling him their troubles in the assurance that he would not betray them.[12]

This particular trait seems to depend upon an unusual capacity to put oneself in other people's shoes, to *identify* oneself with others. It often originates in the kind of premature concern with the feelings of

114

others which Kipling describes himself as having had to develop as a child; a concern which we also observed in Trollope. Kipling became watchful and wary; alert to the changing moods of adults which might presage anger. This prescient awareness of what others were feeling and of how they displayed their emotions probably stood him in good stead when he came to write.

Fear of punishment is not the only reason for this kind of watchful anxiety. Children with depressed mothers, or with mothers whose physical health is a matter for concern, develop the same kind of over-anxious awareness. Such children keep their own feelings to themselves, whilst at the same time taking special note of the feelings of the other person. They are less able than most children to turn to the mother or other care-taker as a resource. In adult life, the watchful, over-anxious child becomes a listener to whom others turn, but who does not make reciprocal relationships on equal terms of mutual self-revelation. The same temperament is not infrequently found in psycho-analysts and doctors, who invite confidences but who are not called upon to reveal themselves.

Kipling knew his confidants better than they were allowed to know him. As often happens with writers, Kipling's revelation of himself was mostly indirect and confined to his fiction. 'Baa, Baa, Black Sheep' is exceptional, in that it appears to be autobiography undiluted.

H. H. Munro, the author 'Saki', is a striking example of a writer whose imagination owed much to bereavement, loss of parental love, and emotional isolation. Saki was born almost exactly five years later than Kipling, on 18 December 1870. Like Kipling, he was born abroad; not in India, but in Burma, where his father was an officer in the British military police. Whilst on furlough in England, in the winter of 1872, his pregnant mother was charged by a runaway cow. She both miscarried and died as a result of this untoward accident. Saki and his elder brother and sister were left behind when their father returned to Burma, to be brought up by their widowed paternal grandmother and her two fearsome daughters, Aunt Charlotte, known as 'Tom', and Aunt Augusta.

These two formidable women were in constant, bickering competition with each other. Both were rigid disciplinarians. Augusta, particularly, was irrationally punitive, adding the threat of divine wrath to her own. Ethel, the eldest of the three Munro children, described her as:

A woman of ungovernable temper, of fierce likes and dislikes, imperious, a moral coward, possessing no brains worth speaking of, and a primitive disposition. Naturally, the last person who should have been in charge of children.[13]

Saki repeatedly revenged himself on his aunts in his stories, of which the most vindictive is 'Sredni Vashtar', in which the guardian of ten-year-old Conradin, who is clearly modelled on Aunt Augusta, is killed by Conradin's pet, a polecat-ferret.

Saki grew up to be a dandy and a homosexual. Like Noël Coward, he concealed his feelings beneath a protective mask of cynicism; and, although beloved by many, was intimate with few. In his perceptive introduction to *The Bodley Head Saki*, J. W. Lambert writes:

Even the tributes of his friends (except perhaps those in the Army) seem to suggest the charming courtesy which is rooted in indifference. Society was for him a breeding-ground of inanity. When he turns from the attack he becomes a celebrant of loneliness. There is no close human relationship in any of his work, except the twisted skein which binds and cripples Francesca Bassington and her son [see *The Unbearable Bassington*].[14]

Saki shared with Kipling and with Lear a preference for the company of children rather than that of adults. All three were animal-lovers and introduced animals into their stories.

Saki and Kipling also shared a certain interest in physical cruelty which sometimes manifests itself distastefully, as in the 'Stalky' stories of Kipling, and in Saki's description of Comus caning a boy at school in *The Unbearable Bassington*. Both men carried with them into adult life a sadistic streak which, as such things often are, was probably derived from a wish for revenge on those who had tormented them in childhood. Fiction provides an acceptable outlet for the discharge of violent feelings. How one wishes that those who act out such emotions by attacking the innocent and helpless were gifted enough to express their feelings in the form of fiction!

A third example is a writer of a very different kind, P. G. Wodehouse. He was born on 5 October 1881. Although he was born in England, he passed most of his first two years in Hong Kong, where his father was a magistrate. At the age of two, Wodehouse and his two brothers, aged six and four, were taken to England by their mother and put in charge of a stranger, a Miss Roper, who was engaged to look after them. After three years of her regime, the boys were moved to a school in Croydon, run by two sisters, and then to a school in Guernsey. Wodehouse himself wrote that he was just passed from hand to hand, and that it was an odd life with no home to go to.

He was not desperately unhappy. In an interview toward the end of his life, he actually claimed to have had a very happy childhood, and contrasted his own fate favourably with that of Kipling. But the lack of any close, abiding affectionate ties in his earliest years inevitably had its effect. His biographer, Frances Donaldson, remarks:

> He simply detached himself from the cold and unrewarding world and retreated into phantasy. From the earliest age he was happiest alone with his own company, and in the absence of any family life or stimulus to the emotions, he cultivated his imagination in solitude. He said he could remember no time when he did not intend to be a writer and he started to make up stories even before he could write.[15]

In an interview which he gave for the *Paris Review* when he was ninety-one, Wodehouse was reported as saying: 'I know I was writing stories when I was five. I don't know what I did before that. Just loafed I suppose.'[16]

After yet another change of school, P. G. Wodehouse was sent to Dulwich College. Here, Frances Donaldson tells us, 'he acquired, for the first time, a degree of permanence and stability'.[17]

For Wodehouse, Dulwich College became the focus for emotions which, in children who have experienced a normal background, usually become attached to 'home'. Forty years after he had left the school, Wodehouse was still following the school's football matches with undiminished emotional intensity. He himself described his years at Dulwich as being like heaven. He was good at games, above average intellectually, and, in the atmosphere of a public school, not required to make close relationships. As Frances Donaldson puts it, 'he could participate without being drawn in'.[18]

Wodehouse's mother re-entered his life when he was fifteen, but he never formed any close relationship with her, and seems to have remained emotionally inhibited and dependent in his later relationships with women. As often happens with the maternally deprived, Wodehouse was drawn to women older than himself. When he married, in 1914, his wife Ethel took entire charge of his financial affairs, and made him a small allowance. She protected him against the world, and, although she sometimes pressed him into social engagements which he shunned, saw that he got the solitude he needed. In these respects, Wodehouse's marriage closely resembled Kipling's.

P. G. Wodehouse continued to dread individual social contacts, hated being interviewed, loathed clubs (though he belonged to a number of them), and lavished on animals the affection which he could not give to his fellow-creatures. When his wife was looking for an apartment in New York he asked her to find one on the ground floor. ' "Why?" she asked, and he replied: "I never know what to say to the lift-boy." '[19]

When he visited his daughter at school, he had to wait outside until she joined him because he was frightened of facing her headmistress without support. He was a sweet, kind, rather childlike character who used his work as a retreat from the world and who was hugely prolific as a result. It is reckoned that he published ninety-six books, as well as writing lyrics for musical comedies and much else besides.

In the ordinary course of life, one usually admires people who make light of their troubles by turning them into jokes; but P. G. Wodehouse made use of humour as a defence to a point at which it distorted his appreciation of reality. His indifference to money, for example, other than the change which he carried for tobacco or a new typewriter ribbon, involved him in recurrent encounters with the tax authorities. Interned in France by the Germans during the Second World War, he did immense damage to his reputation by agreeing to make some light-hearted broadcasts from Germany about his experiences as an internee. Anyone with a normal appreciation of reality, let alone any sense of politics, would have realized that such an act would be looked upon as support for the Nazis, but Wodehouse blithely took it as a chance to keep in touch with his public and to thank his American friends for the parcels which they had sent him, without any suspicion that he would be labelled a traitor.

Kipling, Saki and Wodehouse had in common the experience of being 'farmed out' at an early age, and of lacking the amenities, affection, and support of an ordinary home. As a result, all three suffered subsequently from difficulties in making close relationships and tended to show more affection toward animals or children than they were able to show toward adults.

All three learned to use the imagination, both as a retreat from the world, and also as an indirect way of making a mark upon it. Kipling and Saki expressed in their fiction some of the resentment which they felt toward those who had abandoned them and left them to be mistreated at the hands of strangers. Wodehouse, who was not ill-treated, but merely passed from hand to hand, developed an imaginative world in which there is no violence, no hatred, no sex, and no deep feeling. Although some of Lear's rhymes exhibit a humorous kind of violence, his imaginative world is also sexless and without profound emotion.

It is legitimate to assume that, in these examples, the development of such highly complex imaginative worlds was the consequence of being cut off from the emotional fulfilment which children with more ordinary backgrounds experience in their relations with parents and other care-takers. These writers (and here I include Beatrix Potter and Edward Lear, who were emotionally, but not physically, removed from parental care) compensated for their isolation by their invention, and by, in four instances, partially substituting love of animals for love of people.

However, not every isolated person, even if gifted, turns either to fiction or to the animal kingdom. Nor can difficulties in making relationships necessarily be attributed to adverse circumstances in childhood. As we saw in the previous chapter, people differ, not only in their family backgrounds, but also in inherited temperament. There are those who, however much affection they received as children, never succeed in making close relationships. There are those who compensate for comparative absence of interpersonal relationships by pursuing wealth, rather than by creating fiction. It would be naive to think that the creative activities of man can be subsumed under a single heading. Nevertheless, as these examples show, the gifts which enable a person to become a writer can be set in motion by loss and isolation. We can begin to understand why Simenon, in an interview for the *Paris Review*, said: 'Writing is not a profession but a vocation of unhappiness.'[20]

In the same interview Simenon reveals that, as a young boy, he became acutely aware that complete communication between two people was impossible. He says that this gave him such a sense of solitude, of loneliness, that he would almost scream. It was no doubt this sense of loneliness which fostered his remarkable capacity for inventing stories. It may also be held responsible for his compulsive pursuit of women.

The writers whom we have discussed in this chapter, with the possible exception of P. G. Wodehouse, were unhappy in childhood and had good reason to be so. How far did they continue to be unhappy throughout their lives? Did their early experience prevent them from making the kind of relationships with others which bring happiness? If so, did the exercise of their imaginative gifts bring them happiness of another kind?

These are not easy questions to answer. Edward Lear was prone to severe depression throughout his life, and, in spite of being beloved by many people, seems to have remained emotionally isolated.

Trollope also remained vulnerable to depression, and worked compulsively to stave off melancholy. On the other hand, he made a marriage which he claimed was happy, and which seems to have been so. His middle-aged love for Kate Field in no way contradicts this. He was a sensitive man who strove to conceal his feelings behind a bluff *persona*, but he made many friends, and, as an adult, could certainly not be called isolated. The fame which his novels brought him compensated to a large extent for his early experience of feeling despised and rejected.

Kipling's relationships seem to have been somewhat less intimate than Trollope's, although his passion for privacy makes it difficult to be sure. What is certain is that he had considerable charm, and that this brought him many enduring friendships which were important to him. His marriage gave him security; his fame supported his self-esteem. But, like Trollope, Kipling remained prone to depression, and, so Angus Wilson believes, was plagued by a fear of mental breakdown which made him shy away from introspection. What he attempted in his writing was an art based on external observation, owing as little as possible to self-examination. Angus Wilson concludes that it is this evasion of introspection which prevents Kipling from being amongst the first rank of writers, but which also accounts for his tackling themes which no other writer has undertaken.

Of the writers discussed in this chapter, I think it probable that Saki remained the most isolated. His unhappy childhood had made it difficult for him to form intimate relationships, a difficulty which was compounded by his homosexuality, which was then a crime, and not widely acknowledged or regarded as acceptable in society. His writing brought him some recognition in his lifetime, but its limitations, its exclusion of love, its irony, and its cruelty, precluded Saki from enjoying the fame granted to writers with wider human sympathies.

From his own letters, it appears that the happiest period of his life was during the First World War. At the beginning of the war, Saki was forty-three. His health had not been good, but, in spite of this, he managed to enlist as a private in King Edward's Horse. His letters indicate that he regarded the war as a romantic adventure, enjoyed the male companionship which it afforded, and, perhaps because he did not much care whether or not he survived, relished the danger of nocturnal expeditions to lay mines. Saki was killed by a sniper's bullet on 14 November 1916.

Of the work of the writers discussed so far, that of Wodehouse comes closest to fitting Freud's view of phantasy as primarily escapist. Wodehouse's relationships with other human beings seem to have remained upon a relatively superficial level. The hub around which his life revolved was certainly not intimate attachments, but his work. However, his pleasure in creating his imaginary world, his ingenuity, his verbal skill, and his worldly success, seem to have brought him a kind of happiness which many might envy.

Beatrix Potter, even before she married, succeeded in finding happiness. Provided that she could escape from her oppressive family, and live by herself in the farm which she had bought in the Lake District, country pursuits and her writing made her content. No doubt her marriage brought her even greater fulfilment; but there is no reason to doubt her biographer's opinion that the eight years before her marriage were also a happy time. This was the period when she was able to enjoy the solitary possession of Hill Top Farm and also the period during which she was at her best as a writer.

The idea that the development of imagination and invention in these writers began as compensation for the absence or severance of intimate attachments carries with it the implication that such development is second best; a poor substitute for the close, loving relationships which they should have enjoyed. In early childhood, this is probably the case. Nothing can entirely compensate for the absence of intimate attachments in the very young.

However, what began as compensation for deprivation became a rewarding way of life. All these writers were successful, in spite of the emotional scars they bore. With the possible exceptions of Saki and Lear, all made relationships which, although varying in intensity and closeness, were at least as satisfying as many of those made by people who had not suffered similar childhood deprivations. What began as compensation ended as a way of life which is as valid as any other, and more interesting than most. Even if their intimate attachments were not the hub around which their lives revolved, there is no reason to suppose that these lives were unfulfilled.

9

Bereavement, Depression and Repair

'Writing is a form of therapy; sometimes I wonder how all those who do not write, compose or paint can manage to escape the madness, the melancholia, the panic fear which is inherent in the human situation.'

Graham Greene

'But seriously I wonder whether for a person like myself whose most intense moments were those of depression a cure that destroys the depression may not destroy the intensity – a desperate *remedy.'*

Edward Thomas

In the preceding chapter, we concluded that some writers are impelled to develop their imaginative capacities as a compensation for the absence of, or severance of, intimate relationships with parents. In this chapter, I want to pursue the idea that imagination is able to do more than create compensatory castles in the air, or retreats from unhappiness. Creative imagination, as the quotation from Graham Greene given above suggests, can exercise a healing function. By creating a new unity in a poem or other work of art, the artist is attempting to restore a lost unity, or to find a new unity, within the inner world of the psyche, as well as producing work which has a real existence in the external world. In Chapter 5, reference was made to the fact that people who realize their creative potential are constantly bridging the gap between the world of external reality and the inner world of the psyche. In Winnicott's phrase, 'creative apperception' is what makes individuals feel that life is worth living; and those who are gifted are perhaps more able than most to repair loss in symbolic fashion. The human mind seems so constructed that a new balance or restoration within the subjective, imaginative world is felt as if it were a change for the better in the external world, and vice versa. In thus linking objective and subjective, we are approaching the limits of human understanding; but I believe that the secrets of human creative adaptation are to be found at just those limits. The hunger of imagination which drives men to seek new understanding and new connections in the external world is, at the same time, a hunger for integration and unity within.

Of the writers whose lives were examined in the last chapter, Saki was least able to overcome the traumata of his early childhood. He was also the only one of these particular writers to be permanently deprived of his mother by her death when he was only two years old. In this chapter, I want to examine the relation between creativity and depression. Since bereavement, and specifically early bereavement, is not only a precipitant of depression at the time, but seems often to predispose the sufferer to react to any later losses with particular severity, the complex relation between bereavement, depression and creative achievement will be outlined.

Although separation from both parents is a traumatic event for any young child, we may suppose that, so long as the child knows that they are still alive, he will continue to entertain hopes of being reunited with them. Unless belief in an afterlife prevails, a child who has lost a parent by death can have no such hope. The arbitrary nature of such a deprivation, its unfairness and its inexplicability, are likely to make the world seem an unpredictable, unsafe place over which the child can exert no influence. It is not surprising that loss of a parent in early childhood has often been linked with the development of emotional problems in later life. More especially, parental death has been thought to increase the risk of suffering from episodes of severe depression.

Whether or not early bereavement can by itself produce liability to later depression is a matter of dispute. The effects of such bereavement vary; and, although there is no doubt that early bereavement is traumatic, it may be that it only acts as a trigger for depression in those who are already genetically predisposed.

This supposition is supported by a paper in which the authors compared a group of psychiatric patients who had experienced the death of a parent in childhood with a larger group of psychiatric patients who had suffered no such bereavement. What they concluded was that early loss of a parent affected the severity of later mental illness without determining its type. That is, such a loss was not specifically associated with the development of depression, schizophrenia or other forms of mental illness, but was associated with greater severity of symptoms when the patients were first admitted to hospital.

However, the patients who had experienced childhood bereavement did show greater difficulty in achieving mature, adult attachments.

They also formed intense, unstable interpersonal relationships and complained of chronic feelings of emptiness and boredom.[1]

This latter finding suggests that some, at any rate, of the patients who had suffered early bereavement were chronically depressed, since, as we have seen, complaints of feelings of emptiness are a common feature of depression.

George Brown and Tirril Harris, in their study of depression in working-class women, concluded that, if a woman had experienced the death of her mother before the age of eleven, she was more likely to respond to subsequent losses by developing severe depression. We have already postulated that self-esteem depends upon 'building-in' or incorporating a sense of being unequivocally loved for oneself. Since a mother is, in childhood, the most important source of unequivocal love, it is natural enough that her disappearance should interfere with, or prevent, the incorporation of love, and hence make self-esteem more difficult to attain or preserve.[2]

However, other research workers have questioned whether it is the actual death of the mother which increases vulnerability to depression in later life. A recent study claimed that, in a series of depressed patients of varying types, there was no evidence that parental death before the age of fifteen was a crucial factor.[3] On the other hand, the authors do suggest that lack of a warm relationship with parents in childhood may be an important predisposing factor contributing to the subsequent development of depression in adults, and this fits well with the supposition that absence of built-in self-esteem causes vulnerability to depression. A child cannot incorporate a sense of being loved from a parent who is dead; but neither can he from a parent who is rejecting, absent for long periods, or so disturbed as to be incapable of a warm relationship.

Self-esteem is not only connected with feeling lovable, but also with feeling competent. Depressive personalities, in the face of adversities like divorce or loss by death of a spouse, not only suffer the loss of someone who provided self-esteem by proffering love and care, but also often feel helpless at trying to cope with life alone, at least initially. Brown and Harris write:

> It is certainly not unlikely that loss of mother before eleven may have an enduring influence on a woman's sense of self-esteem, giving her an ongoing sense of insecurity and feelings of incompetence in controlling the good things of the world.

The authors continue:

> Until a child is about eleven the main means of controlling the world is likely to be the mother. Thereafter, the child is more likely to exert control directly and independently. The earlier the mother is lost, the more the child is likely to be set back in his or her learning of mastery of the environment; and a sense of mastery is probably an essential component of optimism. Thus, loss of mother before eleven may well permanently lower a woman's feeling of mastery and self-esteem and hence act as a vulnerability factor by interfering with the way she deals with loss in adulthood.[4]

Another factor linking early loss of a parent with subsequent liability to depression is also connected with feelings of lack of mastery. Some patients who have suffered early bereavement continue to look for the lost parent, and are liable to marry husbands or wives who represent the parent and to whom the patient can turn. Birtchnell found that women who had lost their mothers before the age of ten were significantly more dependent, or, to use Bowlby's terminology, more anxiously attached, than women who had not.[5]

Dependency and a feeling of incompetence, of being unable to cope, are closely connected. Helplessness marches hand in hand with hopelessness in many cases of depression. In Chapter 4, reference was made to Bettelheim's observation that the prisoners in concentration camps who were the first to die were those who had given up any attempt at independent decision-making, and who therefore felt completely helpless in the hands of their persecutors.

Marrying a parent-figure reinforces the sense of being unable to cope. If there is always someone to turn to, someone who will proffer advice and make decisions, the dependent person does not learn competence. The loss of a spouse is more likely to aggravate feelings of helplessness in those who have been particularly dependent upon their spouses than in those who have not. In some instances, the sense of helplessness persists. In others, the bereaved husband or wife, because there is no longer someone to turn to, discovers previously unrealized powers of coping. We have all seen individuals who appear to have taken on a new lease of life after losing a husband or wife; and this is not always because the marriage was unhappy.

Research indicates that undesirable changes in a person's life like death of a spouse, divorce, loss of a job, personal injury, or a prison sentence are correlated with subsequent illness to a significant extent *if they are perceived by the subject as uncontrollable.* It has also been shown that people who feel that their lives are mainly controlled by external forces suffer more from illness in response to stressful events than do those who have a strong sense of control over their lives.[6]

There is general agreement that loss in the present may awaken feelings of loss in the past. This is especially so if the emotions aroused by the original loss have not been completely 'worked through' – a phenomenon referred to in Chapter 3. In cases in which the process of mourning has not been completed, subsequent losses are likely to produce worse effects. It was suggested earlier that the child who had been separated from its parents might retain some hope of being reunited with them, but that the child who had lost a parent by death was deprived of any possibility of consolation. This

127

suggestion implies that death of a parent is likely to have a worse effect on subsequent mental health than separation.

Brown and Harris have produced evidence which goes some way to supporting this hypothesis. They discovered that states of depression in women who had lost a parent by death were more severe, more likely to be diagnosed as psychotic; whereas the types of depression afflicting women who had suffered loss by separation were more likely to be labelled neurotic.

Brown and Harris suppose that someone who has suffered loss by death, when faced with subsequent loss of any kind, is more likely to react to current loss as if it was inevitably irreversible. This may explain some cases in which the loss or failure which acts as a trigger for severe depression seems trivial compared with the reaction which it provokes.[7] For example, an adolescent who has previously lost a parent may become profoundly and inappropriately depressed after failing an examination.

Another factor determining susceptibility may be the importance attached to interpersonal relationships as a source of self-esteem. Young children, unless they are prodigies, will not have had sufficient time to develop the interests and skills which might enhance their sense of competence. As we shall see, those who can turn to creative work have an advantage over those whose self-esteem depends entirely upon close relationships.

Writing and other creative activities can be ways of actively coping with loss, whether this be the loss of current bereavement or the feeling of loss and emptiness which accompanies severe depression originating from other causes. In Chapter 7, it was suggested that a person who was vulnerable to recurrent depression could, if he possessed talent, express in creative work aspects of his true self which he found difficult to manifest in social life. In Chapter 8, we saw that some writers, because of early separation or later isolation and unhappiness, created phantasy worlds into which they could retreat. These are not the only functions which creative work can serve.

The creatively gifted who suffer bereavement, or who experience severe depression for other reasons, can go further than this. As I suggested at the beginning of this chapter, they are often able to use their talents in what can be described as a process of repair or re-creation. This process is an effort to come to terms with loss in which pain is accepted, rather than an attempt to deny loss or to escape from it. Graham Greene, who admits to a manic-depressive temperament and a recurrent need to escape from periods of depression, is right in supposing that writing or composing or painting can be a form of therapy, although this is certainly not their only function. Moreover, this is a form of therapy which does not require any therapist other than the sufferer himself.

We have seen that creative people are used to solitude, and we have explored some of the reasons for this. Instead of seeking friends in whom to confide, or counsellors to whom to tell their troubles, they use their gifts to come to terms with, and to make sense of, their sufferings. Once a work is completed, it can be shared with others; but the initial response to depression is to turn inward rather than outward.

The creative act is one way of overcoming the state of helplessness which, as we have seen, is so important a part of the depressive state. It is a coping mechanism; a way of exercising control, as well as a way of expressing emotion. In fact, the act of expressing emotion itself gives the sufferer some sense of mastery, even if he or she is not particularly gifted. Psychotherapists, especially those trained in the school of Jung, often suggest to their patients that, when feeling overwhelmed by rage or despair, they should attempt to paint or to draw their feelings, or at least write down what they are experiencing. Many patients go through periods of especial stress in which they feel so much at the mercy of their emotions that they fear being unable to tolerate the waiting period between psychotherapeutic sessions. If they can be persuaded to express their feelings in one way or another when alone, they usually lose the sense of being overwhelmed and regain some measure of control.

Tennyson may be cited as one well-known example of a gifted person using his talent as a way of coping with loss. Tennyson began to write *In Memoriam*, his response to the death of his friend Arthur Hallam, within a few days of his first hearing of it. *In Memoriam* was to engross Tennyson intermittently over a period of nearly seventeen years. It was not originally designed for publication, although, when it finally appeared, it was enormously successful.

Hallam had been engaged to the poet's sister, Emily. He had also been Tennyson's closest friend at Cambridge, where both had been members of the exclusive society, the Apostles. Their friendship was intimate and passionate, but neither overtly nor covertly homosexual. Pre-Freudian generations were more fortunate than our own in being able freely to admit 'love' for a member of the same sex, or of the opposite sex, without the implication that all love is necessarily sexual in origin. Hallam died, totally unexpectedly, on 15 September 1833 in Vienna. The cause of death was probably a subarachnoid haemorrhage; that is, a form of stroke due to vascular malformation or aneurysm of the arteries supplying the brain. He was twenty-three years old.

> Unlike Emily, Alfred did not visibly sink under the weight of Hallam's death, although he probably felt it as deeply and it certainly affected him long after she had recovered from it. He kept up the motions of normal daily life, but he had lost his most important anchor to reality. His one remaining resort was to poetry, used as a narcotic for an existence made temporarily meaningless.[8]

Robert Bernard Martin's use of the term 'narcotic' probably originates from Tennyson's own reference to 'dull narcotics' in *In Memoriam*.

> But, for the unquiet heart and brain,
> A use in measured language lies;
> The sad mechanic exercise,
> Like dull narcotics, numbing pain.[9]

It is probably true that any kind of work can serve to diminish the immediate pain of loss. Robert Burton, in his address to the reader which opens *The Anatomy of Melancholy*, writes:

> I write of melancholy, being busy to avoid melancholy. There is no greater cause of melancholy than idleness, 'no better cure than business,' as Rhasis holds.[10]

130

But the exercise of creating poetry does more than anaesthetize the sufferer. It can also restore meaning to life, and a sense of being able to cope. According to Professor Martin, Tennyson not only wrote *In Memoriam* as a direct consequence of his loss, but also a number of other poems which are among his best. Professor Martin cites 'Ulysses', 'Tiresias', 'Morte d'Arthur', 'On a Mourner', 'St Simeon Stylites' and 'O that 'twere possible' from *Maud*, as originating in this way, and specifically refers to their 'therapeutic effect' upon their author, which happily indicates that he realizes that something more than a numbing action is involved.

Tennyson provides a particularly striking example of how genetic endowment interacts with circumstances to produce depression. Tennyson's paternal grandfather was an unstable man, subject to alternating fits of rage and maudlin self-pity. His instability may have been partly related to the fact that he lost his mother when he was five years old. Of his four children, the elder two were girls. Elizabeth, the eldest, was normally cheerful, but 'her health was never a match for her spirits and when she was ill, she sometimes suffered from depression'. Mary, the second child, 'was gloomily and almost spitefully Calvinistic, sadly rejoicing that she was one of the elect, and trying to regret her own family's certain damnation'.[11]

The next child, the poet's father, George Clayton Tennyson, was a severely disturbed clergyman, who not only suffered from recurrent depression, but also from epilepsy, and from addiction to alcohol and laudanum. The fourth child, Charles, was more stable than the others, but was afflicted with epilepsy, from which one of his sons also suffered.

George Clayton Tennyson had twelve children, of whom the poet, Alfred, was the fourth. The first child died in infancy. Of Alfred's ten surviving brothers and sisters, one spent nearly all his life in a mental institution, and was described as dying from exhaustion following mania. Another brother 'suffered from some form of mental illness nearly as incapacitating, a third was an opium addict, a fourth was severely alcoholic, and of the rest of the large family each had at least one bad mental breakdown in a long life'.[12]

Septimus Tennyson, one of the poet's brothers, was recurrently admitted to Dr Matthew Allen's asylum at High Beech, where the poet John Clare was also a patient. Alfred Tennyson himself stayed there, but it is not clear whether or not he was a patient. There is no doubt that he suffered from recurrent periods of depression throughout his life. He was also a heavy smoker and drinker. In a later passage, Professor Martin makes another reference to the role which poetry played in alleviating Tennyson's depression and hypochondria.

> In creating the harmonies and the symbolic order of the poems, he was able to perceive momentarily some kind of unity and wholeness that was applicable to his own life, and so it remained for him until his death.[13]

This perceptive, important statement about the role of creativity in the lives of the distraught goes far beyond Professor Martin's previous reference to poetry as a narcotic. The search for order, for unity, for wholeness is, I believe, a motivating force of signal importance in the lives of men and women of every variety of temperament. The hunger of imagination is active in every human being to some degree. But the greater the disharmony within, the sharper the spur to seek harmony, or, if one has the gifts, to *create* harmony. This is why Edward Thomas, in the remark quoted as one of the epigraphs to this chapter, questions whether ridding himself of depression might not also rid him of the intensity which drove him to write.

Another example of a creative response to loss is furnished by Felix Mendelssohn. His elder sister, Fanny, was almost as gifted a musician as he was himself. They were so devoted to each other that family friends used to say jokingly that they ought to marry. Fanny died suddenly, at the age of forty-one, on 14 May 1847. Although Mendelssohn had married ten years earlier, he was so shattered by the news of his sister's death that he fainted when he read the letter announcing it, and seems never to have recovered from his loss. When he was well enough to travel, Mendelssohn and his family went to Switzerland for a holiday. It was here that he composed his last completed work of chamber music, the Quartet in F minor (Op. 80), which was meant as a memorial to Fanny. It is variously described as passionate, as being his most deeply felt work of chamber music, and as possibly heralding a new phase in Mendelssohn's development as a composer. However, fate did not allow Mendelssohn time to complete his mourning. The composer himself died, only a few months later, on 4 November 1847. Both brother and sister probably died of subarachnoid haemorrhage, the same form of stroke which had killed Arthur Hallam thirteen years earlier.

These are two examples of creative responses to loss in adult life. There are also many examples of creative responses to losses which occurred in early childhood.

Andrew Brink, who is both a Professor of English and an Associate Member of the Department of Psychiatry at McMaster University, has written two books applying object-relations theory to the composition of poetry: the first, *Loss and Symbolic Repair*,[14] the second, *Creativity as Repair*.[15] The first book is a study of the poets Cowper, Donne, Traherne, Keats, and Plath. The second is a sequel to the first, taking into account a wider range of studies connected with the same subject.

Another literary scholar approaching poetry from the same point of view is David Aberbach, author of *Loss and Separation in Bialik and Wordsworth*,[16] *At the Handles of the Lock*,[17] and other papers and books concerned with the same subject. Both authors profess views which deserve detailed exposition which would be inappropriate in this context, but I have drawn on their work and gladly acknowledge my debt to them.

One of the poets studied by Brink is William Cowper, who is also the subject of a biography by David Cecil, *The Stricken Deer*.[18] Cowper is a particularly good example of a poet whose work is closely related with loss of the mother in early childhood. He was also a manic-depressive. As I indicated earlier, I do not accept early bereavement as a cause of manic-depressive psychosis *per se*, but I do incline to the view that such bereavement is likely to make manifest any genetic predisposition to this disorder, and to increase the severity of attacks when they occur.

Cowper was born in 1731, the son of a clergyman. His mother's family was connected with that of the poet John Donne. (It is interesting to record that Donne suffered from depression; that he

133

lost his father when he was four; that he was tempted by the desire to commit suicide whenever he felt afflicted; and that he wrote the first English defence of suicide, *Biathanatos*. Did Donne's family and Cowper's family share a genetic predisposition which early parental loss made actual?)

Cowper's early childhood seems to have been idyllic, and his relationship to his mother particularly close. But when he was nearly six years old, she died, and his world was shattered. He himself wrote:

> What peaceful hours I once enjoy'd!
> How sweet their mem'ry still!
> But they have left an aching void,
> The world can never fill.[19]

His mother remained for him an idealized figure. Forty-seven years after her death he wrote to a friend:

> I can truely say that not a week passes (perhaps I might with equal veracity say a day) in which I do not think of her.[20]

Six years later still, in 1790, he wrote a poem 'On the Receipt of My Mother's Picture Out of Norfolk' which Brink describes as being among his most affecting. He hung the portrait in his bedroom so that it should be the last thing which he saw at night and the first when he woke in the morning. In the poem, Cowper writes of how the portrait has brought back his early loss, but has also stimulated his imagination to bring him temporary comfort; a revealing instance of how the creative act both expresses loss, and also helps the sufferer to overcome it.

> And, while that face renews my filial grief,
> Fancy shall weave a charm for my relief –
> Shall steep me in Elysian reverie,
> A momentary dream, that thou art she.

Cowper ends his poem with this verse:

> And, while the wings of fancy still are free,
> And I can view this mimic shew of thee,

Time has but half succeeded in his theft –
Thyself remov'd, thy power to soothe me left.[21]

After his mother's death, Cowper was sent away to a boarding school at which he was ferociously bullied. He was so frightened of his chief tormentor that he said he only recognized him by his buckled shoes, since he did not dare to look him in the face. Later, he was sent to Westminster School, which was agreeably less traumatic. In 1752, at the age of twenty-one, he took up residence in the Middle Temple. Within a few months he suffered his first severe episode of depression. In 1763, he had another attack. One terrifying poem vividly illustrates a phenomenon referred to in Chapter 7; the degree to which hostility is turned inward against the self during episodes of depression.

LINES WRITTEN DURING A PERIOD OF INSANITY

Hatred and vengeance, my eternal portion,
Scarce can endure delay of execution,
Wait, with impatient readiness, to seize my
    Soul in a moment.

Damn'd below Judas: more abhorr'd than he was,
Who for a few pence sold his holy Master.
Twice betrayed Jesus me, the last delinquent,
    Deems the profanest.

Man disavows, and Deity disowns me:
Hell might afford my miseries a shelter;
Therefore hell keeps her ever hungry mouths all
    Bolted against me.[22]

Feeling as he did about himself when depressed, it is small wonder that he tried to poison himself with laudanum and then to hang himself, albeit unsuccessfully. He had an attack of mania when he was thirty-two. His manic episodes were accompanied by religious ecstasies; transcendent moments of reconciliation, forgiveness, and joy. He tried to make up for the loss of his mother by turning to God. In his Olney Hymn beginning 'Hark my soul! it is the LORD,' Jesus says:

> Can a woman's tender care
> Cease, towards the child she bare?
> Yes, she may forgetful be,
> Yet will I remember thee.[23]

He also found consolation in the contemplation of Nature, but even this failed him when he became severely depressed.

> This glassy stream, that spreading pine,
> Those alders quiv'ring to the breeze,
> Might soothe a soul less hurt than mine
> And please, if any thing could please.

> But fix'd unalterable care
> Foregoes not what she feels within,
> Shows the same sadness ev'ry where,
> And slights the season and the scene.[24]

The experience of being able to recognize beauty intellectually whilst being unable to appreciate it emotionally is a characteristic feature of depression. Coleridge expresses exactly the same deprivation in 'Dejection: An Ode'.

> And those thin clouds above, in flakes and bars,
> That give away their motion to the stars;
> Those stars, that glide behind them or between,
> Now sparkling, now bedimmed, but always seen:
> Yon crescent Moon, as fixed as if it grew
> In its own cloudless, starless lake of blue;
> I see them all so excellently fair,
> I see, not feel, how beautiful they are![25]

At an earlier point in this chapter, reference was made to the tendency of those who have been bereaved in early life to look for the lost parent in those to whom they become attached. Cowper formed dependent attachments to a series of women, but never married, probably because he feared that his original bereavement might be repeated. For many years, Cowper was cared for by an older married woman, Mrs Unwin. After she was widowed, marriage was agreed upon, but, during 1772–3, Cowper suffered another episode of depression in which he expressed the delusion that everyone hated him, including Mrs Unwin. This effectively prevented the marriage from taking place.

Subsequent attacks of depression followed the loss, by death or removal, of other friends upon whom Cowper depended. In 1787, for example, he was depressed from January to June, following the death of a male friend with whom he constantly corresponded, and the removal elsewhere of a valued female friend. However, when he was at his most productive as a poet, he seems to have experienced quite long periods of optimism.

Cowper also provides a striking example of how feelings of helplessness accompany recurrent attacks of depression, perhaps especially when depression is linked with childhood bereavement of the mother, as Brown and Harris noted in the study to which we have frequently referred. In his biography of Cowper, David Cecil points out that

> One of the strongest forces against Cowper's recovery had been his fatalistic submission to evil; and this had been encouraged by his habit of life. For years his whole existence had perforce been one of inert and idle submission to circumstances.[26]

But, at times when Cowper found that he could write, he overcame his sense of helplessness, his belief that he could do nothing to combat forces of evil which, when depressed, he perceived as uncontrollable. One of his women friends, Lady Austen, constantly urged him to undertake new projects. Encouraging the depressed person to do something is a hazardous enterprise. It requires a delicate balance between being sympathetic and being robust. Too much sympathy may reinforce the depressed person's belief in his helplessness and hopelessness. Too much active encouragement makes the depressed person feel that no one understands the depths of his despair.

Lady Austen seems to have struck exactly the right note. When she suggested that Cowper should try blank verse, he responded by saying that he had no subject. 'Write about the sofa,' said Lady Austen; and so he did. The poem became *The Task*, several thousand lines long, in which Cowper poured out all that he felt about the human condition. He recognized the therapeutic effect which writing this long poem had upon him.

> He that attends to his interior self,
> That has a heart, and keeps it; has a mind
> That hungers and supplies it; and who seeks
> A social, not a dissipated life;
> Has business; feels himself engag'd t'achieve
> No unimportant, though a silent, task.[27]

Cowper is not alone amongst poets in having suffered both early bereavement and recurrent episodes of severe depression. We noted above that John Donne lost his father when he was four, and that he was also recurrently suicidal. William Collins, Samuel Coleridge, Edgar Allan Poe, John Berryman, Louis MacNeice, and Sylvia Plath all lost a parent before they reached the age of twelve, and all suffered well-attested periods of depression. Coleridge was addicted to opium; Poe was intermittently alcoholic, used laudanum, and may have been dependent on it; MacNeice was an alcoholic, and both Berryman and Plath committed suicide.

To this list of early bereaved and recurrently depressed poets may be added Michelangelo. It is sometimes forgotten that, as well as painting pictures and creating some of the greatest sculptures in the world, Michelangelo wrote some three hundred poems. Michelangelo's mother died when he was six. As his sonnets demonstrate, he suffered severely from depression throughout his life. Michelangelo's homosexual preference is well-attested. His self-punitive asceticism may have contributed to his depression. It is worth noting that, of his mother's five sons, only one married.

In some of these examples, the genetic contribution to depression is obvious. Parental suicide is one cause of early bereavement. John Berryman's father shot himself when his son was eleven; the poet himself committed suicide on 7 January 1972, at the age of fifty-seven, by throwing himself from a bridge over the Mississippi.

Louis MacNeice's mother developed a severe form of agitated depression when the future poet was five-and-a-half years old. She was admitted to a nursing home in August 1913, and her children never saw her again. She died whilst in hospital in December 1914.

138

Louis MacNeice's sister thought that he was haunted to the end of his life by the memory of his mother walking up and down the garden path in tears. Like many other gifted people prone to depression, Louis MacNeice became an alcoholic.

There are also examples of poets who experienced early bereavement, but who did not, or who are not known to have, suffered from attacks of depression which were so obviously severe as to be labelled mental illness. These poets include John Keats, Thomas Traherne, William Wordsworth, Stephen Spender, Cecil Day-Lewis, and Lord Byron.

Stephen Spender records in his autobiography that his mother was a semi-invalid whose ill-health overshadowed his childhood. She was also an unstable hysteric, given to violent scenes and dramatic gestures. Perhaps this accounts for the fact that, although he was only twelve when his mother died, Spender writes:

If I felt the death of my mother at all, it was as the lightening of a burden and as a stimulating excitement.[28]

In considering bereavement and depression, it is important to remember that even loss of a mother is not always a tragedy!

Byron was certainly unstable, in the sense that he exhibited extreme mood-swings. In Chapter 3, we noted that Keats was preoccupied with death. This is hardly surprising. Keats lost his father when he was eight, his mother when he was fourteen; one brother when he was six, another brother when he was twenty-three. His maternal grandfather died when he was nine; his maternal grandmother when he was nineteen. An uncle died when he was thirteen. He wrote in a letter:

I have never known any unalloy'd Happiness for many days together: the death or sickness of someone has always spoilt my hours.[29]

Perhaps the families of these poets lacked the genetic predisposition to depression which we postulated as being activated by, or combining with, parental loss to produce severe attacks.

139

Nevertheless, loss often produces definable themes in their poetry.

Wordsworth lost his mother when he was eight, his father when he was thirteen. The Zionist poet Chaim Bialik lost his father when he was seven. Both suffered the break-up of their families. In his paper comparing their work, David Aberbach writes:

> The effects of loss and family disruption are reflected in many of the salient characteristics in the poetry of Wordsworth and Bialik: the haunting presences and objects, sometimes obviously a parent or a parent-figure; the yearning for a lost paradise; the emphasis upon feeding; the motif of union with Nature; the general mood of isolation, desertion, depression, guilt; and, finally the hostility. The chief 'Romantic' quality of their poetry – the exploration of the self – can be seen as an attempt to buttress the self made weak by childhood loss and consequent emotional instability.[30]

Thomas Traherne's mother died when he was in about his fourth year. It is uncertain whether or not his father died too, but Traherne and his brother were fostered by relatives, and so effectively lost both parents. Traherne's idealization of Nature and of childhood is seen in similar terms by Andrew Brink, as a reaching out for a bliss that never was. Although Traherne is usually adjudged a poet of happiness and divine love, Brink points out that he also recorded moments of dread and horror. He concludes that

> Traherne's verse and prose give a doctrine of regeneration, of self-change from an unsatisfactory state of life to another better one.[31]

Brink also demonstrates Traherne's dependence upon external objects to achieve the blissful sense of unity for which he is seeking.

> Remarkable in Traherne's art is its ceaseless reaching out to desired objects, natural objects invitingly presented to the sense in unlimited quantity. Desire for fusion with objects, an ever-renewing impulse to acquire them for the mind's satisfaction,

appears in almost everything he wrote . . . The most ordinary sky or tree can move Traherne's spirit to rapture, when he is readied for this transport.[32]

I am inclined to link this, as Brink does, with a lack of 'good objects' within the psyche: a failure, in early childhood, to incorporate the mother's love and thus ensure a continuing source of self-esteem from within.

Boethius, to whose work we referred in Chapter 4, personifies Philosophy as a woman who brings him wisdom from on high. She is at pains to point out to the philosopher that dependence upon external objects for happiness is fraught with risk and illusion. After exposing the emptiness of wealth and delight in precious stones, she goes on to say:

Perhaps, again, you find pleasure in the beauty of the countryside. Creation is indeed very beautiful, and the countryside a beautiful part of creation. In the same way we are sometimes delighted by the appearance of the sea when it's very calm and look up with wonder at the sky, the stars, the moon and the sun. However, not one of these has anything to do with you, and you daren't take credit for the splendour of any of them . . . You are in fact enraptured with empty joys, embracing blessings that are alien to you as if they were your own . . . From all this it is obvious that not one of those things which you count among your blessings is in fact any blessing of yours at all . . . It seems as if you feel a lack of any blessing of your own inside you, which is driving you to seek your blessings in things separate and external.[33]

The ostensibly modern psycho-analytic notion of introjecting 'good objects' or 'blessings' was evidently perfectly familiar in the sixth century AD. In the light of Philosophy's observations, Wordsworth's and Traherne's enraptured worship of Nature takes on a rather different aspect from that of simple pleasure.

As noted already, predisposition to depression and early bereavement are independent variables, although when the former is present,

141

the latter reinforces the tendency to depression and its severity. Early bereavement is certainly common amongst writers, but severe episodes of clinically definable depression, whether or not alternating with mania, are also frequently found in writers without early bereavement as an antecedent. In addition to those already mentioned, poets who suffered from recurrent episodes of depression include Christopher Smart, John Clare, Gerard Manley Hopkins, Anne Sexton, Hart Crane, Theodore Roethke, Delmore Schwartz, Randall Jarrell, and Robert Lowell. Of these poets, Smart, Clare, Sexton, Crane, Roethke, Schwartz, Jarrell, and Lowell all received treatment for depression. Smart and Clare were admitted to 'madhouses'; Lowell was frequently admitted to psychiatric hospitals for periods of mania as well as for depression. Crane, Jarrell, and Sexton all committed suicide.

Few objective studies exist, and those that do are necessarily based on small numbers. But Andreasen and Canter, in 1974, investigated a group of writers at the University of Iowa's Writers' Workshop. The writers interviewed had a much greater prevalence of affective illness (i.e. of severe recurrent depression or of manic-depressive illness) than did a matched control group: 67 per cent compared with 13 per cent. Of fifteen writers, nine had seen a psychiatrist, eight had been treated with drugs or with psychotherapy, and four had been admitted to hospital. Two had suffered from both mania and depression, whilst eight had suffered from recurrent depression only. Six had symptoms of alcoholism. One committed suicide two years after the study was completed. The importance of the genetic factor is attested by the fact that, amongst the relatives of the writers, 21 per cent had a definable psychiatric disorder, usually depression, whereas only 4 per cent of the relatives of the controls were similarly categorized.[34]

In a recent study of forty-seven British writers and artists, selected for eminence by their having won major awards or prizes, Jamison found that 38 per cent had been treated for affective illness. Poets were particularly subject to severe mood-swings, and no less than half the sample studied had been treated with drugs as out-patients, or admitted to hospital for treatment with anti-depressants, electroconvulsive therapy, or lithium.[35]

A person in the throes of mania or deep depression is usually unable to produce work of any value. Restlessness, inability to concentrate, the rapid 'flight of ideas' in mania make sustained work impossible. Retardation of thought processes, feelings of hopelessness and helplessness, the belief that nothing is worthwhile undertaking, the conviction that anything which is produced will be valueless, all serve to prevent the severely depressed person from being creative.

Yet liability to these disorders is particularly common in creative writers. This apparent paradox can be resolved if we accept that this liability acts as a goad, prodding the potential victim into undertaking the solitary, difficult, painful, and often unrewarding work of exploring his own depths and recording what he finds there. As long as he is able to do this, he may escape being overwhelmed. The evidence suggests that, whilst many creative people may be more disturbed than the average person, they are also equipped with greater resources which help them to overcome their conflicts and problems. Psychiatrists experienced in treating creative people know that it is only when their creative powers are paralyzed that they seek help.

We have seen that the extraverted person who tends to lose himself because of over-adaptation to others may be able to recover, and express, his true self in solitude. We have also seen that the man or woman whose development has been impaired by early separation and isolation can find solace in the use of the imagination.

We can now go a step further, and understand that the creative process can be a way of protecting the individual against being overwhelmed by depression; a means of regaining a sense of mastery in those who have lost it, and, to a varying extent, a way of repairing the self damaged by bereavement or by the loss of confidence in human relationships which accompanies depression from whatever cause.

Once again, it is important to emphasize that depression is part of the experience of every human being. There is no hard and fast line to be drawn between depression of the kind which we all experience in response to loss, and the kind of depression which is labelled a psychiatric illness and which requires psychiatric treatment.

Depression varies enormously in depth and severity, but not in its essential nature.

Men and women of genius have at their command talents which loss may mobilize and which manifest themselves in work of lasting interest. The music, the poems, the paintings or other works which loss has inspired may bring increased understanding and solace to others who have suffered similar pangs.

But this does not mean that ordinary men and women who are not so talented have no inner resources, or no imaginative powers. Nor is it implied that the creative response is exclusively set in motion by loss, only that it may be so. Poems are not substitutes for people. Those who write as if they were, and this includes some of the writers quoted in this chapter, do less than justice to the imaginative capacities of the human race. The creative response to loss is only one example of the use of the imagination. Only those who exalt human relationships to an ideal position in the hierarchy of human values could think that creativity was no more than a substitute for such relationships.

10

The Search for Coherence

'It is good that I did not let myself be influenced.'
Ludwig Wittgenstein

In the last two chapters, we were principally concerned with creative individuals whose work was partly derived from loss or separation. Spurred by depression, they strove to create imaginary worlds, to compensate for what was missing in their lives, to repair the damage they had suffered, to restore to themselves a sense of worth and competence. Because of their primary concern with interpersonal relationships, and their struggle to restore, through their work, something which was felt to be missing, many of these individuals could be described as predominantly extraverted, although often driven in upon themselves to a greater extent than extraverted individuals like to be. To use Howard Gardner's terms, we supposed that such individuals were *dramatists* rather than *patterners*. When they retreated into solitude to pursue their creative quests, an element of wishing to restore some blissful union with another person, or with Nature as a surrogate person, was a frequent component of their work.

The exceptions, or partial exceptions, to this generalization are Saki, who was discussed in Chapter 8, and Kafka, some of whose characteristics were outlined at the end of Chapter 7. Both were story-tellers, but their stories are hardly at all concerned with intimate human relationships, and neither man established any prolonged intimate relationship in reality.

145

However, Saki's diary suggests that, damaged though he might have been by his early bereavement and by his childhood experiences, he did engage in a good many sexual encounters with the young men or boys whom he preferred. Although Saki cannot possibly be regarded as predominantly extraverted, there was an extraverted side to his character, manifested in his social life in London, his liking for the fashionable society which he mocked, and his enjoyment of life in barracks before departing for the horrors of the Western Front.

Although he was loved and respected by his friends, Kafka was pathologically introverted: schizoid, as most psychiatrists would label him. He had a few brief sexual encounters, but he contrived that his deepest emotional involvements were almost entirely confined to an exchange of letters. It was only during the last year of his life that he was able to tolerate actually living with a woman.

In this chapter I want to examine some instances of creative individuals whose principal concern was not primarily with human relationships, but with the search for coherence and sense. Such individuals correspond with the people described as introverts by Jung; as convergers by Hudson; as patterners by Gardner; and, when obviously abnormal or disturbed, as schizoid by psychiatrists.

As we have seen, nearly all kinds of creative people, in adult life, show some avoidance of others, some need of solitude. But the individuals I have in mind go further than this. They may, at a superficial level, appear to have better relationships with people than is true of some of the poets mentioned in Chapter 9. But this is often because, unlike the extraverts, and also unlike the type of schizoid personality represented by Kafka, they have learned to relinquish a need for intimacy. They are not so disturbed when relationships go wrong because, for them, the meaning of life is less bound up with intimate relationships than it is in the case of most people.

Let us for a moment assume that the individuals to whom I have just referred showed 'avoidance behaviour' as infants, and let us accept that avoidance behaviour is a response designed to protect the infant from behavioural disorganization. If we transfer this concept to adult life, we can see that an avoidant infant might very well develop into a person whose principal need was to find some kind of meaning

146

and order in life which was *not* entirely, or even chiefly, dependent upon interpersonal relationships. Moreover, such a person would be likely to feel the need to protect the inner world in which this search for meaning and order was going on from interference by others because other people would be perceived as posing a threat. Ideas are sensitive plants which wilt if exposed to premature scrutiny.

In an earlier book, I stressed the need for interpersonal relationships in the maturing of personality. A chapter entitled 'The Relativity of Personality' emphasized the fact that personality is a relative concept.

If by personality we mean a man's 'distinctive personal character' we are obliged to recognize that we can only conceive of such an entity in terms of contrasting it with other personal characters.[1]

I went on to write:

One cannot even begin to be conscious of oneself as a separate individual without another person with whom to compare oneself. A man in isolation is a collective man, a man without individuality. People often express the idea that they are most themselves when they are alone; and creative artists especially may believe that it is in the ivory tower of the solitary expression of their art that their innermost being finds its completion. They forget that art is communication, and that, implicitly or explicitly, the work which they produce in solitude is aimed at somebody.[2]

I still believe this; but I want to add a rider to the effect that maturation and integration can take place within the isolated individual to a greater extent than I had allowed for. The great introverted creators are able to define identity and achieve *self-realization* by *self-reference*; that is, by interacting with their own past work rather than by interacting with other people.

This is clearly impossible for a small child, who must interact both with people and with things in gradually defining its own identity. So

147

far as we can understand it, awareness of being a separate person takes place gradually. We may picture the baby as coming up against objects in the external world; stubbing its toe against the end of the cot, for instance. As it gradually learns to use its limbs and exercise control over their movements, the baby will gain proprioceptive information about the position of its limbs in space, and hence of its own dimensions. It will be recalled that, in Chapter 4, we noted that loss of proprioceptive information from movements of limbs, when imposed by medical immobilization or by interrogation procedures enforcing fixed postures, was a potent force in breaking down the boundaries of self-definition.

The infant must also become aware of its separateness because of its need for care from someone else; for being fed, kept warm, cleaned, and so on. Unless its needs are instantly met, there must be an interval between the realization of a need and its fulfilment, signified by a cry of distress which both summons help and also indicates to itself that there is something or someone 'out there' who provides what it cannot provide for itself. At the beginning of life, self-definition, the awareness of existing as a separate person and the development of a coherent identity must depend upon interaction between baby and mother or mother-substitute. In the ordinary course of events, interaction with others will continue to provide the majority of people with self-definition and coherence throughout life.

Heinz Kohut, one of the most original psycho-analysts of recent years, has based his idea of neurosis and of the cure of neurosis on similar notions. He holds that the development of a healthy, secure, coherent structure of personality depends in the first instance upon the child's repeated experience of being recognized and sustained by what Kohut calls 'empathically resonant self-objects'. That is, the child needs to interact with parents or parent-figures who reinforce the sense of self because they recognize and mirror the child's developing identity as it actually is; empathize with the child's feelings; respond to the child's needs with 'nonhostile firmness and nonseductive affection', neither repudiating the child's demands with aggression, nor yielding to them with undiscriminating sentimentality.[3]

Kohut pictures this need for reinforcement as persistent.

Self psychology [which is the name given to Kohut's revision of psycho-analytic theory] holds that self–selfobject relationships form the essence of psychological life from birth to death, that a move from dependence (symbiosis) to independence (autonomy) in the psychological sphere is no more possible let alone desirable, than a corresponding move from a life dependent upon oxygen to a life independent of it in the biological sphere. The developments that characterize normal psychological life must, in our view, be seen in the changing nature of the relationship between the self and its selfobjects, but not in the self's relinquishment of selfobjects. In particular, developmental advances cannot be understood in terms of the replacement of the selfobjects by love objects or as steps in the move from narcissism to object love.[4]

Kohut believes that the deepest anxiety which a person can experience is what he calls 'disintegration anxiety'. The individuals whom he considers liable to this are those who, because of the immaturity of their parents' responses to them in childhood, or because of the absence of empathic parental understanding, have not built up a strong, coherent personality.

One might compare Kohut's conception with looking in a mirror. A clear, clean, polished mirror will repeatedly reflect the developing person as he actually is, and thus give him a firm and true sense of his own identity. A cracked, dirty, smeared mirror will reflect an incomplete, obscured image which provides the child with an inaccurate and distorted picture of himself.

In Chapter 7, reference was made to the threat of behavioural disorganization which makes infants avoid rejecting mothers. Kohut's perception that certain deprived individuals are threatened by fears of disintegration is surely the same concept in different words. Disintegration anxiety can also be compared with the fears of destruction of the 'inner self' in schizoid subjects which R. D. Laing described so well in *The Divided Self*. Kafka, referred to earlier, is an example of a schizoid individual who felt that his ability to preserve his inner self was threatened by intimacy.

Kohut also believes that the therapeutic effectiveness of psycho-analysis depends upon whether the psycho-analyst can so understand and empathize with his patient that the latter can develop the inner coherence which he was unable to develop in childhood.

This conception of cure is some way removed from that originally advanced by Freud. Freud's model was essentially cognitive. It depended upon the recapture and understanding of the traumas of early childhood, and, more especially, upon undoing repression and making the unconscious conscious.

Kohut's model of cure is a variant of object-relations theory based on transference. The psycho-analyst, if he is doing his job properly, is providing what Franz Alexander used to call 'a corrective emotional experience'. Because the psycho-analyst is able to understand and empathize with the patient's experience and feelings, he is providing repeated reinforcement and repair of the patient's damaged self.

Kohut makes the important point that healing is less dependent upon the theoretical position espoused by the psycho-analyst than the latter probably imagines. That is, provided the psycho-analyst can in fact understand his patient sufficiently well, and convey this understanding to the patient, healing will continue to occur, irrespective of the psycho-analyst's preference for, say, Kleinian theory as opposed to Freudian or Jungian.

Kohut's insistence that self–selfobject relationships are necessary to psychic health throughout life is in line with the ideas of Bowlby and Marris which were discussed in Chapters 1 and 2; namely that intimate attachments or specific loving relationships were alone assumed to give meaning to a person's life. Kohut's position is also similar to that of Fairbairn who, by introducing the term *mature dependence* for the final stage of emotional development, asserted his belief that total autonomy was both impossible and undesirable. 'We must love one another or die,' as Auden put it.[6]

Both Fairbairn and Kohut have made valuable contributions to psycho-analytic theory, but I doubt whether they are right in this particular instance if by 'objects' they invariably mean people, which seems to be the case. Object-relations theory is now too entrenched a term to be abandoned, but it is an inept use of the word 'object', as Rycroft makes clear in his definition in *A Critical Dictionary of Psychoanalysis*.

In psycho-analytical writings, objects are nearly always persons, parts of persons, or symbols of one or the other. This terminology confuses readers who are more familiar with 'object' in the sense of 'thing', i.e. that which is not a person.[7]

It is natural enough that psycho-analysts, who see that much of what is wrong with their patients springs from distortions in their earliest 'object-relationships', and who treat their patients principally through the agency of another form of interpersonal relationship provided by themselves, should assume that object-relationships are the only source of psychic health. I have no doubt whatever that the interaction between the child and its mother and other care-takers is vital in the early years, and that future psychic health and the capacity to make satisfying relationships with others in adult life partly depends on this. I also have no doubt that, as we have seen, disruption of early relationships and hostility or rejection on the part of parents can direct a child more toward the impersonal, or make human relationships very difficult of attainment. But I have also suggested that people can live satisfactory, fulfilled lives without necessarily depending on close or intimate relationships, provided that they have relationships of some kind, and work which engages their interest and ministers to their self-esteem.

Work, especially of a creative kind which changes, progresses, and deepens over the years, can, I believe, provide the integrating factor within the personality, which Kohut assumes comes only from, or chiefly from, the positive reflecting responses of other people.

In his biography of Elgar, Jerrold Northrop Moore writes:

The artist, like the rest of us, is torn by various desires competing within himself. But, unlike the rest of us, he makes each of these desires into an element for use in his art. Then he seeks to synthesize his elements all together to form a style. The sign of a successful synthesis is a unified and unique style plain for all to recognize.[8]

In this view, style is the cement holding the various parts of the personality in balance; an integrating factor which psycho-analysts are aiming to help their patients achieve through empathy and understanding, as explained by Kohut, but which can also be achieved, at any rate by gifted people, working on their own.

If the creation of works of art, or systems of philosophy, or theories of the universe, is, in some instances, an attempt at reparation for early losses or later difficulties in fruitful interaction with other persons, we can see that there is a sense in which a succession of works can represent or substitute for 'objects'. But it is surely absurd to think that all human interests are so derived. Morris N. Eagle, in an important paper, 'Interests as Object Relations', argues that psycho-analytic theory has not done justice to the critical role which interests play in personality functioning.

> In traditional psychoanalytic theory, when interests are considered at all, they tend to be viewed as essentially derivative. Thus, in sublimation – the concept in psychoanalytic theory most germane to an understanding of the development of interests – interests result from 'the instinct's directing itself towards an aim other than, and remote from, that of sexual satisfaction' (Freud, S.E. XIV, p. 94). That is, interests are the product of the diversion of sexual aims to 'higher' pursuits. According to this view, the capacity to develop cultural interests depends on one's ability to sublimate or 'neutralize' sexual energy.[9]

This view still lingers on in the minds of fundamentalist psycho-analysts, but it is out of date, and no longer fits the facts of what we know about human development. Even very young infants show considerable interest in objects which provide novel visual and auditory stimuli; and such stimuli cannot be regarded as anything to do with satisfying basic physical drives like hunger, thirst, or the need for contact and comfort.

In Chapter 5, I referred to Winnicott's concept of 'transitional objects', and suggested that 'these very early manifestations of investing impersonal objects with significance are evidence that man was not born for love alone'. It is also the case, as we have noted, that it is the securely attached child who is most able to leave the mother's side in order to explore the environment and investigate the objects which it contains. Thus, the earliest manifestation of 'interests' cannot be regarded as a substitute for affectional ties, but rather as bearing witness to their adequacy.

In Chapter 4, we saw that, in extreme situations like solitary confinement or the environment of the concentration camp, interests like music or languages, or passionately held religious or political convictions, could serve to prevent mental collapse and consequent death. Eagle quotes the case of a composer

> who, by the usual psychiatric criteria, was quite disturbed. He was frequently paranoid, oversuspicious, chronically over-vigilant, showed extreme mood swings, had periods of intense anxiety, and reported quasi-hallucinations. Yet, in the 26 years that I knew him, he never became seriously disorganized, never was overtly psychotic. It always seemed to me that without his musical gift and passion, which played a central sustaining role in his life, he would have decompensated.[10]

Music evidently played the same part in this man's life as did writing in the life of Kafka. I agree with Eagle's conclusion that

> an interest in objects, as well as the development of affectional bonds, is not simply a derivative or outgrowth of libidinal energies and aims, but is a critical independent aspect of development which expresses an inborn propensity to establish cognitive and affective links to objects in the world.[11]

The ideally balanced person, therefore, might be supposed to find the meaning of his life both in his interpersonal relationships and in his interests. Although interests are not derived from failure in relationships with persons, I shall argue that, in the case of some gifted people who, for one reason or another, do not make close relationships, interests can take over some of the functions more usually performed by intimate relationships.

One of the most interesting features of any creative person's work is how it changes over time. No highly creative person is ever satisfied with what he has done. Often indeed, after completing a project, he experiences a period of depression from which he is only relieved by embarking on the next piece of work. It seems to me that the capacity to create provides an irreplaceable opportunity for *personal develop-ment in isolation*. Most of us develop and mature primarily through interaction with others. Our passage through life is defined by our roles relative to others; as child, adolescent, spouse, parent, and grandparent. The artist or philosopher is able to mature primarily on his own. His passage through life is defined by the changing nature and increasing maturity of his work, rather than by his relations with others.

At an earlier point in this chapter, I suggested that there are some individuals who are particularly preoccupied with a need to discover a meaning and order in life which is not primarily concerned with interpersonal relationships. If the proposals so far advanced are right, we might expect to find examples of creative people who, first, are predominantly introverted; who, second, avoid, or find difficulty in making, close relationships. One might guess that such people would be particularly concerned with developing their own point of view autonomously, protective of their inner worlds against premature scrutiny and criticism by others, and perhaps more than usually impervious to the ideas of others. We should also expect that such people would use their work rather than their interpersonal relationships as their primary source of self-esteem and personal fulfilment.

In addition, we should expect to find that some individuals of this kind were obviously 'neurotic', in the sense of being unhappy, anxious, phobic, or depressed: in other words, showing signs of suffering from that lack of fulfilment in interpersonal relationships which is supposed by object-relations theorists to be the root cause of neurosis. On the other hand, if I am right in supposing that the object-relations theorists have gone too far in this direction, and that interpersonal relationships are not the only source of human stability and happiness, it should be possible to point to other individuals who do not seek fulfilment in this way, but who achieve as much stability and happiness through their work as usually falls to the lot of human beings.

It so happens that one of the most original and important philosophers fulfils all the expectations listed above. In the sketch of Kant's personality which follows, I have drawn upon De Quincey's account of his last days,[12] and upon the references to Kant in *The Philosophers* by Ben-Ami Scharfstein.[13] Philosophers, whilst professionally engaged in expounding, refuting, and disputing the ideas of their colleagues and predecessors, seldom show much interest in their personalities or biographies, and may dismiss any such interest as irrelevant, impertinent, or trivial. Philosophical systems, it may be affirmed, stand or fall in their own right, from whomsoever they may have originated. This is certainly the case; nevertheless, as was suggested in the Introduction, many of the most original philosophers of the Western world were people who were not only unusually intelligent, but unusual in other ways as well.

Immanuel Kant was born on 22 April 1724 at Königsberg, in East Prussia, and spent his entire life there. He was the fourth of nine children, three of whom died in infancy. His father, a saddler, died when Kant was twenty-two. His mother, to whose love and instruction he acknowledged a lasting debt, died when he was thirteen.

Although Kant had nothing but praise for his parents, it seems that his insistence upon complete autonomy displayed itself early, for he showed no inclination to idealize childhood, depicting it as a period when discipline imposed by others must necessarily and regrettably restrict the child's freedom. Indeed, he thought that infants cried at birth because they resented as a constraint their inability to make proper use of their own limbs.

Discipline, however unpleasant it might be, was nevertheless necessary for children. Kant, somewhat severely, believed that novels should be taken away from children since he feared that such reading would encourage romantic phantasy at the expense of serious thoughts. He also considered that children should be taught to endure privation and opposition in order to promote the development of independence.

Kant's insistence upon independence was absolute. According to Bertrand Russell, he asserted that there can be nothing more dreadful than that the actions of one man should be subject to the will of another.[14]

Kant believed that every rational being existed as an end in himself, and that this is how we ought to treat each other.

Kant's correspondence is chiefly concerned with advancing his own philosophical views. He had scant respect for other philosophers, with the exception of Hume, to whom he acknowledged a considerable debt. One of his amanuenses refers to the difficulty which Kant had in identifying himself with the thought of another, attributing this to his inability to extricate himself from his own scheme of thought.

Kant had a number of loyal friends, enjoyed entertaining them to dinner, and, during his latter years, was recognized as a generous host and a fascinating talker. However, he did not form any close relationship with either sex, in spite of the fact that he continued to admire women until well into his seventies. He considered marrying on several occasions, but never took the plunge. Although generous to his relatives, he took care to keep well away from them. He had sisters living in Königsberg, but did not see them for twenty-five years. His surviving brother wrote a touching letter deploring their separation and wishing to be reunited with him. Kant took two and a half years to answer a further letter from his brother, saying that he had been too busy to reply, but that he would continue to think brotherly thoughts of him.

Kant exhibited many obsessional traits of character. His life was ordered with the utmost regularity. Every day, his servant woke him at 4.55 a.m. At 5 a.m. he took breakfast, and then spent the morning writing or lecturing. At 12.15 p.m. he would dine. During most of his life, the solitary constitutional which followed dinner was so exactly timed that the inhabitants of Königsberg could set their clocks by it. In later years, when Kant entertained friends every day, the timing must have varied, since we are told that conversation might run on through the afternoon, till four or five o'clock. After this he would read till 10 p.m. when he went to bed.

Kant showed the obsessional person's typical impatience and intolerance of matters which he cannot himself immediately control.

This is another aspect of the desire to be free of constraints imposed by others. In his latter years, he could not bear the smallest delay when, after dinner, he wanted coffee. At his dining table, he could tolerate no interruptions to the flow of talk, and chose a wide variety of guests in order that there should be no shortage of topics of conversation. His own talk was wide-ranging. Kant was well-informed, not only in mathematics and the sciences, but also in the field of politics, which formed a chief subject of conversation at his table. He seldom talked of his own work, partly no doubt from modesty, but possibly also from a reluctance to expose his ideas to the intrusive rough-and-tumble of dinner-table talk.

And what may seem still more singular, it was rarely or never that he directed the conversation to any branch of philosophy founded by himself. Indeed he was perfectly free from the fault which besets so many *savans* and *literati*, of intolerance towards those whose pursuits might happen to have disqualified them for any special sympathy with his own.[15]

Kant was fanatically preoccupied with physical health, both his own and that of others. He took great pains never to sweat, and developed a technique of breathing only through his nose, night and day, because only thus could he get rid of catarrh and cough. So much was this the case that he refused to take a companion on his daily walk in case conversation forced him to breathe through his mouth whilst in the open air. His bedroom was never heated, even in the coldest weather; but his study was kept at 75 degrees Fahrenheit.

As might be expected, Kant was ascetic, never over-indulging himself even in the things of which he was particularly fond, namely, coffee and tobacco. He boasted of his health, took a great interest in medicine, and, when his friends were ill, became very disturbed about them, making perpetual enquiries. However, once they were dead, he dismissed them from his mind and immediately regained his composure. Kant wrote that anxious fear at the thought of death nourished the fancies of the hypochondriac; but, in old age, he affirmed his readiness to die with resignation and courage.

Kant attributed his tendency to hypochondria to the flatness and narrowness of his chest. He admitted that, at times, he had been plagued with irrational fears about illness to the extent of becoming depressed and weary of life. However, his obsessional rituals seem to have acted as efficient defences against his tendency toward depression, and the impression left is that, by middle life, he was predominantly cheerful in a calm and rational fashion. Although Kant certainly exhibited neurotic anxieties, it was not until near the time of his death, at the age of seventy-nine, that he again became overtly unhappy.

It is clear that he developed cerebral arteriosclerosis. His memory for recent events began to fail, although he continued to recall remote events with accuracy, and could repeat long passages of poetry. His obsessional concern increased, and he became disturbed if any furniture or other object was removed from its proper place. He developed strange delusions about electricity, to which he attributed the headaches from which he suffered. He became reluctant to see strangers, for, like many patients with arteriosclerotic dementia, Kant retained insight into his own disabilities, and was reluctant to reveal to others the decline in his mental powers. Toward the end of his life, Kant was plagued with nightmares; again, a not uncommon accompaniment of hardening of the cerebral arteries.

Kant died on 12 February 1804, just over two months before his eightieth birthday. His fame ensured that Königsberg had never before seen so magnificent a public funeral.

Kant was a university professor of a type familiar in the older academies of the Western world. Although his gifts and his achievements are hard to match, there are plenty of examples of dons with similar personalities and interests. Meticulous, obsessional scholars whose lives are dedicated to their work, and for whom interpersonal relationships take second place, find Oxford and Cambridge college life particularly attractive. As residents, they are well looked after. The need for solitude and private study is taken for granted; whilst companionship, without the emotional demands of family life, is available when needed. The warmth of human passion was absent from Kant's life, but he was universally respected, and evidently regarded with affection by his friends. His personality was characteristically obsessional, but his defences against anxiety and depression worked well for the greater part of his life. Although some psycho-analysts might disagree, it would be a mistake to regard such a life as neurotically unhappy.

To the non-philosopher, and perhaps to some philosophers also, philosophy appears to be a very odd subject. It is not an empirical study: that is, it is not concerned, as are the hard sciences, with building an edifice of knowledge to which each generation adds, as it were, a new story. The problems with which philosophers generally concern themselves are not susceptible of final, permanent solutions. All that most philosophers claim in the way of advance in their subject is that, because certain questions have been clarified, some former ways of approaching those questions can now be discarded.

Although philosophers are like scientists in trying to be as objective as possible, philosophy does not closely resemble the empirical sciences. On the other hand, philosophy is unlike the arts in that it is not concerned with making obviously personal statements or express-ing human emotions. Yet, in some ways, it resembles both the arts and the sciences. As science progresses, the new knowledge added by each generation becomes incorporated into the general structure. This means that no modern physicist, for example, need study the original papers of Newton, or even of Einstein. What they added to physics and cosmology has been assimilated, and the way in which they reached their conclusions, although interesting historically, is only interesting historically, not relevant to future progress. The ideas of even the greatest and most original scientists are inevitably superseded.

In the arts, there is generally no question of the present replacing or superseding the past. Beethoven uses a larger orchestra than does Mozart; and Wagner uses one which is larger still. Although the range of expressive possibilities of the orchestra has been extended, this does not mean that Beethoven's music is greater than Mozart's or that Wagner's music is greater than Beethoven's, whatever some nineteenth-century critics may have supposed. Beethoven's music, however much it may depend upon Mozart's previous achievement, does not supersede or replace that achievement. Mozart's music, Beethoven's music and Wagner's music are all supreme examples of composition and all irreplaceable.

159

The same is true in painting. Although technical discoveries in perspective and the like have sometimes been taken to indicate the superiority of Renaissance painters to their 'primitive' counterparts, we recognize that the paintings of Cimabue and Giotto were concerned with the values of their own time, and are irreplaceable masterpieces without which we should be the poorer.

In this sense, philosophy resembles the arts more than it does the sciences. The writings of Plato and Aristotle are still studied and must be studied by anyone trying to understand philosophy. Books continue to be written about them, as they do about Descartes, Hume, Kant, or Wittgenstein. Although progress analogous to that made in the sciences may be achieved by pointing out flaws in particular philosophical arguments, philosophical systems often remain as distinct statements; points of view which may be in conflict with one another, which are not reducible to one another, but which co-exist as a plurality in the way described by Isaiah Berlin. This incompatibility seems to me to be linked with the fact that so many philosophers insist upon autonomy at all costs, are reluctant to acknowledge debts to others, and sometimes assert that they are almost incapable of reading the work of other philosophers. Although science progresses by criticism of what has gone before, by the adoption of hypotheses which explain a wider range of phenomena, scientists are always building on the past. The mental stance adopted by philosophers is quite different from that employed by most scientists, however original they may be.

Kant, Leibniz, Hume and Berkeley all insisted that their contributions to philosophy depended upon their having freed themselves from the influences of their predecessors and pursued their own autonomous paths irrespective of the past. So did Wittgenstein, who is another example of a philosopher who was introverted, who particularly prized solitude, who claimed that he was largely impervious to influence, and who certainly found his main source of self-esteem in his work. He is generally accounted to be the most original and influential philosopher of the twentieth century.

Wittgenstein was born on 26 April 1889 in Vienna. He was the youngest of five brothers and three sisters. One of his brothers was

160

Paul Wittgenstein, the pianist who lost his right arm in the First World War, for whom Ravel composed his piano concerto for the left hand alone. Ludwig Wittgenstein was himself passionately fond of music, and, in adult life, learned to play the clarinet. After being privately educated till the age of fourteen, he went to school in Linz, and then to study engineering in Berlin.

According to G. H. von Wright's biographical sketch of Wittgenstein, the years from 1906, when Wittgenstein left school, to 1912, when he was at Cambridge studying with Bertrand Russell, were a period of anxious searching and considerable unhappiness.[16] His interest shifted from aeronautical engineering to mathematics; and this brought him into contact with Frege, who advised him to go to Cambridge to work with Russell. In the second volume of his autobiography, Russell paints a vivid picture of Wittgenstein:

> He was perhaps the most perfect example I have ever known of genius as traditionally conceived, passionate, profound, intense, and dominating. He had a kind of purity which I have never known equalled except by G. E. Moore ... His life was turbulent and troubled, and his personal force was extraordinary.[17]

Russell describes him as coming to his rooms at midnight, pacing up and down for hours, and announcing that when he left he was going to commit suicide. A predominantly gloomy outlook and a tendency to depression persisted throughout Wittgenstein's life.

Wittgenstein must have been one of the most profoundly introverted men of genius who have ever existed. What was taking place in his own mind was, to him, far more important than anything taking place in the external world. His first major work, *Tractatus Logico-Philosophicus*, was written during the First World War, when Wittgenstein was a serving officer in the Austrian Army. Bertrand Russell writes:

> He was the kind of man who would never have noticed such small matters as bursting shells when he was thinking about logic.[18]

Wittgenstein was indifferent to social conventions, disliked the small talk of academic life, and hated social pretensions. From 1920 to 1926, he was an elementary school teacher in various remote village schools in Austria. Although stimulating, he was an irritable, impatient schoolmaster. He was accused of cruelty to the children, and, in spite of being acquitted, gave up his teaching career. He later confessed that he had once struck a little girl in one of his classes, and was ashamed that he had denied doing so when she complained to the principal.

His father had died in 1912, leaving a great deal of money. When Wittgenstein returned to Vienna after the war, he distributed his wealth amongst his brothers and sisters. When it was arranged that he should meet Russell in The Hague to discuss the *Tractatus*, Russell had to sell some of the possessions which Wittgenstein had left in Cambridge in order to get him enough money to pay his fare from Vienna to Holland.

From 1926 to 1928, Wittgenstein occupied himself in designing and building a house in Vienna for his sister Gretl. Hermine Wittgenstein, another sister, describes the obsessional way he went to work, overseeing every detail, and insisting that every fitting should be precisely engineered to the last millimetre.

The strongest proof of Ludwig's relentlessness with regard to precise measurements is perhaps the fact that he decided to have the ceiling of a hall-like room raised by three centimetres just as the cleaning of the completed house was to commence. His instinct was absolutely right and his instinct had to be followed.[19]

As we have seen, Kant also displayed obsessional traits, a characteristic which one would expect in those who are primarily *patterners*, concerned with making sense and order out of their experience. Wittgenstein also shared with Kant an imperviousness to the ideas of others. Norman Malcolm writes:

Wittgenstein had done no systematic reading in the classics of philosophy. He could read only what he could whole-heartedly assimilate. We have seen that as a young man he read Schopenhauer. From Spinoza, Hume and Kant he said that he could get only occasional glimpses of understanding.[20]

Wittgenstein was far less socially inclined than Kant, never dined in his college, and was ascetically indifferent to food. When staying in Ireland, he considered that the first meal which his host provided was too elaborate. What he wanted was porridge for breakfast, vegetables for lunch, and a boiled egg in the evening. Accordingly, this was provided each day for the rest of his visit.[21]

He was extremely secretive about his private life. His earliest notebooks are partly written in code. His passion for privacy may have been connected with his homosexuality, which manifested itself in attachments to men like David Pinsent, to whom he dedicated the *Tractatus*, or to the much younger Francis Skinner. At least two of his male friends were lame; a condition which constitutes a particular form of compulsive attraction for some natures. But some who knew Wittgenstein best seemed sure that he was physically chaste.

Whether or not this is the case, there is no doubt that he was predominantly solitary. Indeed, he spent months at a time entirely alone in a hut which he had bought in Norway, and another period in 1948 in a hut beside the sea in Galway.

Wittgenstein was a much more tormented character than Kant: more prone to depression, perpetually threatened with fears about his own sanity, intolerant, dogmatic, suspicious of others, and sure that he was right. His was a nature close to paranoia. Yet his proud indifference to worldly considerations, his dedication to the discovery of truth at all costs, his disdain of compromise, and his intellectual passion, deeply impressed all those who encountered him.

In spite of their differences, Wittgenstein and Kant share a number of the character traits and attitudes which, at an earlier point in this chapter, were postulated as likely to be found in predominantly introverted creative people who had turned away from human relationships. Neither man founded a family or formed any continuing close personal ties. Both were ascetic, shunning self-indulgence of any kind. Both were largely impervious to the ideas of other philosophers. Both were passionately concerned with preserving autonomy. Both based their self-esteem on their work, rather than upon the love of other human beings.

Both these men of genius displayed a compulsive drive to discover order, coherence, and sense by means of abstract thought, and it was this search for truth that gave meaning to their lives. It is likely that the motive power which spurs such passionate intensity is derived from an awareness of potential chaos within: the 'disintegration anxiety' or fear of 'behavioral disorganization' referred to earlier. Wittgenstein, especially, was haunted by fears of breakdown. Kant's obsessional need for order reveals anxiety which, though not as intense as that shown by Wittgenstein, is nevertheless comparable.

There are many examples of men of genius whose intense preoccupation with the search for order was probably motivated by similar anxieties; although one must remember that, even when such a search is originally sparked by fears of disintegration, it can later become self-propelled by the intrinsic interest of the subject, or by the reward which the individual gains from being recognized as proficient or original.

Newton is an example of a man of genius who began life with considerable disadvantages, who grew up to be an eccentric, who suffered a mental illness in middle age, and who then became more stable though remaining isolated. I have written about Newton at some length elsewhere, but the links between his abnormal personality and his exceptional achievements are so evident and so interesting that, in the context of this chapter, they deserve especial notice.[22]

Newton was born prematurely on Christmas Day 1642. His father, an illiterate yeoman, had died three months previously. So far as is known, neither his mother's family nor his father's had previously produced anyone of particular distinction. For his first three years, Newton enjoyed the undivided attention of his mother without suffering any competition; indeed, he was such a tiny baby that it can be assumed that he received even more care than was customary. This idyll was rudely shattered when, on 27 January 1646, just after Newton's third birthday, his mother remarried. She not only presented him with an unwanted stepfather, but also moved house, leaving Newton to be reared by his maternal grandmother. We know that Newton passionately resented this as a betrayal. At the age of twenty, he wrote a confession. Amongst the fifty-eight sins of which he found himself guilty was 'Threatning my father and mother Smith to burne them and the house over them'.[23]

The psycho-analyst Erik Erikson has postulated basic trust versus basic mistrust as the earliest nuclear conflict which the developing human being encounters. Although all of us probably carry with us into adult life some sense of paradise lost, most of us experience sufficient continuity of maternal care for long enough to establish basic trust in other human beings as the norm, mistrust only as the exception. But, if a child enjoys a particularly close relationship with the mother which is suddenly terminated before he is old enough to understand any possible reasons for such a betrayal, he is likely to mistrust all other human beings whom he later encounters and only gradually be persuaded that anyone at all is trustworthy. This was certainly true of Newton. Whiston, Newton's successor in the Lucasian chair of mathematics at Cambridge, said that Newton was 'of the most fearful, cautious, and suspicious temper that I ever knew'.[24]

From 1661, when he first went to Trinity College, Cambridge, until he left for London in 1696, Newton remained predominantly a recluse, preoccupied with his work to the exclusion of almost everything else, with little social contact with other human beings, and no close relations with either sex. Newton's distrust of others is attested by his reluctance to publish his work. He feared that critics would harm him and that others would lay claim to his discoveries. One biographer, Brodetsky, writes:

He was always somewhat unwilling to face publicity and criticism, and had on more than one occasion declined to have his name associated with published accounts of some of his work. He did not value public esteem as desirable in itself, and feared that publicity would lead to his being harassed by personal relationships – whereas he wished to be free of such entanglements . . . Apparently Newton hardly ever published a discovery without being urged to by others: even when he had arrived at the solution of the greatest problem that astronomy has ever had to face he said nothing about it to anybody.[25]

Newton was touchy about questions of priority, as his bitter quarrels with Leibniz, Flamsteed and Hooke bear witness. He was extremely reluctant to own that he was indebted to other men's work. Newton is clearly another example of an introverted creator who fulfils all the criteria postulated at an earlier point in this chapter. That is, he was avoidant of personal relationships, protective of his work against scrutiny, intensely concerned with autonomy, and used his work as his primary source of self-esteem and personal fulfilment. In addition, he suffered overt mental illness.

When he was just over fifty, Newton became transiently psychotic. Some have claimed that his illness was the result of poisoning with mercury, which Newton used in his experiments. But whether or not his psychosis had a toxic origin, it resulted in an exaggeration of his suspiciousness to the point where he broke with his friend Pepys, and believed that the philosopher Locke was endeavouring to 'embroil' him with women. This paranoid episode was succeeded by a period of depression in which he wrote to Locke begging his forgiveness for having had uncharitable thoughts of him. Newton appears to have made a good recovery. He moved from Cambridge to London, became Warden and then Master of the Mint, and was also elected President of the Royal Society. He remained celibate, but his fame brought him considerable satisfaction and a wide acquaintance. George II and Queen Caroline are said to have often entertained him. He continued to revise his scientific publications and to work on his theological studies and his *Chronology of Ancient Kingdoms Amended*. He died in his eighty-fifth year.

Kant, Wittgenstein and Newton were all men of genius who, however different they may have been in other ways, shared a vast capacity for original, abstract thought with a lack of close involvement with other human beings. Indeed, it could reasonably be argued that, if they had had wives and families, their achievements would have been impossible. For the higher reaches of abstraction demand long periods of solitude and intense concentration which are hard to find if a man is subject to the emotional demands of a spouse and children.

Psycho-analysts will point to the obvious fact that these three men were technically 'abnormal', and I concede that all three exhibited more than the usual share of what is generally deemed 'psycho-pathology'. Nevertheless, all three survived and made important contributions to human knowledge and understanding which, I consider, they could not have made if they had not been predominantly solitary. Would they have been happier if they had been able, or more inclined, to seek personal fulfilment in love rather than in their work? It is impossible to say. What should be emphasized is that mankind would be infinitely the poorer if such men of genius were unable to flourish, and we must therefore consider that their traits of personality, as well as their high intelligence, are biologically adaptive. The psychopathology of such men is no more than an exaggeration of traits which can be found in all of us. We all need to find some order in the world, to make some sense out of our existence. Those who are particularly concerned with such a search bear witness to the fact that interpersonal relationships are not the only way of finding emotional fulfilment.

11

The Third Period

'In our novels, it is music, among all the arts, that isolates the individual from the society of his contemporaries, makes him aware of his separateness and, finally, provides a personal significance to his life regardless of his social or even personal loyalties. It is the one measure of survival which never fails ...'

Alex Aronson

At the beginning of life, survival depends upon 'object-relationships'. The human infant cannot care for itself, and is dependent upon the care of others throughout many long years of childhood. Toward the end of life, the opposite condition obtains. Although illness or injury may make the elderly physically dependent, emotional dependence tends to decline. The old often show less interest in interpersonal relationships, are more content to be alone, and become more preoccupied with their own, internal concerns. It is not my intention to suggest that old people do not continue to be interested in their spouses, children, and grandchildren; but rather to point out that the intensity of this interest somewhat declines. There is often an increase in objectivity toward others combined with a decrease in identification with them. This may be why relationships between grandparents and grandchildren are often easier than between parents and children. The grandchild does not feel that as much is expected of him by grandparents as is expected by parents, and may thus establish an easier, less reciprocally demanding relationship with them.

This change in intensity of involvement is partly determined by a decline in the insistence of the sexual impulse which, until middle age or later, compels most men and women to engage in intimacy. It may also be a merciful provision of Nature, designed to lessen the pain of the inevitable parting from loved ones which death brings in its train. Man is the only creature who can see his own death coming; and, when he does, it concentrates his mind wonderfully. He prepares for death by freeing himself from mundane goals and attachments, and turns instead to the cultivation of his own interior garden. Both Jung and Freud exemplify this change. They each survived into their eighties, and both almost abandoned interest in psychotherapy in favour of ideas and theories about human nature. In old age, there is a tendency to turn from empathy toward abstraction; to be less involved in life's dramas, more concerned with life's patterns.

This change, like other aspects of human nature, can be most clearly seen in the productions of those who have left behind a series of works of abiding interest. When men and women of genius live long enough, changes in style become so apparent that it is customary to divide their work into periods, often designated 'first', 'second', and 'third', or 'early', 'middle', and 'late'. The third or late period is relevant to the main theme of this book, since it is a time when communication with others tends to be replaced by works depending more upon solitary meditation.

The significance of the first two periods in the life of an artist is not difficult to determine. Even the most gifted men and women have to learn their craft, and they are bound to be influenced by their teachers and predecessors. The first period, therefore, although it may be characterized by works of undoubted genius, is one in which the artist has usually not fully discovered his individual voice. Bernard Berenson defined genius as 'the capacity for productive reaction against one's training',[1] and as an artist becomes more confident, he gains the courage to dispense with whatever aspects of the past are irrelevant to himself, and enters upon his second period, in which both his mastery and his individuality are clearly manifest. In this period, the need to communicate whatever he has to say to as wide a public as possible is usually evident.

The second period may occupy the greater part of an artist's life, and many of the greatest geniuses have not lived long enough to enter upon a third phase in their creative output. Amongst composers, for example, Mozart, Schubert, Purcell, Chopin, and Mendelssohn lived such brief lives that, in spite of their astonishing precocity, they did not have time to show the kind of change which is manifest in the works of Beethoven and Liszt.

Beethoven lived until the age of fifty-seven: not an advanced age by modern standards, but sufficiently so for his works to provide a good example of the three periods referred to. (This is, of course, a simplification to which musical scholars can find exceptions; but, in broad terms, the ordinary music-lover can at once hear what is meant.) Beethoven's string quartets divide naturally into three groups. The first set of six, op. 18, were embarked upon during Beethoven's twenty-eighth year and preoccupied him during 1798 and 1799. The first three of the set were published in June 1801, the second three four months later. Although no one else could have composed them, Kerman writes that 'they reveal some clear traces of Haydn and some remarkably strong traces of Mozart'.[2] They are certainly enjoyable, but not *echt* Beethoven in the sense in which the later quartets are.

The three quartets dedicated to Count Razumovsky, op. 59, nos. 1–3, plus the so-called 'Harp' Quartet op. 74 and the Quartet in F minor op. 95, are generally grouped together as the 'middle' quartets. The Razumovsky quartets were written during the years 1804–6; op. 74 in 1809, and op. 95 in 1810. The early 1800s were years of immense activity for Beethoven. The 'Eroica' Symphony of 1803–4 represents an entirely new dimension in symphonic music. The Waldstein and Appassionata sonatas, composed mainly in 1804 and 1805, are quite different from any piano sonatas which had gone before. It is worth recalling that these 'heroic' works were composed after the Heiligenstadt Testament which, as we saw earlier, was written in 1802. Beethoven's deafness was already severe, and later changes in his style cannot be attributed to increasing withdrawal into himself on that account alone.

The Razumovsky quartets also illustrate this new departure. They reveal Beethoven's power, energy and confidence as well as his capacity for depicting the deepest emotion. (Compare, for example, the moving adagios of op. 59 no. 1 and op. 59 no. 2 with the exhilaration of the finale of op. 59 no. 3.) These wonderful quartets are both entirely individual and also in a different category from the op. 18 set, enjoyable as those early quartets certainly are.

Between 1806 and 1809, Beethoven completed the Fourth, Fifth, and Sixth symphonies, the Violin Concerto and the Fourth and Fifth piano concertos, as well as a number of smaller works. In 1809 came the 'Harp' Quartet, so-called because of the pizzicato exchanges between the instruments in the first movement. It is a beautiful work, but perhaps should be regarded as a transitional piece which attempts no striking innovation. The same is not true of its successor, the F minor quartet op. 95. This is an extremely compressed, powerful, almost violent work. Beethoven himself named it *quartetto serioso*. Coming as it does at the end of the series of 'middle' quartets, some commentators have thought it closer in spirit to the series of the five 'last' quartets. Kerman writes:

> In the opinion of the present writer, and not his alone, certainly, the Quartet in F minor stands at the highest summit of Beethoven's artistic achievement up to the end of the second period.[3]

The next group of quartets, the five 'last' quartets, were not embarked upon until the 1820s. It is probable that the first of the group, op. 127 in E flat, was begun in 1822, but laid aside until 1824 to allow Beethoven to complete the Ninth Symphony. The last of the five, op. 135 in F major, was composed during August and September 1826. The substitute last movement of op. 130, written at the insistence of his publisher as an alternative to the Great Fugue, was completed later that autumn, and was the last music which Beethoven composed. He died on 24 March 1827.

Martin Cooper writes of Beethoven's late style:

> Nothing is conceded to the listener, no attempt is made to capture his attention or hold his interest. Instead the composer communes with himself or contemplates his vision of reality, thinking (as it were) aloud and concerned only with the pure

essence of his own thoughts and with the musical processes from which that thought itself is often indistinguishable.[4]

The middle three of these last quartets, op. 132 in A minor, op. 130 in B flat major and op. 131 in C sharp minor, were for a long period considered unintelligible. They certainly show a considerable departure from conventional sonata form. The A minor quartet has five movements; the B flat major quartet has six movements; and the C sharp minor quartet has seven movements. There are frequent, sudden changes of tempo, unexpected juxtapositions of themes, and unpredictable interruptions to the flow of the music. Kerman gives the illuminating title 'Dissociation and Integration' to his chapter on opp. 130 and 131. After discussing that extraordinary and violent piece of music, the Great Fugue, which was the original finale to op. 130, Kerman writes:

> In all this, it seems to me indicated that Beethoven was working toward some new idea of order or coherence in the cyclic composition, an order markedly different from the traditional psychological sequence that he had developed in the earlier music. This new order is not easy to comprehend, because on the evidence of the Quartet in B flat, the idea was not entirely realized.[5]

There is an interesting parallel to be found in J. W. N. Sullivan's book, *Beethoven*, first published in 1927. After discussing the significance and usefulness of conventional sonata form to express psychological processes, he goes on to write:

> But in the quartets we are discussing, Beethoven's experience could not be presented in this form. The connection between the various movements is altogether more organic than that of the four-movement sonata form. In these quartets the movements radiate as it were, from a central experience. They do not represent stages in a journey, each stage being independent and existing in its own right. They represent separate experiences, but the meaning they take on in the quartet is derived from their

relation to a dominating, central experience. This is characteristic of the mystic vision, to which everything in the world appears unified in the light of one fundamental experience.[6]

Wilfrid Mellers writes in similar terms about the Diabelli Variations, Beethoven's longest piano work, which was published in 1823. He calls them

a circular rather than linear work ... Like Bach's Goldberg Variations, and despite the difference between the two composers' approach, they rather see 'a world in a grain of sand', making us aware that experience is a totality in which the trivial and the sublime coexist.[7]

In the last chapter of this book, we shall see that Sullivan's and Mellers's delineation of a central experience uniting opposites has parallels in the work of Jung.

Sullivan is more convinced than Kerman that Beethoven fully expressed the new vision toward which he was striving. As an amateur, my own guess is that he did not completely achieve this. Had he lived longer, we might have had works which more perfectly exemplified the synthesis of elements, the unity which he was seeking. Most people would agree that he came nearest to it in the C sharp minor quartet, which Beethoven himself considered his greatest. As Maynard Solomon points out,

A continuity of rhythmic design adds to the feeling that this is one of the most completely integrated of Beethoven's works. But there are many pressures toward discontinuity at work in this Quartet: six distinct main keys, thirty-one changes of tempo (ten more than in opus 130), a variety of textures, and a diversity of forms within the movements – fugue, suite, recitative, variation, scherzo, aria and sonata form – which makes the achievement of unity all the more miraculous.[8]

The last quartet of all, op. 135 in F major, seems to be a return to an earlier genre, perhaps a relaxation after intense spiritual effort, or an expression of peace attained. The question and answer 'Muss es sein? Es muss sein', which is the epigraph of the finale, probably had a trivial origin. Schindler connects it with Beethoven's unwillingness to hand out money for housekeeping. But the fact that Beethoven placed it where he did may also be interpreted as a sign that this habitual rebel had reached some kind of reconciliation with fate.

Beethoven's last quartets strikingly exemplify the main features of the third period in a creative person's life. Third period works share certain characteristics. First, they are less concerned with communication than what has gone before. Second, they are often unconventional in form, and appear to be striving to achieve a new kind of unity between elements which at first sight are extremely disparate. Third, they are characterized by an absence of rhetoric or any need to convince. Fourth, they seem to be exploring remote areas of experience which are intrapersonal or suprapersonal rather than interpersonal. That is, the artist is looking into the depths of his own psyche and is not very much concerned as to whether anyone else will follow him or understand him. These features are plainly to be discerned in the last quartets of Beethoven; but they are also to be found in the work of other composers, provided they lived long enough.

Liszt, for example, died in his seventy-fifth year. For about fifteen years before his death, his music shows a remarkable change. There is none of the old flamboyance, and no more transcendental virtuosity – or at least no virtuosity for its own sake. Instead, there is a preoccupation with Hungarian folksong; the genuine, peasant variety, not the *ersatz* kind to be found in the early rhapsodies. There is also a partial abandonment of conventional tonality, which anticipates Schoenberg and Bartók. Instead of using the habitual system of stating a theme, developing it through various keys, recapitulating it, and finally arriving at a goal, Liszt experiments with violent contrasts and clashes, and with impressionistic effects achieved by the sustaining pedal. Humphrey Searle writes:

The style has become extremely stark and austere, there are long passages in single notes and a considerable use of wholetone chords, and anything resembling a cadence is avoided; in fact, if a work does end with a common chord it is more often in an inversion than in root position. The result is a curiously indefinite feeling, as if Liszt was launching out into a new world of whose possibilities he was not quite sure. For the majority of these works he returned to his first love, the piano; but in general the old pianistic glitter is absent – Liszt was now writing for himself, and no longer for his public.[9]

Searle's comments on Liszt's late style are strikingly similar to Martin Cooper's remarks on Beethoven's late style which were quoted above. Beethoven and Liszt have comparatively little in common as composers, but both, in their early and middle periods, used rhetoric to convince their listeners, and both abandoned it in their last compositions.

There are, of course, other examples of artists turning more and more toward some kind of inner development as they grow older. Bach's *Art of Fugue*, which was his last major composition, may not have been primarily aimed at an audience. It is not even certain for what instrument or combination of instruments *The Art of Fugue* was written, or whether it may have been a purely theoretical work, not designed for performance at all. Malcolm Boyd is certain that

performance alone can never result in a complete apprehension of Bach's last-period works. Even with the most thoughtful performance and the most attentive listening the augmentation canons in the *Musical Offering* and the *Art of Fugue* will sound dry, academic and even ungainly if experienced in the same way as one might experience the *Orgelbüchlein* or the '48'. But to the score reader, able to follow and to ponder on their cold logic, they offer an insight into the mysteries of infinity every bit as teasing in its mathematical beauty as Zeno's paradox of Achilles and the tortoise . . . One would not, of course, willingly forgo the degree of comprehension and enjoyment that performance of this music can offer, but only through study can we hope to arrive at a complete perception of it, and after study, contemplation; for it exists in a world far removed from the *musica humana* of our own, where music, mathematics and philosophy are one.[10]

Once again, we see that, toward the end of life, interest becomes increasingly directed toward pattern-making and the impersonal.

Even in so lushly romantic a composer as Richard Strauss, something of the kind can be detected. Between the age of seventy-eight and his death at the age of eighty-four, Strauss composed the Second Horn Concerto, the First and Second Sonatina for wind instruments, *Metamorphosen* for twenty-three strings, the Concerto for Oboe, the Duet Concertino for clarinet and bassoon, and the Four Last Songs. Mosco Carner comments that, with the exception of *Metamorphosen*, these are slight works, but that

> a classical tendency, manifest in the young Strauss, showed itself again in the octogenarian, yet greatly enriched and mellowed by the artistic and human experiences of a life-time. The neo-classical tendency is displayed in a number of features: in the turn to pure instrumental music; in the avoidance of an emotionally charged expression and the emphasis on exquisitely refined and polished workmanship; in the symmetrical cut of thematic ideas (mostly in regular four and eight bars) and 'old-fashioned' cadences; in the marked preference for simple diatonic writing, and in the transparent scoring, whose sparseness and economy – already to be found in *Daphne* and *Capriccio* – is in strong contrast with the sumptuousness and lavishness of Strauss's symphonic poems and the majority of his operas. *Metamorphosen*, which is the most important of Strauss's late compositions, shows all these features at their most characteristic, to say nothing of a formidable skill displayed in the polyphonic interweaving of the parts.[11]

Brahms, like Mozart, was inspired by a brilliant clarinet player toward the end of his career as a composer. He first heard Richard Mühlfeld in 1891 in Meiningen; and the latter's skill as a performer inspired Brahms to write the Clarinet Trio, the Clarinet Quintet, and two sonatas for clarinet (or viola) and piano. Although Brahms himself preferred the Trio, most critics agree that the Quintet is the greatest of these works, but disagree about the feelings which it evokes. Some find it characterized by nostalgia tempered with resignation; 'autumnal' is a favourite adjective. Robert Simpson finds it permeated with an underlying melancholy. William Murdoch found it 'rapturous';

> a work that is intimate, yet full of warm colour, the clarinet adding such a glow that one can hardly believe that the composer is not a young man full of the joy of life, with all the exuberance of youth and the glamour of a passionate love.[12]

In 1893, Brahms published his last set of pieces for solo piano, op. 119. Composers often write music in a minor key but end in the major. It is one way of reaching 'home' in triumph or in happiness. It is worth noting that the E flat Rhapsody which concludes op. 119, and which is the last piece which Brahms composed for solo piano, reverses the usual order. It is written in the major key but ends in the minor.

Brahms, as Richard Strauss was to do over fifty years later, wrote four last songs: the Four Serious Songs which he composed in 1896, the year before he died. The settings are of words from the Lutheran Bible, but carefully chosen so that none conflict with Brahms's agnosticism. The first song, of which the words are taken from Ecclesiastes 3:19–22, is so relevant to one theme in this book that I cannot forbear to quote it. After declaring that men have no pre-eminence above the beasts, for all must die, the author of Ecclesiastes goes on:

> Who knoweth the spirit of man that goeth upward, and the spirit of the beast that goeth downward to the earth? Wherefore I perceive that there is nothing better, than that a man should rejoice in his own works; for that is his portion: for who shall bring him to see what shall be after him?

Brahms's very last composition was a set of eleven Chorale Preludes for Organ, which remind both Denis Arnold and Fuller Maitland of Bach. The former refers to them as 'tranquilly introspective in a manner reminiscent of Bach'.[13] The latter, commenting on the last of the set, writes:

it must be admitted that none of the great composers has given the world a final utterance of more exquisite and touching beauty. The last few bars have a cadence of such fresh and expressive beauty as even Brahms himself never surpassed, and once again we are reminded of Bach . . .[14]

Both Richard Strauss and Brahms showed some of the characteristics of third period works in their late compositions: lack of rhetoric, lack of any need to persuade or convince, and some inclination toward the impersonal rather than the personal. But their late music also exhibits a nostalgic trend which is absent from the compositions of Beethoven and Liszt. I am inclined to link this with the fact that both men, in their private lives, were cautious, hesitant individuals, uncommitted to living life to the full. Nostalgia, which is close to sentimentality, seems usually to be an expression of regret for opportunities missed, rather than regret for actual past accomplishments or pleasures. Brahms was a cautious man of whom Nietzsche wrote: 'His is the melancholy of incapacity.'[15] Although he was seriously in love with Clara Schumann (who was fourteen years his senior), and had a number of emotional attachments to other women, he never whole-heartedly committed himself and remained a bachelor. He destroyed all his apprentice compositions and many later works which he felt did not come up to standard. Peter Latham writes: 'It is as though he feared that they might somehow be produced later in evidence against him.'[16]

Following the disappointment of his hopes of a life with Clara Schumann, Brahms became involved with Agathe von Siebold, but broke his engagement to her when the question of marriage became urgent. It was noticed by everyone who knew him that, as he became older, Brahms became more and more reserved and withdrawn, concealing his true feelings behind a wall of abruptness and sarcasm. By nature, Brahms had a warmer, more emotional temperament than the philosophers discussed in the last chapter; but disappointment and rejection prevented his emotions from finding fulfilment. No wonder his later music is tinged with nostalgia and regret.

Richard Strauss's life was also incomplete. He was married to a singer who, as she grew older, became more and more dominating, grasping, snobbish, and waspish. One has only to look at their wedding photograph to guess their relationship. Pauline Strauss seems to have been heartily disliked by all who knew her. She was clearly a severely obsessional character. She required her husband to wipe his feet on three sets of doormats before entering the house, and lost her temper with the servants if the linen closets were not ordered with mathematical precision. Strauss may have taken a masochistic pleasure in being so imperiously dominated, but five of his operas revolve around the theme of fidelity, and he is said to have had an affair with one of the prima donnas who sang *Salome*. He was a weak man who welcomed the rise of Hitler, supported Goebbels's attack on Hindemith and Furtwängler, substituted for Bruno Walter as a conductor when the latter was threatened by the Nazis, and also substituted for Toscanini when the latter refused to conduct in Germany. He wrote to Hitler apologizing for his connection with the Jewish writer, Stefan Zweig, who had written a libretto for him. For twenty-five years before the Indian summer which produced his last group of works, Strauss composed little of consequence. Strauss was an egotist whose main interest lay in money and the promotion of his own works. Toscanini once said to him, 'For Strauss the composer, I take my hat off. For Strauss the man, I put it on again.'[17] The composer whose *Elektra* and *Salome* are full of horror, violence and perverse sexuality, was himself an inhibited weakling. It is not surprising that his last works, beautiful as they are, evoke more feelings of nostalgia than of reconciliation or integration.

Henry James is an author whose 'third period' presents features of particular interest. His last three novels, *The Ambassadors*, *The Wings of the Dove*, and *The Golden Bowl*, are even more densely complex in style than his early and middle work. Partly because they were dictated, rather than handwritten, revision was more easily accomplished, and constant revision became habitual. Perhaps we should be grateful that, during James's lifetime, the word-processor had not yet been invented. James's anxiety to avoid the expected sometimes results in prose which is opaque and difficult to understand. The reader finds that he needs to concentrate more intensely than most readers of novels wish to do if he is to follow the twists and turns of James's tortuous writing.

179

What is interesting is that James, in *The Ambassadors*, exhibits the preoccupation with pattern and order already noted as characteristic of the third period, combined with a determination to preach the gospel of living life to the full which, in other artists, would be more typically associated with earlier periods in their work. Henry James was fifty-seven when he wrote *The Ambassadors*, the age at which Beethoven died. James himself picks out as the core of the book the speech given to Lambert Strether in chapter 2 of Book Fifth.

> Live all you can; it's a mistake not to. It doesn't so much matter what you do in particular, so long as you have your life. If you haven't had that, what *have* you had?[18]

It was an injunction which James himself had singularly failed to follow. But, in 1899, while staying in Rome, James had met a young American sculptor of Norwegian origin, called Hendrik Andersen. James bought one of his busts, and exacted a promise that Andersen would come and stay with him, which, for three days, he later did. Leon Edel comments that James became aware that he had deeper feelings for Andersen than he had ever had before for anyone outside his own family. Moreover, James's letters to Andersen contain far more references to physical affection than had previously been evident in James's correspondence. Henry James was sexually inhibited. He had

> exalted the intellectual and emotional rather than the physical in human relations ... We must remind ourselves also, in weighing this delicate and ambiguous evidence, that James had hitherto tended to look at the world as though through plate glass. Andersen seems to have helped James emerge from behind that protective wall. If we let our fancy run, we might think of him as opening James up to sensory feeling to a greater degree than had been the case earlier; perhaps the touch of those strong fingers of the sculptor's hand may have given James a sense of physical closeness and warmth which he had never allowed himself to feel in earlier years; and it is this which we read in his letters.[19]

So James's third period is out of kilter. Instead of the physical being less evident as he became older, it suddenly impinges upon him as a valid, albeit irrational, part of love; something which he himself had failed to grasp in earlier days and which made him feel, rightly, that he had missed something in life of signal importance.

Although the main theme of *The Ambassadors* is Strether's injunction to 'live all you can', the novel also displays a symmetrical pattern. The inhibited, fifty-five-year-old Lambert Strether is despatched from America to rescue a young American, Chad Newsome, from the supposedly bad influence of Parisian life and, more especially, from the clutches of Madame de Vionnet. However, after meeting Madame de Vionnet, and himself succumbing to the liberating influence of Europe, Strether abandons his rescue mission, and urges the young man to stay. Meanwhile, Chad's attitude has changed. After at first refusing to leave France, he then eagerly embraces the idea of returning to America and engaging in business. Thus, the two main protagonists of the novel change places.

Ralf Norrman, who has studied such patterns in Henry James's fiction, refers to this switch as an example of 'chiastic inversion': 'A changes and becomes what B has been; while B changes and becomes what A has been.'[20] Chiasmus refers to a crossing over, as in the case of the optic chiasm at the base of the brain, in which some of the fibres of the optic tracts cross over to join those from the other side. The novel which precedes the last three, *The Sacred Fount*, derives from this device in such an artificial way that I find it unreadable. In Notebook III, on 17 February 1894, James records two ideas suggested to him by Stopford Brooke. The second runs as follows.

> The notion of the young man who marries an older woman and who has the effect on her of making her younger and still younger, while he himself becomes her age. When he reaches the age that *she* was (on their marriage), she has gone back to the age that *he* was. – Mightn't this be altered (perhaps) to the idea of cleverness and stupidity? A clever woman marries a deadly dull man, and loses and loses her wit as he shows more and more . . .[21]

However, this type of pattern-making does not necessarily result in artificiality. James's last novel, *The Golden Bowl*, which is one of his greatest, depends upon multiple chiastic inversion, as Ralf Norrman points out. The four main characters are the widowed American, Adam Verver, and his daughter Maggie; Prince Amerigo and Charlotte Stant. Maggie marries the Prince, and persuades her father to marry Charlotte in order to compensate for her loss. However, the tie between father and daughter is so persistent that they continue to spend a great deal of time together, which revives a former attachment between Charlotte and the Prince. Maggie eventually brings this situation to an end by despatching her father and Charlotte to America, whilst she remains in Europe with the Prince. The four characters encounter each other, form new partnerships, revert to the former pattern (with the addition of what is now adultery), and finally settle for the partnerships made after their original encounters.

What is extraordinary is that this apparently artificial pattern does not kill the human emotions involved as I think it does in *The Sacred Fount*. The aesthetic pursuit of symmetry is tempered with a real appreciation of human passion, and, as Edel makes clear, for the first time James conceives as possible, and actually brings off, a marriage between the Old World of Europe and the New World of America.

Henry James seems archetypally an ambiguous figure; sympathetic, and deeply concerned with human feelings, yet somehow always detached from them. To revert to Howard Gardner's oft-used classification, James is both a dramatist and a patterner. As he grew older, his awareness of the physical aspect of love grew more rather than less, because of his feeling for Andersen. This awareness both saddened and enlarged him. I think it made possible the synthesis between opposites which is apparent in *The Golden Bowl*, and prevented that rich and daring novel from being overwhelmed by the aesthetic patterns from which it originated.

'The Beast in the Jungle', written toward the end of 1902, is James's most powerful and most tragic tale, and is also clearly autobiographical, in that it expresses his bitter regret for what he had missed in life, and his shame at having been so enclosed within the prison of his own egotism that he had not dared fully to love.

It will be recalled that this is the story of John Marcher, who, all his life, has been sure that a particular, unusual experience was lying in wait for him, which he pictures as a beast tracking him in the jungle, awaiting its chance to spring. He has confided his secret to a woman, May Bartram. When, after a ten-year interval, they meet again, she reminds him of his confidence, and asks him if anything has happened. It has not; and when he goes on to describe what he is still anticipating, something which may suddenly break out in his life, something which, he thinks, might annihilate him or alter everything in his world, May Bartram hazards the guess that what he is expecting but cannot describe is what is familiar to many people as the danger of falling in love. John Marcher dismisses the idea.

During the many years to come, they continue to spend much of their time together. Eventually, May Bartram dies. Marcher has failed to respond to, failed even to recognize, the offer of love which, at one point, she clearly makes him. Only when she is dead does he realize that the beast in the jungle sprang at that moment.

> The escape would have been to love her; then, *then* he would have lived. *She* had lived – who could say now with what passion? – since she had loved him for himself; whereas he had never thought of her (ah how it hugely glared at him!) but in the chill of his egotism and the light of her use.[22]

Marcher, kneeling on May Bartram's grave,

> saw, in the truth, in the cruelty of his image what had been appointed and done. He saw the Jungle of his life and saw the lurking Beast; then, while he looked, perceived it, as by a stir of the air, rise, huge and darkened – it was close; and, instinctively turning in his hallucination to avoid it, he flung himself, face down, on the tomb.[23]

In a letter to Hugh Walpole, James wrote:

> I think I don't regret a single 'excess' of my responsive youth, I only regret in my chilled age certain occasions and possibilities I *didn't* embrace.[24]

Henry James's last novels exhibit at least some of the characteristics of third period works to which reference was made earlier. His elaborate style makes no concessions, so that it is fair to say that he is less directly concerned with communication or with trying to woo or convince the reader. Pattern and order, although evident throughout his work, are even more insistently present in *The Ambassadors* and *The Golden Bowl*. However, James is not so concerned as some of the artists mentioned in this chapter with exploring remote areas of experience beyond the personal. His late acceptance of the physical element in love actually enriches his work at a time in life when those artists who, like Bach, had fully experienced this aspect of life, seem to be reaching out beyond it. In this sense, he is also achieving a new unity between disparate elements. Leon Edel writes:

'Live all you can,' had been central to *The Ambassadors*: man had to learn to live with the illusion of his freedom. Life without love wasn't life – this was the conclusion of *The Wings of the Dove*; and having found love James had come to see at last that art could not be art, and not life, without love. He had become his own Sphinx; he was answering his own riddles.[25]

12

The Desire and Pursuit
of the Whole

'Dust as we are, the immortal spirit grows
Like harmony in music; there is a dark
Inscrutable workmanship that reconciles
Discordant elements, makes them cling together
In one society.'

William Wordsworth

In Plato's *Symposium*, Aristophanes takes it upon himself to initiate his friends into the secret of love's power. He begins by recalling the myth that there were originally three sexes: hermaphrodite, male, and female. The male originated from the sun, the female from the earth, and the hermaphrodite from the moon which partakes of the nature of both sun and earth. Each human being was a rounded whole, with four legs and four arms, able to walk upright in either direction, or to run by turning over and over in circular fashion.

These original human beings were so arrogant, so insolent, and so powerful that they constituted a threat to the gods, who debated how best to restrain them. Zeus decided that they should be bisected, and later arranged matters so that reproduction took place by means of sexual intercourse rather than by emission on to the ground, as had happened previously.

The consequence of this bisection of the human race was that each half-being felt compelled to seek out a partner who would restore its former wholeness. The male sought another male, the female another female, and the hermaphrodite a contrasexual partner

'Love', says Aristophanes, 'is simply the name for the desire and pursuit of the whole.'[1]

Plato's myth is a potent one. Down the centuries, the notion that we attain wholeness and complete ourselves by merging sexually with another person has been the chief inspiration of romantic literature and the climax of thousands of novels. There is enough truth in the myth for most of us still to be powerfully affected by it. In youth, especially, sexual union with a beloved person does bring with it, however ephemerally, a sense of completion which few other experiences can match. But sex is only one out of a variety of ways of attaining unity.

Although Freud continued to regard sexual fulfilment as the main source of satisfaction in the lives of both men and women, and to think that neurotic problems were the consequence of psychological blocks preventing the attainment of sexual maturity, he did retain some doubts as to whether complete emotional fulfilment was actually possible. In a comparatively early paper Freud wrote:

> It is my belief that, however strange it may sound, we must reckon with the possibility that something in the nature of the sexual instinct itself is unfavourable to the realization of complete satisfaction.[2]

In spite of this, and in spite of the fact that, at this time, Freud thought that cultural achievements were the result of sublimation of aspects of the sexual impulse which could not find direct expression when trammelled by the restrictions of civilization, sexual fulfilment continued to represent an ideal both for Freud and his followers.

However, there is more to the experience of falling in love than the desire for, or achievement of, sexual union. Falling in love is, for the majority, one of the most compelling emotional experiences which anyone can encounter. Whilst the state of being in love persists, the person experiencing it usually feels an ecstatic sense of unity both with the world outside and also within the self: a sense of unity which was initiated by encountering the beloved person, and which may continue to depend upon the existence of the beloved person, but which does not necessarily require his or her actual physical

186

presence. Being in love is usually thought of as the closest, most intimate form of interpersonal relationship; but it is a state of mind which, once triggered, may persist for some time independently of any actual encounter with the beloved. The earth assumes a smiling countenance; and, although this may be no more than a projection of the inner bliss of the subject, there is a sense in which feeling that all is right with the world may actually promote a better adjustment to it. All the world loves a lover, and a lover loves all the world.

In Chapter 5, I anthropomorphically assumed that creatures who were more or less perfectly adjusted to the environment could be called 'happy'. It seems to me that those in love experience happiness because, for a brief period, they feel a sense of being perfectly adjusted to the world around them as well as a sense of ecstatic peace and unity within. Whilst the state of being in love persists, there appears to be no discrepancy between actuality and the world of the imagination. The 'hunger of imagination' is temporarily sated. This is something other than sexual infatuation. Although sexual intercourse can sometimes be an immensely fulfilling experience which brings in its train a sense of peaceful relaxation, the state of being 'in love' is a different condition. Ecstasy is not the same as sexual orgasm; and being in love is a state of mind closer to ecstasy than it is to orgasm. As Marghanita Laski points out in her book *Ecstasy*, sexual imagery is used to describe ecstasy only by those who have no experience of a normal sex life.[3]

Freud certainly appreciated the difference between sexual fulfilment and the sense of unity which accompanies the state of being in love, but he exalted the former experience and denigrated the latter. In Chapter 3, brief reference was made to Freud's discussion with Romain Rolland of the 'oceanic feeling'. It will be recalled that Freud designated the oceanic feeling as 'a feeling of an indissoluble bond, of being one with the external world as a whole'.[4] Freud goes on to compare this feeling with that of being in love.

At the height of being in love the boundary between ego and object threatens to melt away. Against all the evidence of his senses, a man who is in love declares that 'I' and 'you' are one and is prepared to behave as if it were a fact.[5]

In Chapter 3, I suggested that Freud was right in seeing a similarity between the feeling of unity with the universe and the feeling of unity with a beloved person, but wrong to dismiss such experiences as merely regressive illusions.

The sense of perfect harmony with the universe, of perfect harmony with another person, and of perfect harmony within the self are intimately connected; indeed, I believe them to be essentially the same phenomena. The triggers for these experiences are of many different kinds. Marghanita Laski lists 'nature, art, religion, sexual love, childbirth, knowledge, creative work, certain forms of exercise',[6] as being the most common. Admiral Byrd's description of feeling at one with the universe, which was given in Chapter 3, is a characteristic example for which the triggers were solitude, silence, and the majesty of the Antarctic. Experiences of this kind can also occur spontaneously in solitude without the aid of any external stimulus. Such transcendental experiences are closely connected with aspects of the creative process; with suddenly being able to make sense out of what had previously appeared impenetrable, or with making a new unity by linking together concepts which had formerly seemed to be quite separate.

Plato's myth is an accurate account of the human condition in that it depicts man as an incomplete creature constantly in search of wholeness or unity; but confines itself to describing unity in terms of a sexual relationship. In fact, transcendental experiences of things suddenly coming together or making sense of life can even be triggered by something as impersonal as mathematics. Bertrand Russell describes such a moment.

At the age of eleven, I began Euclid, with my brother as my tutor. This was one of the great events of my life, as dazzling as first love. I had not imagined that there was anything so delicious in the world.[7]

Einstein was likewise transported by Euclid at the age of twelve, when, at the beginning of the school year, he received a book expounding Euclidean plane geometry.

There is a good example of the oceanic feeling being triggered by scientific discovery in an early novel by C. P. Snow. The same example is used by Marghanita Laski in *Ecstasy*, and underlines her contention that, although orgasmic experiences may share some features with ecstatic experiences, the latter are of a different order. In Snow's novel, which is clearly autobiographical, the young scientist has just received confirmation that some difficult work he has been doing on the atomic structure of crystals has turned out to be correct.

Then I was carried beyond pleasure. I have tried to show something of the high moments that science gave to me; the night my father talked about the stars, Luard's lesson, Austin's opening lecture, the end of my first research. But this was different from any of them, different altogether, different in kind. It was further from myself. My own triumph and delight and success were there, but they seemed insignificant beside this tranquil ecstasy. It was as though I had looked for a truth outside myself, and finding it had become for a moment part of the truth I sought; as though all the world, the atoms and the stars, were wonderfully clear and close to me, and I to them, so that we were part of a lucidity more tremendous than any mystery.

I had never known that such a moment could exist. Some of its quality, perhaps, I had captured in the delight which came when I brought joy to Audrey, being myself content; or in the times among friends, when for some rare moment, maybe twice in my life, I had lost myself in a common purpose; but these moments had, as it were, the tone of the experience without the experience itself.

Since then I have never quite regained it. But one effect will stay with me as long as I live; once, when I was young, I used to sneer at the mystics who have described the experience of being at One with God and part of the Unity of things. After that afternoon, I did not want to laugh again; for though I should interpret it differently, I think I know what they meant.[8]

Freud dismissed the oceanic feeling as an illusion based on

regression to an infantile emotional state. The notion that a kind of union or 'wholeness', which was not rooted in the body, could be a valid and vital experience, an ideal toward which men strive, would have seemed to Freud to be an evasion of the harsh facts of man's physicality. Freud was always inclined to dismiss as unreal psychological experiences which could not easily be traced to, or linked with, the body. It is a limitation of his thought which we have already encountered when discussing his attitude to phantasy.

When psycho-analysis was first developed as a method of treatment, Freud advised against taking on patients of fifty or older, on the grounds that, in most cases, the elasticity of the mental processes needed for change was lacking. Since psycho-analytic technique demanded scrupulous reconstruction of the past, Freud also felt that the mass of material which had accumulated during a life of this length would prolong treatment interminably. Although modern Freudians often treat patients of middle-age and over, the principal thrust of psycho-analysis has always been toward understanding childhood, youth, and the emancipation of the individual from emotional ties to parents. This is also the period of life when the sexual impulse is most urgently compelling, and when solution of sexual problems proves most rewarding.

But, however sincerely one subscribes to the evolutionary view that man's prime biological task is to reproduce himself, the very fact that the lifespan extends for so long beyond the period at which, at least for women, reproduction is possible, raises doubts as to whether the act subserving reproduction entirely deserves this pride of place. What Jung calls 'the second half of life' must surely have some other meaning and purpose.

It was left to Jung and his followers to pay attention to the problems of the middle-aged. Jung's major contribution to psychology and to psychotherapy is in the field of adult development. He paid relatively little attention to childhood, believing that, when children exhibited neurotic distress, the answer to their problems should usually be sought in studying their parents' psychology rather than their own.

Jung's interest in the problems of adult development originated from the crisis which he himself experienced between 1913 and the end of the First World War. Reference was made to this period of distress at the beginning of Chapter 7. In July 1913, Jung reached the age of thirty-eight. By this time, he had married, fathered a family, and established himself as a psychiatrist of world renown. His hope had been that, together with Freud, he could develop a new science of the mind. But some force within him, against his own inclination, compelled him to develop his own individual point of view. The first fruits of this was the book originally known, in English translation, as *The Psychology of the Unconscious*, which was published in 1912.* In his autobiography, Jung describes how, for two months, he was unable to write the final chapters, because he knew that Freud would regard his divergence from him as a betrayal. The sad story of the estrangement between the two pioneers which followed can be traced in *The Freud–Jung Letters*.†

Jung was the first psychiatrist to draw attention to what is now familiarly known as the 'mid-life crisis'. His distress forced him into a long period of self-analysis in which he recorded his own visions and dreams, many of which were alarmingly threatening. But, out of this dangerous period, Jung forged his own, individual point of view. He wrote:

> The years when I was pursuing my inner images were the most important in my life – in them everything essential was decided.[9]

Jung's self-analysis convinced him that, whereas the young individual's task was primarily to emancipate himself from his original family, establish himself in the world, and found a new family in his turn, the middle-aged individual's task was to discover and express his own uniqueness as an individual. Jung defined personality as 'the supreme realization of the innate idiosyncrasy of a living being'.[10]

This quest was not primarily egotistical since, in Jung's view, the essence of individuality could only be expressed when the person concerned acknowledged the direction of a force within the psyche which was not of his own making. Men became neurotic at the mid-point of life because, in some sense, they had been false to

---

* Now published as *Symbols of Transformation*: Collected Works, V (London, 1956).

† *The Freud–Jung Letters*, edited by William McGuire, translated by Ralph Manheim and R.F.C. Hull (London, 1974).

themselves, and had strayed too far from the path which Nature intended them to follow. By scrupulous attention to the inner voice of the psyche, which manifested itself in dreams, phantasies, and other derivatives of the unconscious, the lost soul could rediscover its proper path, as Jung himself succeeded in doing. The attitude or 'set' required of the patient is really a religious one, although belief in a personal God or adherence to a recognized religious creed is not part of the undertaking.

Jung himself discovered, in childhood, that he could no longer subscribe to the orthodox Protestant faith in which he had been reared by his father, who was a pastor in the Swiss Reformed Church. It might be alleged that the whole of Jung's later work represents his attempt to find a substitute for the faith which he had lost. Such a speculation may be interesting but is ultimately unimportant. Whether or not Jung's ideas originate from personal conflict neither confirms nor invalidates them. As he puts it in one of his best-known statements:

> Among all my patients in the second half of life – that is to say, over thirty-five – there has not been one whose problem in the last resort was not that of finding a religious outlook on life . . . This of course has nothing whatever to do with a particular creed or membership of a church.[11]

Because Freud dismissed religion as an illusion, Freudian analysts have tended to regard such statements as evidence of Jung's unregenerate obscurantism. However, as the Freudian analyst Charles Rycroft has pointed out,

> there would seem to be no necessary incompatibility between psychoanalysis and those religious formulations which locate God within the self. One could, indeed, argue that Freud's Id (and even more Groddeck's It), the impersonal force within which is both the core of oneself and yet not oneself, and from which in illness one becomes alienated, is a secular formulation of the insight which makes religious people believe in an immanent God.[12]

192

Jung came to specialize in the treatment of middle-aged individuals.

> The clinical material at my disposal is of a peculiar composition: new cases are decidedly in the minority. Most of them already have some form of psychotherapeutic treatment behind them, with partial or negative results. About a third of my cases are not suffering from any clinically definable neurosis, but from the senselessness and aimlessness of their lives. I should not object if this were called the general neurosis of our age. Fully two thirds of my patients are in the second half of life. This peculiar material sets up a special resistance to rational methods of treatment, probably because most of my patients are socially well-adapted individuals, often of outstanding ability, to whom normalization means nothing.[13]

The path of self-development upon which such individuals embarked under Jung's guidance was named by him 'the process of individuation'. This process tends toward a goal called 'wholeness' or 'integration': a condition in which the different elements of the psyche, both conscious and unconscious, become welded together in a new unity. Wordsworth describes just such a process in the lines from *The Prelude* which form the epigraph to this chapter. The person who approaches this goal, which can never be entirely or once and for all time achieved, possesses what Jung called

> an attitude that is beyond the reach of emotional entanglements and violent shocks – a consciousness detached from the world.[14]

This new integration is essentially an internal matter; a change in attitude taking place within the psyche of the individual, promoted by the analyst, but not primarily occurring because of the patient's changing relation with the analyst in the way described earlier when psychotherapy based upon 'object-relations' theory was discussed. Indeed, when Jung's more advanced patients were embarked upon the individuation process, he would encourage them to pursue their

193

quest alone, as he himself had done, only bringing the material of their dreams and visions to him when his especial comment was needed, or when the material appeared particularly obscure.

Jung encouraged his patients to set aside part of the day for what came to be known as 'active imagination'. This is a state of reverie, in which judgement is suspended, but consciousness is preserved. The subject is required to note what phantasies occur to him, and then to let these phantasies pursue their own path without conscious intervention. In this way, the subject may be able to rediscover hidden parts of himself as well portray the psychological journey on which he is embarking.

When I was a psychotherapist in practice, I sometimes adopted an approach derived from this technique with middle-aged patients suffering from depression. Such patients are often people who, because of the demands of their careers and families, have neglected or abandoned pursuits and interests which, at an earlier point in time, gave life zest and meaning. If the patient is encouraged to recall what made life meaningful to him in adolescence, he will begin to rediscover neglected sides of himself, and perhaps turn once again to music, or to painting, or to some other cultural or intellectual pursuit which once enthralled him, but which the pressure of life's business had made him abandon.

Persistence with active imagination not only leads to the rediscovery of aspects of the personality which have been neglected, but to a change of attitude in which the subject comes to realize that his own ego or will is no longer paramount, but that he must acknowledge dependence upon an integrating factor which is not of his own making. Jung wrote:

> If the unconscious can be recognized as a co-determining factor along with consciousness, and if we can live in such a way that conscious and unconscious demands are taken into account as far as possible, then the centre of gravity of the total personality shifts its position. It is then no longer in the ego, which is merely the centre of consciousness, but in the hypothetical point between conscious and unconscious. This new centre might be called the Self.[15]

Jung describes reaching this point as achieving peace of mind after what may have been long and fruitless struggles. He wrote:

If you sum up what people tell you about their experiences, you can formulate it this way: They came to themselves, they could accept themselves, they were able to become reconciled to themselves, and thus were reconciled to adverse circumstances and events. This is almost like what used to be expressed by saying: He has made his peace with God, he has sacrificed his own will, he has submitted himself to the will of God.[16]

This is not healing through insight, nor through making a new and better relationship with another person, nor even through solving particular problems, but healing by means of an inner change of attitude.

Jung quotes a letter from a former patient which illustrates the change to which he is referring.

Out of evil, much good has come to me. By keeping quiet, repressing nothing, remaining attentive, and by accepting reality – taking things as they are, and not as I wanted them to be – by doing all this, unusual knowledge has come to me, and unusual powers as well, such as I could never have imagined before. I always thought that when we accepted things they overpowered us in some way or other. This turns out not to be true at all, and it is only by accepting them that one can assume an attitude towards them. So now I intend to play the game of life, being receptive to whatever comes to me, good and bad, sun and shadow forever alternating, and, in this way, also accepting my own nature with its positive and negative sides. Thus everything becomes more alive to me. What a fool I was! How I tried to force everything to go according to the way I thought it ought to![17]

Something very similar is described by William James:

The transition from tenseness, self-responsibility, and worry, to equanimity, receptivity, and peace, is the most wonderful of all those shiftings of inner equilibrium, those changes of the personal centre of energy, which I have analyzed so often; and the chief wonder of it is that it so often comes about, not by doing, but by simply relaxing and throwing the burden down.[18]

The state of mind which these three writers are describing is clearly more than constructive resignation, although it is not identical with the intensity of ecstatic states which are suddenly triggered and usually brief. William James wrote:

Mystical states cannot be sustained for long. Except in rare instances, half an hour, or at most an hour or two, seems to be the limit beyond which they fade into the light of common day. Often, when faded, their quality can but imperfectly be reproduced in memory; but when they recur it is recognized; and from one recurrence to another it is susceptible of continuous development in what is felt as inner richness and importance.[19]

The end-point of individuation shares with ecstatic states the experience of a new unity within, described by Jung as being a new reciprocity between conscious and unconscious. The sense of peace, of reconciliation with life, of being part of a greater whole, is closely similar. Jung's concept of the subject accepting dependence upon an integrating factor which is within, but which is not the ego, is paralleled by the more passive attitude of 'waiting upon God' so often found in the accounts given by the religious mystics.

In his chapter 'The Divided Self', William James considers the process of unification.

It may come gradually, or it may occur abruptly; it may come through altered feelings, or through altered powers of action; or it may come through new intellectual insights, or through experiences which we shall later have to designate as 'mystical'. However it comes, it brings a characteristic sort of relief; and never such extreme relief as when it is cast into the religious mould . . . But to find religion is only one out of many ways of

196

reaching unity; and the process of remedying inner incompleteness and reducing inner discord is a general psychological
process, which may take place with any sort of mental material,
and need not necessarily assume the religious form.[20]

Whether or not these experiences of unification occur suddenly or
gradually, they are so impressive that they generally seem to leave
permanent effects within the mind. However, it would be naive to
suppose that people who reach this state of peace maintain it
uninterruptedly or for ever. We noted, in Chapter 3, the association
of ecstatic states of mind with death. If life is to continue, one cannot
linger for ever in a state of oceanic tranquillity. One of the major
themes of this book has been that man's adaptation to the world is the
result, paradoxically, of *not* being perfectly adjusted to the environment, of *not* being in a state of psychological equilibrium. The
ecstatic sense of wholeness is bound to be transient because it has no
part in the total pattern of 'adaptation through maladaptation' which
is characteristic of our species. Boeotian bliss is not conducive to
invention: the hunger of imagination, the desire and pursuit of the
whole, take origin from the realization that something is missing,
from awareness of incompleteness.

Jung's concept of integration is not in fact that of a static mental
condition, although it is sometimes misinterpreted as being so. In
Jung's view, the development of the personality toward integration
and mental health is an ideal which is never entirely reached or, if
temporarily attained, is bound to be later superseded. Jung thought
that the achievement of optimum development of the personality
was a lifetime's task which was never completed; a journey upon
which one sets out hopefully toward a destination at which one never
arrives.

The new attitude gained in the course of analysis tends sooner
or later to become inadequate in one way or another, and
necessarily so, because the flow of life again and again demands
fresh adaptation. Adaptation is never achieved once and for all
. . . In the last resort it is highly improbable that there could ever
be a therapy which got rid of all difficulties. Man needs

197

difficulties; they are necessary for health. What concerns us here is only an excessive amount of them.[21]

The path of individuation and the changes of attitude which take place can be closely matched with accounts of the creative process given by men and women of genius. First, the mental state during which new ideas arise or inspiration occurs is exactly that which Jung recommended to his patients and which he called 'active imagination'. Although, occasionally, the germ of a new composition or hypothesis occurs in a dream, by far the greater number of new ideas occur during a state of reverie, intermediate between waking and sleeping. Poets, like Yeats and Wordsworth, sometimes describe this state as being both asleep and awake. It is a state of mind in which ideas and images are allowed to appear and take their course spontaneously; but one in which the subject is sufficiently awake and conscious enough to observe and note their progress. Both the patient engaging in 'active imagination' and the creator seeking inspiration need to be able to be passive, to let things happen within the mind.

Many writers have described how characters which they have invented seem to take on an independent life of their own, or of how their pens seem sometimes to be guided by some directing agency other than by their own volition. For example, Thackeray recorded:

I have been surprised at the observations made by some of my characters. It seems as if an occult Power was moving the pen. The personage does or says something, and I ask, how the dickens did he come to think of that?[22]

George Eliot told J. W. Cross

that, in all she considered her best writing, there was a 'not herself' which took possession of her, and that she felt her own personality to be merely the instrument through which this spirit, as it were, was acting.[23]

Nietzsche wrote of his *Thus Spoke Zarathustra*:

Has anyone at the end of the nineteenth century a distinct conception of what poets of strong ages called *inspiration*? If not, I will describe it now. – If one had the slightest residue of superstition left in one, one would hardly be able to set aside the idea that one is merely incarnation, merely mouthpiece, merely medium of overwhelming forces.[24]

Second, creativity usually consists of forming new links between formerly disparate entities, the union between opposites described by Jung. This linking process is obvious in scientific creativity, in which a new hypothesis reconciles or supersedes ideas which were previously thought to be incompatible. Kepler had been able to describe the motions of the planets round the sun; Galileo had described the motions of bodies upon the earth. Until Newton, the sets of laws governing these two types of motion had been regarded as quite separate. But Newton's idea that gravity could operate at vast distances enabled him to combine the discoveries of Kepler and Galileo in such a way that the motions of bodies in the heavens and bodies upon the earth could be seen to obey the same universal laws.

Combining opposites can also be demonstrated in the visual arts and in music. The aesthetic impact of a painting usually depends upon the skill with which the painter has balanced and combined opposing forms and colours. Sonata form in music usually consists of an exposition stating two distinct themes, the first and second subjects, which are then juxtaposed and combined in various ways in the development section. Our delight in this kind of music is related to the skill with which the composer creates a new unity out of themes which at first appeared quite separate.

Third, the creative process continues throughout life. No creator is ever satisfied with what he has done. New problems constantly occur which compel him to seek new solutions. Completed works are but halts on the way; staging posts on a journey which, as in Jung's picture of the development of personality, is never completed. Indeed, the works of an artist are the outward and visible signs of his inner development as a person. We have already discussed some of the changes which tend to occur as creative people become older.

Fourth, the creative process and the process of individuation are both phenomena taking place largely in solitude. Although Jung's account of the individuation process derived from what he observed in patients undergoing analysis, who were therefore under his scrutiny and in some sort of relation with him, he regarded individuation as a natural path of psychological development which took place independently of the analyst's influence. Indeed, as I wrote earlier, Jung was at pains to make his 'more advanced' patients as independent of him as possible, and encouraged them to pursue their own path of psychological discovery by themselves, only intervening when the material produced was particularly obscure.

The human mind seems to be so constructed that the discovery, or perception, of order or unity in the external world is mirrored, transferred, and experienced as if it were a discovery of a new order and balance in the inner world of the psyche. This may seem an improbable hypothesis, but aesthetic appreciation, as well as the creation of works of art, depend upon it. The quotation given earlier, from C. P. Snow, beautifully illustrates how a new scientific discovery, a new truth 'outside', becomes something with which the scientist identifies himself, and which is therefore also felt as being 'inside'. Outer happenings and inner experience interact with one another; which is why seeing the perfect balance of colours and masses in a painting, or hearing the integration of opposing themes in a piece of music gives the observer or the listener the marvellous experience of a new unity as if it were within his own psyche. Similarly, the process of reducing inner discord and reaching a degree of unification within the psyche has a positive effect upon the subject's perception of, and relation with, the external world.

Apart from Jung, the only psychologist to pay very much attention to experiences of unity or to their healing effects is Abraham Maslow, who has written extensively about what he calls 'peak experiences'. In his view, the ability to have such experiences is a sign of psychic health; an attribute of the 'self-actualizing' person.

My feeling is that the concept of creativeness and the concept of the healthy, self-actualizing, fully human person seem to be coming closer and closer together and may perhaps turn out to be the same thing.[25]

200

Maslow continues his investigation of the creative attitude by observing that

> the creative person, in the inspirational phase of the creative furor, loses his past and his future and lives only in the moment. He is all there, totally immersed, fascinated and absorbed in the present, in the current situation, in the here-now, with the matter-in-hand ... This ability to become 'lost in the present' seems to be a *sine qua non* for creativeness of any kind. But also certain *prerequisites* of creativeness – in whatever realm – somehow have something to do with this ability to become timeless, selfless, outside of space, of society, of history. It has begun to appear strongly that this phenomenon is a diluted, more secular, more frequent version of the mystical experience that has been described so often as to have become what Huxley called *The Perennial Philosophy*.[26]

Moreover, Maslow realizes that the creative attitude and the ability to have peak experiences depends upon being free of other people; free, especially, from neurotic involvements, from 'historical hangovers from childhood', but also free of obligations, duties, fears and hopes.

> We become much more free of other people, which in turn means that we become much more ourselves, our Real Selves (Horney), our authentic selves, our real identity.[27]

Maslow's attitude is thus very different from that of the object-relations theorists who tend to assume that the meaning of life is invariably bound up with interpersonal relationships.

This book began with the observation that many highly creative people were predominantly solitary, but that it was nonsense to suppose that, because of this, they were necessarily unhappy or neurotic. Although man is a social being, who certainly needs interaction with others, there is considerable variation in the depth of the relationships which individuals form with each other. All human beings need interests as well as relationships; all are geared toward

201

the impersonal as well as toward the personal. The events of early childhood, inherited gifts and capacities, temperamental differences, and a host of other factors may influence whether individuals turn predominantly toward others or toward solitude to find the meaning of their lives.

The capacity to be alone was adumbrated as a valuable resource, which facilitated learning, thinking, innovation, coming to terms with change, and the maintenance of contact with the inner world of the imagination. We saw that, even in those whose capacity for making intimate relationships had been damaged, the development of creative imagination could exercise a healing function. Examples were also given of creative individuals whose chief concern was with making sense and order out of life rather than with relationships with others; a concern with the impersonal which, we suggested, tended to increase with age. Man's adaptation to the world is largely governed by the development of the imagination and hence of an inner world of the psyche which is necessarily at variance with the external world. Perfect happiness, the oceanic feeling of complete harmony between inner and outer worlds, is only transiently possible. Man is constantly in search of happiness but, by his very nature, is precluded from finally or permanently achieving it either in interpersonal relationships or in creative endeavour. Throughout the book, it was noted that some of the most profound and healing psychological experiences which individuals encounter take place internally, and are only distantly related, if at all, to interaction with other human beings.

The happiest lives are probably those in which neither interpersonal relationships nor impersonal interests are idealized as the only way to salvation. The desire and pursuit of the whole must comprehend both aspects of human nature.

The epigraph of this chapter is taken from *The Prelude.* It is fitting that Wordsworth should also provide its end.

> When from our better selves we have too long
> Been parted by the hurrying world, and droop,
> Sick of its business, of its pleasures tired,
> How gracious, how benign, is Solitude.[28]

202

References

INTRODUCTION

1. Edward Gibbon, *Memoirs of My Life and Writings*, edited by G. Birkbeck Hill (London, 1900), pp. 239–41.
2. Lytton Strachey, *Portraits in Miniature* (London, 1931), p. 154.
3. Edward Gibbon, *op. cit.*, p. 236, note 3.
4. *Ibid.*, p. 244.

CHAPTER 1

1. Ernest Gellner, *The Psychoanalytic Movement* (London, 1985), p. 34.
2. Sigmund Freud, *Letter to Pfister* (1910), quoted in Ernest Jones, *Sigmund Freud*, II (London, 1955), p. 497.
3. Sigmund Freud, 'Transference', Lecture XXVII in *Introductory Lectures on Psycho-Analysis*, Standard Edition, edited by James Strachey, 24 volumes, XVI (London, 1963), pp. 431–47.
4. Peter Marris, 'Attachment and Society', in *The Place of Attachment in Human Behavior*, edited by C. Murray Parkes and J. Stevenson-Hinde (London, 1982), p. 185.
5. Robert S. Weiss, 'Attachment in Adult Life', in *The Place of Attachment in Human Behavior, op. cit.*, p. 174.
6. John Bowlby, *Loss, Sadness and Depression; Attachment and Loss*, III (London, 1980), p. 442.

CHAPTER 2

1. Bernard Berenson, *Sketch for a Self-Portrait* (Toronto, 1949), p. 18.
2. A.L. Rowse, *A Cornish Childhood* (London, 1942), pp. 16–18.
3. Donald W. Winnicott, 'The Capacity to be Alone', in *The Maturational Processes and the Facilitating Environment* (London, 1969), p. 29.
4. *Ibid.*, p. 33.
5. *Ibid.*, p. 34.
6. *Ibid.*, p. 34.
7. William C. Dement, *Some Must Watch While Some Must Sleep* (San Francisco, 1972), p. 93.
8. Stanley Palombo, *Dreaming and Memory* (New York, 1978), p. 219.

9. David Stenhouse, *The Evolution of Intelligence* (London, 1973), p. 31.
10. *Ibid.*, p. 67.
11. *Ibid.*, p. 78.

CHAPTER 3

1. Colin Murray Parkes, *Bereavement*, second edition (Harmondsworth, 1986), pp. 158–9.
2. Loring M. Danforth, *The Death Rituals of Rural Greece* (Princeton, 1982), pp. 143–4.
3. *Ibid.*, p. 144.
4. Richard E. Byrd, *Alone* (London, 1958), p. 7.
5. *Ibid.*, p. 9.
6. *Ibid.*, pp. 62–3.
7. *Ibid.*, p. 206.
8. William James, *The Varieties of Religious Experience* (London, 1903), p. 419.
9. Sigmund Freud, *Civilization and Its Discontents*, Standard Edition, edited by James Strachey, 24 volumes, XXI (London, 1961), pp. 64–5.
10. *Ibid.*, p. 67.
11. *Ibid.*, p. 72.
12. *Ibid.*, p. 72.
13. Richard Wagner, in *Wagner on Music and Drama: A Selection from Richard Wagner's Prose Works*, arranged by Albert Goldman and Evert Sprinchorn, translated by H. Ashton Ellis (London, 1970), pp. 272–3.
14. Glin Bennet, *Beyond Endurance* (London, 1983), pp. 166–7.
15. Christiane Ritter, translated by J. Degras, *Woman in the Polar Night* (London, 1954), p. 144.
16. John Keats, 'Ode to a Nightingale', Noel Douglas replica edition (London, 1927) of Taylor and Hessey edition (London, 1820), pp. 110–11.

CHAPTER 4

1. Norval Morris, *The Future of Imprisonment* (Chicago, 1974), p. 4.
2. Ida Koch, 'Mental and Social Sequelae of Isolation', in *The Expansion of European Prison Systems*, Working Papers in European Criminology No. 7, edited by Bill Rolston and Mike Tomlinson (Belfast, 1986), pp. 119–29.
3. Lawrence E. Hinkle and Harold G. Wolff, 'Communist Interrogation and Indoctrination of "Enemies of the States", *AMA Archives of Neurology and Psychiatry* (1956), Vol. 76, pp. 115–74.
4. *Ibid.*, p. 12.
5. *Ibid.*, p. 25.
6. Edith Bone, *Seven Years Solitary* (London, 1957).
7. Christopher Burney, *Solitary Confinement* (London, 1952).
8. Bruno Bettelheim, *Surviving and Other Essays* (London, 1979), p. 103.
9. Yehudi Menuhin, *Theme and Variations* (New York, 1972), p. 103.
10. Quoted in Maynard Solomon, *Beethoven* (London, 1978), p. 117.
11. *Ibid.*, p. 124.
12. André Malraux, *Saturn: an Essay on Goya* (London, 1957), p. 25.
13. Francisco Goya, quoted in Kenneth Clark, *The Romantic Rebellion* (London, 1973), p. 95.

14. Stanley Cohen and Laurie Taylor, *Psychological Survival* (New York, 1972), p. 110.
15. Joseph Frank, *Dostoevsky: The Years of Ordeal, 1850–1859*, 5 volumes (Princeton, 1983), II, p. 122.
16. *Hitler's Secret Conversations, 1941–44* (New York, 1953), p. 235. Quoted in William L. Shirer, *The Rise and Fall of the Third Reich* (London, 1964), p. 119, note.
17. Arthur Koestler, *Kaleidoscope* (London, 1981), pp. 208–15.

CHAPTER 5

1. Samuel Johnson, *The History of Rasselas*, in *Samuel Johnson*, edited by Donald Greene (Oxford, 1984), p. 387.
2. Sigmund Freud, 'Creative Writers and Day-Dreaming', Standard Edition, edited by James Strachey, 24 volumes IX (London, 1959), p. 146.
3. *Ibid.*, p. 145.
4. Sigmund Freud, 'Formulations on the Two Principles of Mental Functioning', Standard Edition, XII (London, 1958), p. 219.
5. Francisco Goya, Epigraph to *Los Caprichos*.
6. Sigmund Freud, *op. cit.*, XII, p. 224.
7. Donald W. Winnicott, 'Transitional Objects and Transitional Phenomena' (1951), in *Through Paediatrics to Psycho-Analysis* (London, 1975), pp. 229–42.
8. S. Provence and R. C. Lipton, *Infants in Institutions: A Comparison of their Development with Family-Reared Infants during the First Year of Life* (New York, 1962).
9. Donald W. Winnicott, *Playing and Reality* (New York, 1971), p. 65.

CHAPTER 6

1. Anthony Storr, 'The Concept of Cure', in *PsychoAnalysis Observed*, edited by Charles Rycroft (London, 1966), p. 72.
2. Germain Bazin, translated by F. Scarfe, *A Concise History of Art* (London, 1962), p. 11.
3. Herbert Read, *Icon and Idea* (London, 1955), p. 27.
4. Germain Bazin, *op. cit.*, p. 24.
5. Raymond Firth, *Elements of Social Organization*, third edition (London, 1961), p. 173.
6. Colin Morris, *The Discovery of the Individual* (London, 1972), p. 88.
7. Jacob Burckhardt, *The Civilization of the Renaissance in Italy*, second edition (Oxford, 1981), p. 81.
8. Edward O. Wilson, *Sociobiology: The New Synthesis* (Cambridge, Mass., and London, England, 1975), p. 564.
9. Raymond Firth, *op. cit.*, p. 171.
10. Edmund Leach, edited by F. Kermode, *Social Anthropology* (London, 1982), pp. 139–40.
11. Peter Abbs, 'The Development of Autobiography in Western Culture: from Augustine to Rousseau' (unpublished thesis, University of Sussex, 1986), p. 130.
12. *Ibid.*, pp. 131–2.
13. Bruno Bettelheim, *The Children of the Dream* (London, 1969), p. 212.

205

14. Urie Bronfenbrenner, *Two Worlds of Childhood: US and USSR* (London, 1971), pp. 10–11.
15. Matthew 22: 37, 38.
16. Christopher Brooke, *The Monastic World, 1000–1300* (London, 1974), pp. 114–15.

CHAPTER 7

1. C. G. Jung, *Memories, Dreams, Reflections*, edited by Aniela Jaffe, translated by Richard and Clara Winston (London, 1963), p. 170.
2. C. G. Jung, *Two Essays on Analytical Psychology*, *Collected Works*, edited by Herbert Read, Michael Fordham and Gerhard Adler, translated by R. F. C. Hull, 20 volumes, VII (London, 1953), p. 40.
3. *Ibid.*, p. 41.
4. *Ibid.*
5. Wilhelm Worringer, *Abstraction and Empathy*, translated by Michael Bullock (London, 1963), p. 5.
6. *Ibid.*, p. 4.
7. *Ibid.*, p. 36.
8. Howard Gardner, *Artful Scribbles* (New York, 1980), p. 47.
9. Sigmund Freud, 'Mourning and Melancholia', Standard Edition, edited by James Strachey, 24 volumes, XIV (London, 1957), pp. 243–58.
10. Mary Main and Donna R. Weston, 'Avoidance of the Attachment Figure in Infancy: Descriptions and Interpretations' in *The Place of Attachment in Human Behavior*, edited by Colin Murray-Parkes and Joan Stevenson-Hinde (London, 1982), p. 46.
11. *Ibid.*, p. 46.
12. *Ibid.*, p. 52.
13. Franz Kafka, *Letters to Felice*, translated by James Stern and Elizabeth Duckworth, edited by Erich Heller and Jürgen Born (London, 1974), p. 271.
14. *Ibid.*, pp. 155–6.
15. Erich Heller, *Franz Kafka* (New York, 1975), p. 15.
16. Quoted by Allan Blunden in 'A Chronology of Kafka's Life', in *The World of Franz Kafka*, edited by J. P. Stern (London, 1980), p. 28.
17. W. B. Yeats, 'The Second Coming', *The Collected Poems of W. B. Yeats*, second edition (London, 1950), p. 211.

CHAPTER 8

1. Anthony Trollope, *An Autobiography* (London, 1946), pp. 54–5.
2. C. P. Snow, *Trollope* (London, 1975), p. 9.
3. Humphrey Carpenter, *Secret Gardens* (London, 1987), pp. 138–41.
4. Margaret Lane, *The Tale of Beatrix Potter* (London, 1970), p. 9.
5. *Ibid.*, p. 38.
6. *Ibid.*, p. 50.
7. Humphrey Carpenter, *op. cit.*, p. 138.
8. Vivien Noakes, *Edward Lear* (London, 1985), p. 14.
9. *Ibid.*, p. 107.

10. Charles Carrington, *Rudyard Kipling* (Harmondsworth, 1970), p. 50.
11. Angus Wilson, *The Strange Ride of Rudyard Kipling* (London, 1977), p. 18.
12. *Ibid.*, p. 276.
13. A. J. Languth, *Saki* (Oxford, 1982), p. 14.
14. *The Bodley Head Saki*, edited by J. W. Lambert (London, 1963), p. 59.
15. Frances Donaldson, *P. G. Wodehouse* (London, 1982), p. 46.
16. *Writers at Work*, fifth series, edited by George Plimpton (Harmondsworth, 1981), p. 11.
17. Frances Donaldson, *op. cit.*, p. 44.
18. *Ibid.*, p. 50.
19. *Ibid.*, p. 3.
20. *Writers at Work*, first series, introduced by Malcolm Cowley (London, 1958), p. 132.

CHAPTER 9

1. Paul V. Ragan and Thomas H. McGlashan, 'Childhood Parental Death and Adult Psychopathology', *American Journal of Psychiatry*, 143:2 (February 1986), pp. 153–7.
2. George W. Brown and Tirril Harris, *Social Origins of Depression* (London, 1978), p. 240.
3. C. Perris, S. Holmgren, L. von Knorring and H. Perris, 'Parental Loss by Death in the Early Childhood of Depressed Patients and of their Healthy Siblings', *British Journal of Psychiatry* (1986), 148, pp. 165–9.
4. George W. Brown *et al.*, *op. cit.*, p. 240.
5. John A. Birtchnell, 'The Personality Characteristics of Early-bereaved Psychiatric Patients', *Social Psychiatry*, 10, pp. 97–103.
6. Roger Brown, *Social Psychology, The Second Edition*, (New York, 1984), pp. 644–5.
7. George W. Brown *et al.*, *op. cit.*, p. 285.
8. Robert Bernard Martin, *Tennyson: The Unquiet Heart* (Oxford, 1980), p. 184.
9. Alfred Tennyson, *In Memoriam*, v, in *The Works of Alfred, Lord Tennyson* (London, 1899), p. 248.
10. Robert Burton, *The Anatomy of Melancholy*, edited by Holbrook Jackson (London, 1972), p. 20.
11. Robert Bernard Martin, *op. cit.*, p. 4.
12. *Ibid.*, p. 10.
13. *Ibid.*, p. 140.
14. Andrew Brink, *Loss and Symbolic Repair* (Ontario, 1977).
15. Andrew Brink, *Creativity as Repair* (Ontario, 1982).
16. David Aberbach, *Loss and Separation in Bialik and Wordsworth*, Prooftexts (Johns Hopkins University Press, 1982), Vol. 2, pp. 197–208.
17. David Aberbach, *At the Handles of the Lock* (Oxford, 1984).
18. David Cecil, *The Stricken Deer, or The Life of Cowper* (London, 1943).
19. William Cowper, *The Poetical Works of William Cowper*, edited by H. S. Milford (Oxford, 1934), Olney Hymn I, lines 9–12, p. 433.
20. William Cowper, *The Letters and Prose Writings of William Cowper*, edited by James King and Charles Ryskamp, 5 volumes, II (Oxford, 1981), letter to Joseph Hill, November 1784, p. 294.
21. William Cowper, *Works*, *op. cit.*, lines 17–20, lines 118–21, p. 39, p. 396.

22. William Cowper, 'Lines Written During a Period of Insanity', lines 1–12, *Works, op. cit.*, pp. 289–90.
23. William Cowper, *Works, op. cit.*, Olney Hymn XVIII, lines 9–12, p. 444.
24. William Cowper, *Works, op. cit.*, 'The Shrubbery', lines 5–12, p. 292.
25. Samuel T. Coleridge, 'Dejection: An Ode', lines 31–8. *The Portable Coleridge*, edited by I. A. Richards (Harmondsworth, 1977), p. 170.
26. David Cecil, *op. cit.*, p. 206.
27. William Cowper, *Works, op. cit.*, The Task, III, lines 373–8, p. 172.
28. Stephen Spender, *World Within World* (London, 1951), p. 6.
29. John Keats, *The Letters of John Keats*, edited by M. B. Forman (Oxford, 1935), letter 134, p. 353.
30. David Aberbach, *Loss and Separation in Bialik and Wordsworth*, Prooftexts (1982) Vol. 2, p. 198.
31. Andrew Brink, *Loss and Symbolic Repair* (Ontario, 1977), p. 115.
32. *Ibid.*, p. 117–18.
33. Boethius, *The Consolation of Philosophy*, translated by V. E. Watts (Harmondsworth, 1969), pp. 66–7.
34. N. J. C. Andreasen and A. Canter, 'The Creative Writer', *Comprehensive Psychiatry*, 15 (1974), pp. 123–31.
35. Kay R. Jamison, 'Mood Disorders and Seasonal Patterns in top British Writers and Artists', unpublished data.

CHAPTER 10

1. Anthony Storr, *The Integrity of the Personality* (London, 1960), p. 24.
2. *Ibid.*, p. 27.
3. Heinz Kohut, *How Does Analysis Cure?*, edited by Arnold Goldberg with the collaboration of Paul Stepansky (Chicago, 1984), p. 109.
4. *Ibid.*, p. 43.
5. Ronald D. Laing, *The Divided Self* (London, 1960).
6. Wystan H. Auden, *The English Auden: Poems, Essays and Dramatic Writings, 1927–1939*, edited by Edward Mendelson, XLI, 'September 1, 1939', line 88 (London, 1977), p. 246.
7. Charles Rycroft, *A Critical Dictionary of Psychoanalysis* (London, 1968), p. 100.
8. Jerrold N. Moore, *Edward Elgar* (Oxford, 1984), p. vii.
9. Morris N. Eagle, 'Interests as Object Relations', in *Psychoanalysis and Contemporary Thought* (1981), 4, pp. 527–65.
10. *Ibid.*, p. 532, note 2.
11. *Ibid.*, pp. 537–8.
12. Thomas De Quincey, 'The Last Days of Kant', in *The English Mail-Coach and Other Essays*, introduced by John Hill Burton (London, 1912), pp. 162–209.
13. Ben-Ami Scharfstein, *The Philosophers, Their Lives and the Nature of their Thought* (Oxford, 1980).
14. Bertrand Russell, *History of Western Philosophy* (London, 1946), p. 731.
15. Thomas De Quincey, *op. cit.*, p. 170.
16. Norman Malcolm, *Ludwig Wittgenstein, A Memoir*, with a Biographical Sketch by Georg Henrik von Wright (Oxford, 1958), p. 4.
17. Bertrand Russell, *The Autobiography of Bertrand Russell, 1914–1944*, Vol. II (London, 1968), pp. 98–9.

18. *Ibid.*, p. 99.
19. Hermine Wittgenstein, 'My Brother Ludwig', in *Ludwig Wittgenstein, Personal Recollections*, edited by Rush Rhees (Oxford, 1981), p. 9.
20. Norman Malcolm, *op. cit.*, p. 20.
21. M. O'C. Drury, 'Conversations with Wittgenstein', in *Ludwig Wittgenstein*, edited by Rush Rhees (Oxford, 1981), p. 140.
22. Anthony Storr, 'Isaac Newton', *British Medical Journal* (21–28 December 1985), 291, pp. 1779–84.
23. Richard S. Westfall, 'Short-writing and the State of Newton's Conscience, 1662', *Notes and Records of the Royal Society*, 18 (1963), p. 13.
24. J. M. Keynes, 'Newton the Man', in G. Keynes (ed.), *Essays in Biography* (London, 1951), p. 311.
25. S. Brodetsky, *Sir Isaac Newton* (London, 1972), pp. 69, 89.

CHAPTER 11

1. Bernard Berenson, *The Italian Painters of the Renaissance* (London, 1959), p. 201.
2. Joseph Kerman, *The Beethoven Quartets* (Oxford, 1967), p. 12.
3. *Ibid.*, p. 184.
4. Martin Cooper, *Beethoven: The Last Decade* (London, 1970), p. 11.
5. Joseph Kerman, *op. cit.*, p. 322.
6. J. W. N. Sullivan, *Beethoven* (London, 1927), p. 225.
7. Wilfrid Mellers, *Beethoven and the Voice of God* (London, 1983), p. 402.
8. Maynard Solomon, *Beethoven* (London, 1978), p. 325.
9. Humphrey Searle, *The Music of Liszt* (New York, 1966), p. 108.
10. Malcolm Boyd, *Bach* (London, 1983), p. 208.
11. Mosco Carner, 'Richard Strauss's Last Years', in *The New Oxford History of Music*, X, edited by Martin Cooper (Oxford, 1974), p. 325.
12. William Murdoch, *Brahms* (London, 1933), p. 155.
13. Denis Arnold, 'Brahms', in *The New Oxford Companion to Music* (Oxford, 1983), p. 254.
14. J. A. Fuller Maitland, 'Brahms', in *Grove's Dictionary of Music and Musicians*, 5 volumes, third edition, edited by H. C. Colles, I, p. 452.
15. Friedrich Nietzsche, *The Case of Wagner*, translated by Walter Kaufmann (New York, 1967), p. 187.
16. Peter Latham, *Brahms* (London, 1966), p. 87.
17. Quoted in George R. Marek, *Richard Strauss* (London, 1967), p. 323.
18. Henry James, *The Ambassadors*, 2 volumes (London, 1923), I, p. 190.
19. Leon Edel, *The Life of Henry James*, 2 volumes (Harmondsworth, 1977), II, pp. 333–4.
20. Ralf Norrman, *The Insecure World of Henry James's Fiction* (London, 1982), p. 138.
21. *The Notebooks of Henry James*, edited by F. O. Matthiessen and Kenneth B. Murdock (Chicago, 1981), pp. 150–51.
22. Henry James, 'The Beast in the Jungle', in *The Altar of the Dead* (London, 1922), p. 123.
23. *Ibid.*, p. 114.
24. Quoted in Leon Edel, *op. cit.*, II, p. 694.
25. *Ibid.*, p. 538.

CHAPTER 12

1. Plato, *The Symposium*, translated by W. Hamilton (Harmondsworth, 1951), p. 64.
2. Sigmund Freud, *On the Universal Tendency to Debasement in the Sphere of Love*, Standard Edition, edited by James Strachey, 24 volumes, XI (London, 1957), pp. 188–9.
3. Marghanita Laski, *Ecstasy* (London, 1961), p. 148.
4. Sigmund Freud, *Civilization and Its Discontents*, Standard Edition, edited by James Strachey, 24 volumes, XXI (London, 1961), p. 65.
5. *Ibid.*, p. 66.
6. Marghanita Laski, *op. cit.*, p. 206.
7. Bertrand Russell, *The Autobiography of Bertrand Russell*, 3 volumes (London, 1967–9), I, p. 36.
8. C. P. Snow, *The Search* (London, 1934), pp. 126–7.
9. C. G. Jung, *Memories, Dreams, Reflections* (London, 1963), p. 191.
10. C. G. Jung, 'The Development of Personality', *Collected Works*, XVII (London, 1954), p. 171.
11. C. G. Jung, 'Psychotherapists or the Clergy', in *Psychology and Religion: Collected Works*, XI (London, 1958), p. 334.
12. Charles Rycroft, 'Introduction: Causes and Meaning', in *Psychoanalysis Observed* (London, 1966), p. 22.
13. C. G. Jung, 'The Aims of Psychotherapy', in *The Practice of Psychotherapy: Collected Works*, XVI (London, 1954), p. 41.
14. C. G. Jung, 'Commentary on "The Secret of the Golden Flower" ', in *Alchemical Studies: Collected Works*, XIII (London, 1967), p. 46.
15. *Ibid.*, p. 45.
16. C. G. Jung, *Psychology and Religion: Collected Works*, XI (London, 1958), pp. 81–2.
17. C. G. Jung, 'Commentary on "The Secret of the Golden Flower" ', *op. cit.*, pp. 47–8.
18. William James, *The Varieties of Religious Experience* (London, 1903), p. 289.
19. *Ibid.*, p. 381.
20. *Ibid.*, p. 175.
21. C. G. Jung, *The Transcendent Function: Collected Works*, VIII (London, 1969), p. 73.
22. W. M. Thackeray, Roundabout Papers, *The Works of William Makepeace Thackeray with Biographical Introductions by his daughter, Anne Ritchie* (London, 1903), XII, pp. 374–5.
23. J. W. Cross, *George Eliot's Life as related in her Letters and Journals* (Edinburgh and London, 1885), III, pp. 421–5.
24. Friedrich Nietzsche, *Ecce Homo*, translated by R. J. Hollingdale (Harmondsworth, 1979), p. 48.
25. Abraham Maslow, *The Farther Reaches of Human Nature* (Harmondsworth, 1973), p. 59.
26. *Ibid.*, pp. 63–4.
27. *Ibid.*, p. 67.
28. William Wordsworth, *The Prelude: The Complete Poetical Works of William Wordsworth*, introduced by John Morley (London, 1950), p. 261.

Epigraphs

INTRODUCTION

Edward Gibbon, *The History of the Decline and Fall of the Roman Empire*, edited by J. B. Bury, 7 volumes. (London, 1898), V, p. 337.

CHAPTERS

1. John Milton, *Paradise Lost*, Book 8, line 364.
2. Michel De Montaigne, *Of Solitude*, from *The Essays of Montaigne*, translated by E. J. Trechmann (New York, 1946), p. 205.
3. Charles de Gaulle, *Memoires de Guerre*, Vol. III (Paris, 1959), p. 288.
4. Francis Bacon, *De Dignitate et Augmentis Scientiarum* (ed. 1640, translated by Gilbert Watts), vii, 37.
5. Samuel Johnson, *Boswell's Life of Johnson*, edited by G. Birkbeck Hill, 6 volumes. (Oxford, 1887), III, p. 341.
6. Thomas De Quincey, *The Collected Writings of Thomas De Quincey*, edited by David Masson, 14 volumes. (Edinburgh, 1889–1890), p. 235.
7. Carl G. Jung, *The Psychology of the Unconscious*, in *The Collected Works of C. G. Jung*, 20 volumes. (London, 1953–79), VII, p. 58.
8. Walt Whitman, *Song of Myself*, stanza 32, lines 684–5, in *Leaves of Grass*, edited by Emory Holloway (London, 1947), p. 52.
9. Graham Greene, *Ways of Escape* (Harmondsworth, 1981), p. 211. Edward Thomas, quoted in *Edward Thomas*, by R. George Thomas (Oxford, 1985), p. 162.
10. Quoted in Ben-Ami Scharfstein, *The Philosophers* (Oxford, 1980), p. 89. [Refers to L. Wittgenstein, *Vermischte Bemerkungen* (Oxford, 1978), p. 11 (1929).]
11. Alex Aronson, *Music and the Novel* (New Jersey, 1980), p. xiii.
12. William Wordsworth, *The Prelude*, from *The Complete Poetical Works of William Wordsworth*, introduced by John Morley (London, 1950), p. 239.

Index

213

214

215